ON THE
TRAIL
OF
HARRY
POTTER

By

VERA G. LEE

ON THE TRAIL OF HARRY POTTER

Copyright © 2011 by Vera G. Lee
All rights reserved.
Published in the United States
by
Pitapat Press
P.O.Box 333
New Town, MA 02458
www.pitapatpress.com
pitapatpress@verizon.net

Cover & Book Design by
Arrow Graphics, Inc.
info@arrow1.com
Printed in the United States of America

ISBN 978-0-615-43326-4
Library of Congress Control Number: 2010936881

Again, to my fabulous family

CONTENTS

INTRODUCTION

———•◆•———

In spite of an avalanche of blogs, newspaper and magazine articles about *Harry Potter*, few books have been written on all seven volumes of the cycle. And to date, no one has published a book-length study of Rowling's work from a literary perspective. Most studies that treat part or all of the series focus instead on aspects such as magic and fantasy, philosophy, morality, myth, religion or spirituality.[1]

Unlike such works, mine is the first to analyze the whole *Harry Potter* cycle through the lens of literary criticism. Rather than explain *what* Rowling has created in *Harry Potter*, I propose to demonstrate *how* she has created it. And why, thanks to that *how*, the series has had an astounding success.

To use the phrase "literary criticism" in connection with this popular tale for children and young adults presupposes that the story is, indeed, a work of literature. Such an idea might induce teeth gnashing among critics who disdain *Harry Potter* and dismiss it as inferior, unworthy reading. Eminent writers like Professor Harold Bloom and the late William Safire voiced their objections having read only the first volume of the cycle, *The Sorcerer's Stone*.[2]

Bloom held that the story was "not well written," that it would not survive as a masterpiece but would eventually lose its appeal. Still, its immediate popularity bothered him deeply, since it represented a "dumbing-down" of the reading public.[3] As for Safire, he allowed that it was well and good for children to be drawn in by this tale of adventure, but "the trouble is that grown-ups are buying these books ostensibly to read to kids, but actually to read for themselves." Why is that bad? Because it leads to "the infantilization of adult culture...not just dumbing down [but] growing down."[4] These authors propose alternatives, classics such as *The Wind and the Willows, Huckleberry Finn* and *Alice in Wonderland,* as more suitable for children and adults as well.

A third example of similar anti-Potter criticism is found in an online article of 2006 by Jennie Bristow, who writes that although it's true that the cycle has led children to read books, in the past kids were supposed to read "good" books. She adds that *Harry Potter* books have achieved popularity because of "their readability, not their quality." As for adults who love the series, theirs is clearly a case of "a generation that does not want to grow up."[5]

For these critics, as for some others, *Harry Potter*'s seduction of adult readers would seem more shocking than children tuning in to sex-and-violence TV shows. One can almost imagine grown-up Pottermaniacs sneaking their books onto planes and trains in brown paper bags. What is less imaginable is how, exactly, *Harry Potter* can cause a "dumbing-down" of our civilization. Does reading it really leave us with a diminished intellectual capacity? I, for example, who have devoured the cycle a number of times, am still capable of reading Cervantes and Tolstoy.

Although Bloom, Safire and others have complained of adults reading a children's book, they are obviously judging *Harry Potter* as if it were, in fact, an adult work. Nevertheless, some of their objections should be addressed. One of their major complaints concerns the quality of Rowling's writing. Needless to say, they have a low opinion of it. Safire counted seven clichés on page four of the first book. One can, indeed, find phrases like "in broad daylight," "gazed open-mouthed" and "stretch his legs." (In reality, such ordinary expressions work in context. They are perfectly suited to Rowling's ironic description of the very mediocre Vernon Dursley, whose ordinary life is suddenly upended by the extraordinary.)

Others have called the series "derivative." Perhaps because young Harry goes off to Hogwarts in the English boarding school tradition, as in *Tom Brown's Schooldays*. Or because Harry is not the first fictional hero to perform magic. Or because previous stories have also featured an ancient Merlin, or Gandalf, figure.

Harry Potter may well contain elements found elsewhere. It would be hard to find writers who did not build on the art of their predecessors–including, of course, Shakespeare and seventeenth-century classic playwrights who cannibalized entire plots from the ancients. Still, as the following chapters will demonstrate, Rowling is inventive rather than imitative.

As for wanting young readers to turn to "better" books, that makes no sense at all. The books on the critics' proposed reading list are different, rather than better, and (to use a cliché) one might as well compare apples to oranges. *Harry Potter* is oceans apart from *The Wind in the Willows*, a leisurely, poetic story of animals conversing in the style of adults. It is light years away from Twain's homespun tale about the adventures of an engaging backwoods boy.[6] And Rowling's brand of humor bears no resemblance to the sprightly whimsy of *Alice in Wonderland*. Whether these books would be more beneficial to children is beside the point, for the very young would find them too difficult to read, understand and absorb and would have to postpone the pleasure until later. Fortunately, however, in the meantime they have *Harry Potter*.

It would seem that what has most offended critics is the huge popularity engendered by the cycle. Because it caught on so spectacularly–and because of the great hype lavished on it–they have undoubtedly dismissed it as commercial, therefore bad. According to the third critic, above, the story's popularity was due to its "readability," not its "quality"—as if the two were mutually exclusive. As we shall see, besides being readable and accessible, Rowling's work has quality aplenty.

The masterful comic playwright, Molière, responding to negative criticism of his work, said, "My greatest sin is pleasing my public."[7] Undoubtedly, Rowling could say the same thing.

* * *

In this study, I shall begin by discussing four main characters, their function, their originality, evolution and interaction with each other. This will be followed by an examination of Rowling's plotting, with an emphasis on structure and techniques. I shall then offer a detailed analysis of her humor and style. To end with, my study will reach beyond the cycle itself to consider Rowling's spin-offs, *Tales of Beedle the Bard*, *Quidditch Through the Ages* and *Fantastic Beasts And Where To Find Them*, and, finally, to compare the *Harry Potter* films with the books themselves.

My book is intended for a general public. I hope it will interest not only *Harry Potter* fans but also those who have never read the work but might be curious to know about it. This presents a problem: how to give necessary background information to the uninitiated without boring those familiar with every aspect of the story? I have tried to strike a compromise, that is, to clarify points for neophytes without plaguing seasoned readers with information overload. My apologies if I have erred in either direction.

In creating *Harry Potter*, J. K. Rowling has conjured up a wide variety of ingredients, some familiar, others new and exotic, and distilled them lovingly in her own distinctive cauldron. With a wand fashioned of experience, imagination and taste, she transformed her concoction into a classic. I propose to demonstrate in the following pages how and why Rowling's mix of disparate ingredients is a success–one that will endure long after the initial media hype and film flurry have subsided.

* * *

My deep gratitude to Frank Dill of Charles Rose Architects for his careful reading and incisive comments on my manuscript. A

Harry Potter fan himself, in the midst of designing, writing and teaching, he took precious time to provide me with his highly valuable criticism.

I am greatly indebted to Professor Judith Wilt, of Boston College's Department of English, for graciously consenting to read chapters of my book and for her very useful observations and suggestions.

My heartfelt thanks to two other Potterphiles for studying and giving me their views on specific chapters: Bruce Leymaster helped greatly in getting me off on a good footing. And my own daughter, Amanda Gees–as always, there when I needed her–has proved unfailingly on target in her reading and assessment.

Finally, I am deeply grateful to Charles Eichhorn for the hours he devoted to proofreading the manuscript and to mi querida sobrina tanguera, Susan Lax, for her astute and useful observations.

I am truly blessed.

---

[1] A good percentage of them are guides or compilations of essays.

[2] Published originally in the UK as *The Philosopher's Stone*.

[3] "Can 35 Million Book Buyers Be Wrong? Yes." *Wall Street Journal*, July 11, 2000.

[4] "Besotted with Potter," *New York Times*, January 27, 2000. Safire is quoting Philip Henshaw in his use of the word "infantilization." More recently, the phrase "cultural infantilization" with reference to *Harry Potter*'s effect on readers has been attributed to Joel Rickett, news editor of *Bookseller.com*.

[5] "Harry Potter and the Meaning of Life," *Spiked-Online.com*. June 19, 2003.

[6] It is significant that both *The Wind in the Willows* and *Huckleberry Finn* received their share of negative reviews upon publication. Children's author, Arthur Ransome, for one, called *Willows* a "failure." *The Boston Herald* described *Huckleberry Finn* as "pitched in but one key, and that is the key of a vulgar and abhorrent life." February 20, 1885. Others saw the book as commercial and coarse.

[7] In *The Impromptu of Versailles*.

PART I

FOUR KEY CHARACTERS

Introductory Note

The four characters I have chosen to discuss here are among the most richly developed ones in the story: Harry and three friends who supported him throughout the series, Hermione, Ron and Dumbledore. Other important members of Harry's inner circle—Hagrid, Sirius and Luna, for example—will be featured later in this book (along with less likeable characters, such as Snape).

As for Harry, Hermione and Ron, believably differentiated, interacting with complete naturalness, they are portrayed far more realistically than pre-teens and teens found in other fantasy stories geared to children and young adults.[1] On the one hand, we have three characters who perform feats of heroism in a mythical, impossible world. On the other, the very same three resemble kids you could run across any day in your own hometown.

Harry, of course, is the most important one, and everything centers around him. It is only with Harry that Rowling allows herself omniscience, reading his mind, conveying his feelings, analyzing his reactions and moods. With all the others she explains nothing. Yet she deftly manages to communicate their thoughts and feelings to readers through their actions, reactions, gestures, facial expressions, what they say and what they do not say. This is a master at work.

1

HARRY

—————◆·◆·◆—————

"True heroism consists in being superior
to the ills of life in whatever shape they
may challenge us to combat."

—Napoleon Bonaparte

"Life is the sum of all your choices."

—Albert Camus

We have far more information about Harry than about any
other character in his story. Unlike the others, he is
onstage throughout, playing a part in nearly every episode
of every book. Not only that, readers are made privy to his private
thoughts and feelings from beginning to end. He is indisputably the
most developed figure in the cycle. Yet beyond his circular glasses,
his famous scar and unruly hair, one would be hard put to describe
Harry Potter in a sentence, a paragraph or a whole chapter. For he
is also the most complex of the cast of characters, ever changing, at
times contradictory or conflicted, and certainly a far cry from such
classic, uncomplicated and predictable all-American heroes as Tom
Swift or the Hardy Boys.

Still, it is possible to discover clues, to gather evidence and gain
some understanding of this most extraordinary—and ordinary—
protagonist. So let us start from square one, at the beginning of *The
Sorcerer's Stone*, with eleven-year-old Harry living with the Dursleys
at 4 Privet Drive.

Suspension of Disbelief

Consider his past. At age one, brutally deprived of both parents. For the next decade, cruelly treated by his Uncle Vernon Dursley and Aunt Petunia who relegate him to a small cupboard under the stairs, while their spoiled, obese son Dudley enjoys two bedrooms. Because his dreadful relatives insist that his parents, James and Lily Potter, died in an automobile accident, Harry has no idea they were gifted and admired sorcerers, murdered by evil Lord Voldemort. Nor that he himself somehow survived Voldemort's attack with only a scar on his forehead, and that he is now celebrated throughout the magic world as "The Boy Who Lived." Instead, ten formative years of his life have been spent in a blatant lie and under the most painful conditions.

But suddenly, miraculously, a new and wonderful future opens to him. At age eleven Harry discovers he has magic powers. And he learns that except for summers with the Dursleys (ordinary non-magic people, or "Muggles"), he will board at a school of wizardry, where he will develop magic skills with boys and girls of his own age. He will even have a private stash of gold at his disposal. And that's just for starters. During the course of seven years—the time span of his story—Harry Potter will become a hero, experiencing adventure after adventure, winning the admiration, even adulation, of his peers. And captivating readers of all ages.

So readers are faced with two completely disparate stages of Harry's life: the early decade of stultifying gloom followed by seven exciting years of impressive feats crowned by success. Is there any possible connection between his tormented childhood and his brilliant career as a pre-teen and teenager?

Some critics have seen a causal relationship between Harry, the abused child, and Harry, the hero of the novel. One writer explains that "By abusing Harry, [the Dursleys] predispose him to identify with the abused."[2] Another source stresses Harry's "resilience," his ability to adapt and form attachments despite his miserable upbringing.[3] But more pessimistically, a third states that because of

Harry's horrid home life he is unable to connect with others and represents "a case study in avoidance" when it comes to romance.[4]

Such analyses are logical and convincing on many levels. But seeking a cause-and-effect relationship between Harry's wretched past and his charmed future can lead us astray. For instance, if we view his long history of childhood mistreatment through the lens of modern psychology, we might well diagnose the boy as prone to "dissociation." That is, as a means of coping with prolonged cruelty he would very likely stifle his feelings and become emotionally disconnected with himself and others.[5] However, if that were applied to Harry Potter, he would not be Harry Potter.

For Harry is not a case study but a fictional invention. He does not gradually bridge some psychological chasm and become "normal." He merely performs according to a grander design—a destiny imposed on him by his creator, J. K. Rowling. And in *Harry Potter*, she makes no significant link between Harry's childhood at the Dursleys' and his behavior and actions in the story. The part of his past she does grant importance to—one that will continually obsess and inspire her protagonist—centers instead on the murdered parents he lost in the first year of his life. And throughout the seven volumes, if Harry behaves like boys his age, forms friendships, falls in love and is loved in return, again, that is not the end product of a psychological evolution. It is simply his story—or, more accurately, Rowling's.

So readers are bidden to suspend incredulity and accept the fiction, as they must do with *Cinderella*[6], *Snow White*, *David Copperfield* and other stories with insufferable stepparents. The young protagonists of such tales not only survive their ill treatment but, freed of their tormentors, find success and romance, ending up in a fine marriage and, of course, living happily ever after.

Meet Harry Potter

According to one young reader, "Everyone can identify with Harry. Everyone would love to go from a plain nothing to an amazing hero who will save the world. He's popular one minute and made fun of the next. He's cool but he's dorky, he has cool friends and nerdy friends, he's smart but he makes mistakes...">[7]

Who is Harry Potter and what is he made of?

Early on, during his stay with the Dursleys, we have precious little insight into his character, his personality or potential. Under the domination of his foster parents, his role with them is necessarily limited, and only a few traits come to light. We can see that though ill-used by his relatives, he is not a powerless or mute victim. He occasionally expresses his anger in sassy remarks to his uncle and taunts his cousin Dudley. Passively aggressive, he disobeys on the sly. When the Dursleys leave the house he runs to the kitchen to raid the refrigerator or sneaks into Dudley's room to use his computer. On rare occasions, if pushed to the limit, Harry can fly into a rage: at one point he actually uses physical force, grabbing his uncle by the neck when the man refuses to let him have an important letter. But when faced with great stress or danger, his counteroffensive moves are not conscious acts of aggression. For at such times he unknowingly, automatically, releases magic that saves him from catastrophe.

Beyond such information, at that point a curious reader has little to go on. It is clear that Harry is both excited and bewildered when he learns he's a wizard about to train at an institution for sorcerers. And that he's uncomfortable, not inflated or smug, when people lavish attention on him as a celebrity. But he only truly begins to reveal himself a third of the way into *The Sorcerer's Stone*, on the express train taking him away from the Dursleys' to Hogwarts School of Magic. There, he immediately demonstrates a lively consideration for others, decency and tact.

His first instinct is to share, and he takes obvious pleasure in having someone to share with: his new acquaintance, Ron Weasley. All the more so since Ron has only dry sandwiches to eat, so Harry can help tactfully by offering him his own tastier food as a "swap." When forgetful Neville Longbottom enters their compartment, lamenting the loss of his pet toad, Harry immediately assures him, "He'll turn up." (I, 104)

Later, at age twelve, aware that Ron Weasley's younger sister Ginny has a huge crush on him, he pretends not to notice she accidentally knocks things over whenever he's near. And when Ron seems embarrassed about showing Harry his family's cramped and messy house, Harry—a hundred times happier there than at the Dursleys' immaculate home—says, "This is the best house I've ever been in." (II, 41)

However, while caring and thoughtful throughout his story, Harry is no pushover and nobody's fool. In Book One, after the pretentious snob, Draco Malfoy, enters their train compartment and delivers a nasty insult to Ron, he tells Harry pointedly: "You don't want to go making friends with the wrong sort. I can help you there" and starts to leave, reaching to shake hands with Harry. But Harry, ignoring Draco's hand, replies coolly "I think I can tell who the wrong sort of friends are for myself, thanks." (pp. 108-9)

Harry is instinctively helpful and protective. Seeing someone wronged or in danger automatically ignites a fuse propelling him into action. When Malfoy spitefully snatches Neville Longbottom's Remembrall (a magic device that helps people remember things) and flies in the air with it, Harry, incensed, mounts his broom and captures the ball. And seeing a snake poised to attack another student, Justin, Harry acts instantaneously to stop the animal in its tracks.

His generosity and fairness are not limited to his friends. In fact, they extend even to his adversaries. A case in point: Chapter I of *The Order of the Phoenix*, in which Harry saves his hateful cousin Dudley from a dementor.[8] Terrified by the creature, Dudley, convinced that Harry has aimed some sort of dark magic at him, hits his cousin and nearly knocks him out. But Harry casts a spell with his wand, ridding them of the dementor, then immediately runs to Dudley, manages to lift up his huge body and drags him all the way home.

Even where potentially dangerous people are concerned, Harry gives proof of humaneness. He saves the life of odious Draco Malfoy twice toward the end of *The Deathly Hallows*. In *The Prisoner of Azkaban* Sirius and Lupin point their wands at Peter Pettigrew, the traitor responsible for betraying Harry's parents to villainous Voldemort. They are about to utter the magic killing curse, *Avada Kedavra!* when Harry shouts "NO!…He can go to Azkaban [prison] but don't kill him." And when Pettigrew slobbers over Harry in relief, Harry tells him in disgust, "I'm not doing this for you. I'm doing it because—I don't reckon my dad would've wanted them to be killers—just for you." (p. 376)

In helping and rescuing others, Harry has no idea whether his kindness will elicit thanks and admiration or snubs and harassment. Occasionally the results are positive. After he flies up on his broom to save Neville's Remembrall from Malfoy's clutches, he imagines he will be punished for underage flying. Instead, the Headmistress, Professor McGonagall, seeing his expertise at capturing the ball, rewards him by letting him perform as Seeker in the all-important game of Quidditch.[9]

However, more often than not, Harry's good instincts lead to disastrous results. When he prevents a snake from attacking Justin by communicating with the animal, Justin is terrified by Harry rather than grateful to him. His saving of Dudley from the dementor earns him only anger and berating from the Dursleys. Draco Malfoy, although rescued twice by Harry, remains as hostile as ever towards him. Sparing Pettigrew's life turns out to be a mixed blessing. On the one hand it permits Pettigrew to sneak away and join Voldemort. On the other, later, when the traitor is about to strangle Harry, Harry reminds him that he spared his life, so Pettigrew hesitates one brief instant before finishing Harry off. As a result, Pettigrew himself is strangled through Voldemort's magic and Harry escapes. However, Harry's gallantry in sharing the coveted Triwizard Tournament cup with his rival, Cedric Diggory, results in a disaster: it leads Cedric to his death.

But whatever the consequences, Harry will retain his fundamental sense of justice. In fact, much as he reveres the memory of his dead father, his discovery that, as a student, James Potter played a cruel and demeaning practical joke on Harry's current professor and nemesis, Severus Snape, leaves him not amused but aghast. When his godfather Sirius explains that Harry's father was, after all, only fifteen years old at the time, Harry replies heatedly, "I'm fifteen!" (V, 670) And on the subject of Dumbledore's dictatorial beliefs as a teenager, when Ron tries to excuse him on the basis of his youth, Harry replies simply, "Our age." (VII, 391) In both cases, just two words strongly indicate that he himself would never think or behave similarly.

Interestingly, even in the throes of battle and threatened with death, Harry will not—cannot—kill a soul. In the direst of situations, even face to face with Voldemort, not once does he pronounce the killing curse, *Avada Kedavra!* In *The Goblet of Fire* and *The Deathly Hallows*, Voldemort traps Harry mercilessly, inflicting pain and misery on him. In both instances, when Voldemort decides to finish Harry off, raising his wand and uttering the lethal *Avada Kedavra!* Harry (who escapes in both cases), will not follow his example. He limits himself instead to milder magic, such as his signature curse, *Expelliarmus!*, which disarms (diswands) opponents without taking their lives.

How to explain all that? What is the source of Harry's capacity for empathy, his sense of fairness, his aid to those in distress and unwillingness to inflict harm, the mercy he shows a traitor like Pettigrew? None of that stems from a Christian belief or some conventional moral code. His "upbringing" by the Dursleys—without a single edifying role model—would hardly have furnished him with a standard of ethical behavior. And religion plays no part at all in his life during the seven years we know him. To view his morality as a reaction against the Dursley's or as some sort of throwback to the admirable parents he never knew would seem a bit of a stretch. In the last analysis, Harry's instinctual decency can only be explained by a non-explanation: he is Harry Potter.

And yet, with all his kindly impulses, our hero is not virtue personified. For he is not only humane but human, exhibiting the anxieties, crankiness and occasional lack of control found in your average growing boy. This becomes particularly evident in the fifth volume, *The Order of the Phoenix*. If that book is the most somber of the series, it is mainly because Harry's mood is at its lowest ebb. He is obsessed with Voldemort's murder of Cedric Diggory, and he has a good chance of being expelled from Hogwarts for using magic at home.

Worst of all, in the course of this book he learns his mind is inhabited by Voldemort and that when Voldemort failed to murder him along with his parents, he left part of his soul in Harry. As a result, the boy experiences scar pains, blackouts and nightmares in which he sees and feels what Voldemort says and does. Before *The Order of the Phoenix*, Harry had his painful moments of unhappiness and frustration but never so acutely stultifying and prolonged as in the fifth volume, where his anger and hostility come constantly to the fore.

Like most of the other books, *The Order of the Phoenix* starts in late summer, with Harry at the Dursleys'—not a pleasant situation at best. But this time, unlike the others, we find him sloppy and surly, in the throes of a prolonged depression and steeped in self-pity. So he baits his cousin Dudley, knowing full well that Dudley can't get back at him, since he's afraid Harry might hex him in some way. Harry accuses his cousin of beating up a younger boy, and when Dudley uses the excuse that the boy was sassy ("cheeky") to him, Harry answers, "Yeah? Did he say you look like a pig that's been taught to walk on its hind legs? 'Cause that's not cheek, Dud, that's true." This commentary follows: "It gave Harry enormous satisfaction to know how furious he was making Dudley; he felt as though he was siphoning off his own frustration into his cousin, the only outlet he had." (p. 13)

But even away from the Dursley family and united with those who love him, anger continues to well up in Harry, and he takes it out on his closest friends. Resentful that Ron and Hermione have spent time together while he languished at 4 Privet Drive, he throws away the birthday presents they sent him. Infuriated that they have been enjoying each other's company at Sirius's house and privy to news he himself is ignorant of, when he sees them he first remains remote, then lets his fury build, asking, "How come I have to stay at the Dursleys' while you two get to join in everything that's going on here?" When they explain that they haven't been allowed inside information, rather than calm down, he shouts, each word capitalized:

> "SO YOU HAVEN'T BEEN IN THE MEETINGS, BIG DEAL!...YOU'VE STILL BEEN TOGETHER. ME, I'VE BEEN STUCK AT THE DURSLEYS' FOR A MONTH AND I'VE HANDLED MORE THAN YOU TWO HAVE EVER MANAGED...WHO SAVED THE SORCERER'S STONE? WHO GOT RID OF RIDDLE? WHO SAVED BOTH YOUR SKINS FROM THE DEMENTORS?" (p. 65)

Later, when Harry hears Ron and Hermione bickering, he becomes enraged, rails at them, telling them to shut up, then leaves abruptly. The author comments: "The vision of Ron and Hermione's shocked faces afforded him a sense of deep satisfaction." (pp. 235-6) Even being allowed back at Hogwarts does not revive the old Harry. Resentment and self-pity continue to fuel his anger. To put it mildly, he is not the most pleasant person to be around.

A most logical explanation of volume five's chronically depressed Harry is that he has just turned fifteen, that is, about the right age for a teenager to start acting—or acting up—like a teenager. At one point in the book Harry is anxiously awaiting a word from his mentor, Dumbledore, when Phineas Nigellus appears on the scene. Nigellus is a former Hogwarts headmaster, deceased, but like other bygone headmasters, he actively wanders in and out of his magic portrait and is capable of speech. When Nigellus gives Harry the message that Dumbledore wants him to stay put, Harry, furious, bursts out with:

> "So that's it, is it? *Stay there?*...Just stay put while the grown-ups sort it out, Harry! We won't bother telling you anything, though, because your tiny little brain might not be able to cope with it!"

Phineas promptly derides Harry for his self-centeredness, calls him a "puffed-up popinjay" and nails him with the exit line: "Now, if you will excuse me, I have better things to do than to listen to adolescent agonizing…" (p. 496)

Still despite his bouts of moodiness and surliness in this book, Harry remains overall loyal, dependable and as capable as ever of heroism. Whenever needed, he rises to the occasion, as in the shining example of "Dumbledore's Army." When villainous Dolores Umbridge refuses to teach Hogwarts students how to defend themselves against the lethal magic of Voldemort and his supporters, Harry accepts Hermione's suggestion to teach a clandestine course in Defense Against the Dark Arts to fellow students. He attracts a large, enthusiastic following, with the group calling itself "Dumbledore's Army," in honor of their much esteemed Headmaster. Harry does a superb job of teaching and is pleased to find himself popular with his schoolmates. One of the few bright spots of the volume, at least it indicates that Harry's admirable qualities have not diminished or evaporated into some adolescent black hole.

A year later, in Book Six, *The Half-Blood Prince*, we find Harry a lot less prone to self-pity and sounding more like a man than a teenager. Although he still gets riled at times, at sixteen he has far greater control and can handle an unpleasant encounter maturely, without the rudeness and sarcasm of the past. Witness his meeting with Rufus Scrimgeour, the newly appointed Minister of Magic. Harry disapproves of the Ministry, which has impeded Dumbledore's efforts to rid the world of Voldemort. When Scrimgeour shows up at Ron's home, Harry's friends there suspect he has not come just for a friendly visit and are concerned when the Minister asks Harry to go with him for a walk around the garden. Although Harry, too, mistrusts the man, he leaves with him. On his way out, to allay his friends' anxieties, he quietly tells them not to worry.

Once alone with Scrimgeour, he understands why the Minister is there. Harry now has a reputation throughout the magic community for being the only one to foil Voldemort and to escape death from his onslaughts. So Scrimgeour thinks that if he can convince Harry to visit the Ministry often, the boy's presence would give that questionable institution credibility, a certified stamp of approval. A lesser person than Harry might have been flattered by the invitation and proud to be seen in such illustrious company. But Harry does not need or want points with the Ministry or the Minister. During their talk he becomes angry, not only because of the man's attempts to use him but especially because he knows the Ministry is still sending innocent people into the clutches of the dementors at Azkaban prison. In speaking with Scrimgeour, however, Harry demonstrates a control he sorely lacked in Book Five. Now, though increasingly upset and indignant during their dialogue, his statements are neither screamed in capital letters nor followed by a trail of exclamation marks.

At the beginning of their conversation Scrimgeour does all the talking, while Harry remains largely silent, in the classic power position, waiting to see what the man will come up with. When the Minister finally starts asking questions, Harry deliberates before answering. After asking himself how much he should reveal, he delivers only the minimum, without falsifying the facts. If he is unsure, he asks the Minister to clarify his question and mulls it over before answering. When Scrimgeour goes too far, grilling Harry directly about Dumbledore's doings, he simply replies, "Sorry, but that's between us." But rather than adopt an aggressive tone, Harry "kept his voice as pleasant as he could."

Scrimgeour finally comes to the real object of his visit, suggesting that Harry "stand alongside" the Ministry, and the young man replies, slowly, with careful deliberation, "I don't understand what you want…'Stand alongside the Ministry'…What does that mean?" When Scrimgeour explains it would mean Harry's "popping in and out of the Ministry from time to time to give people "the right impression," Harry's anger begins bubbling up. He remembers the injustices he himself suffered at the hands of the Ministry's sadistic Dolores Umbridge. But he keeps calm. The text reads: "So basically," he said, as though he just wanted to clarify a few points, "You'd like to give the impression that I'm working for the Ministry?" Then when Scrimgeour doesn't deny that, Harry refuses the offer—but replies, still in a calm and pleasant tone of voice: "No, I don't think that'll work." And he gives his reasons candidly.

These are the closing words of their interview:

> **Scrimgeour:** "Still Dumbledore's man through and through, aren't you, Potter?"
> **Harry:** "Yes I am…Glad we straightened that out."
> (VI, 343-8)

It is interesting that Scrimgeour, who has used Harry's first name up to this point, now addresses him as "Potter." And though he has just reminded Harry he's only sixteen, he refers to him as Dumbledore's "man." For with everything he has seen and experienced, Harry has, indeed, come of age.

Yet he does not miraculously transform into a model of perfection or an idealistic hero, à la Tom Brown. For even at seventeen, he still occasionally acts up. But with this difference: as he matures, he thinks about his behavior, analyzes it, reacts to it. In the final book of the series, *The Deathly Hallows*, Harry blows up at Remus Lupin, his former Hogwarts professor and an old friend of his father. Here is the situation: Harry plans to leave Hogwarts in order to find and destroy a number of dangerous "Horcruxes," bewitched objects that contain pieces of Voldemort's soul and keep the fiend alive. Remus Lupin offers to join him on his quest. But the offer does not please Harry. Instead it infuriates him because he knows that Lupin's wife, Tonks, is about to give birth. Harry—an orphan who would give anything to have his parents again—accuses Lupin of wanting to abandon his unborn baby to go off on an "adventure."

Lupin tries to explain. He was bitten by a werewolf as a child and is himself a werewolf. He can't bear the thought of making his new family outcasts by his presence and letting his child be an object of embarrassment and shame. Harry, however, replies insultingly, even calling Lupin—a kindly man who has always supported and befriended him—a coward for wanting to leave with him.

Now, however, we find a conspicuous change in Harry's reactions. Rather than the boy of fifteen feeling pleased with his display of righteous indignation, the more mature Harry is conflicted. First he feels a "sickening sense of remorse." Remembering Lupin's tortured white face, he tells his friends "I know I shouldn't have called him a coward." When they agree, he tries to justify himself, saying first that Lupin deserved it, then asking, unable to keep the plea out of his voice, "But if it makes him go back to Tonks, it'll be worth it, won't it?" Yet Harry wonders if his father would have been supportive of his stance with Lupin or angry at how his son had treated a close old friend of his. (VII, 213-6)

Uneasy at times about his own behavior, he now recognizes with some discomfort that he doesn't always act according to his own standards of honesty and decency. In Book VII a recalcitrant troll, Griphook, reluctantly consents to sneak Harry into a vault at Gringotts Bank to find one of Voldemort's Horcruxes, the golden Hufflepuff Cup. In exchange he demands the valuable Sword of Gryffindor, currently in Harry's possession. The troll undoubtedly wants the sword immediately after Harry obtains the cup from Gringotts. On the other hand, Harry knows he will need it for an indefinite period of time, in order to destroy Voldemort's other Horcruxes.

So he fudges. He agrees to hand over the sword once he is successful. But he doesn't say exactly *when*. And he is most uncomfortable with his "solution." Although his mission to undermine Voldemort's power is all-important, does the end justify his less-than-honest means? His answer: what choice does he have? Yet he can't help thinking about the entrance to a prison erected by the tyrannical Grundelwald—an institution evocative of a World War II concentration camp—and the words over the gateway: "For The Greater Good."

Harry's self-searching, his efforts to sort out and evaluate his own motives, add up to a rare quality: a willingness to make a stab at self-honesty. Although, inevitably, his actual behavior is sometimes less than ideal, at least he does not delude himself. As with any and all human beings, his acts and comportment will be inconsistent. But where he remains consistent throughout the novel is in his desire for authenticity and his search for the right answers.

Harry needs, hungers for, the truth, for himself and for his mission in life. In the last three books, much of his anger is directed at his idol, Dumbledore, because the man, a good many times, will not communicate with him and give him direct answers. Dumbledore has his reasons, but nothing could hurt Harry more than being in the dark, unknowing. Even when Harry has nightmares that not only pain him physically and mentally but also leave him vulnerable to Voldemort, he cannot use available means of blocking them, because they inform him; they can lead him to understand what is really happening, where it is happening and what will happen to him.

So our Quidditch Seeker ever seeks understanding, enlightenment, the knowledge to steer him toward his ultimate goal: victory. For a Quidditch player, victory means catching the Snitch and winning the 150 points. On a far grander scale for Harry, it means saving the world from evil personified: Voldemort. In view of that enemy's mastery of the dark arts, mere physical prowess cannot suffice for the challenge. What mental skills can Harry call on to help him meet it?

The Mind of the Seeker

As a student at Hogwarts, Harry is not particularly impressive. That might be partly because he has a lot on his mind outside of classes: Quidditch practice, numerous adventures that take him away from school grounds and continual pain and anxiety related to Voldemort. Besides, only a handful of the Hogwarts professors teach effectively, and some of the lot are pure sham. As a result, very few of the magic charms Harry uses throughout the series are learned in a classroom. In Book Four, Professor "Mad-Eye" Mooney (or, more accurately, the person impersonating him) does teach a swelling spell, *Engorgio!* in class, giving Harry the means of inflating a detestable aunt the following year. But the all-important Patronus spell that defeats deadly dementors is taught to him by Professor Lupin outside of the classroom. And he first witnesses his much-used *Expelliarmus!* spell outside of class, in a Dueling Club demonstration by Professors Snape and Lockhart.

In general, Harry learns charms and spells non-academically, for instance, by observing adults perform them or through tutoring by Hermione and intensive sessions with her to prepare him for the Triwizard Tournament *(Goblet of Fire)*. And if he scores well on the O.W.L. exams[10] in Snape's subject, Potions, it is certainly no thanks to Snape's dismaying classes where Harry absorbs next to nothing. It just happens he has been cribbing answers from a tattered old potions book. It contains scrawled marginalia providing ingenious solutions, along with brilliant spells and hexes invented by the student who originally owned the book. (It also happens that that former student was none other than Severus Snape.)

Unlike Hermione, who studies, memorizes and performs to perfection, Harry simply gets through his courses as best he can; although a tad better than his buddy Ron, he is no shining star. In *The Order of the Phoenix*, we read: "It came as no surprise to [the class] that Harry and Ron were given additional practice of the Silencing Charm for homework." (V, 376) And one year later, failing miserably in the same class, he is told, "For homework...*practice.*" (VI, 515)

Clearly, if Harry had to depend on his academic skills to achieve his goal, he would fall far short of the mark. Fortunately, another, keener and more impelling brand of intelligence comes to his rescue. Harry is instinctively alert. A fast thinker whether on his feet or in the air pursuing the Snitch, he can see things before others do, and his brain transmits messages instantaneously to his body.

We see this as early as Book I, *The Sorcerer's Stone*. Harry, Ron and Hermione are desperately trying to find a key to get through a locked door. Dismayed because hundreds of winged keys are flying above them, the three of them mount broomsticks to try to find the right one. Again, the Quidditch metaphor comes into play: "Not for nothing, though, was Harry the youngest Seeker in a century.

He had a knack for spotting things other people didn't." (p. 280) He sees a silver key, concludes it's the right one (unlike the others, it has a bent wing, so he surmises it must have been used in the door) and captures it. This same alertness and rapid-fire thinking come into play in Harry's encounters with his arch foes. Faced with an obstacle or caught in a trap, his mind races, "far beyond Ron's and Hermione's." (VII, 429) As a result, more often than not, he manages to find a way of foiling the enemy—at least temporarily.

He does it principally through imagination, intuition or instinct. Without consciously or rationally working problems out, he senses the answers "somehow." When he flies in the air for the first time in order to retrieve Neville's Remembrall from Malfoy, "Harry knew, somehow, what to do." (I, 149) When he saves Justin from the snake, "Harry wasn't sure what made him do it. He wasn't even aware of deciding to do it." (II, 194) And later, sheer instinct provides Harry with the only means of countering Tom Riddle's death curse: "Then, without thinking, without considering, as though he had meant to do it all along, Harry seized the basilisk fang..." (II, 322) Similarly, in every volume of the work, we find explanations—or non-explanations—of his decisions, such as, "He did not know what made him say it but...." (VI, 297) and "He could not even explain satisfactorily why he had decided against it." (VII, 503)

Although Harry's brand of sixth sense does not always prove effective or on the mark, in the majority of cases it serves him well. So in *The Deathly Hallows*, when he is hiding out in a bleak, anonymous location, Lupin, who sends him a message via underground radio, advises Harry "to follow his instincts, which are good and nearly always right." (p. 441)

Largely because of these qualities of alertness, radar-like identification of objects and objectives and instinctive understanding, Harry assumes the role of leader. His friends Hermione and Ron are helpful, at times, indispensable. Hermione, a quick thinker, has great organizational skills and, especially, the ability to research solutions enabling them to meet the challenges they face. Ron, who contributes mainly through friendship and bravery, occasionally saves the day by fortuitous acts and discoveries. But most often both friends defer to Harry, who, quite naturally, takes charge. "Where are we going?" "What'll we do?" they each ask him at various times, waiting for—and acting on—his decision. Even after a long period of inaction on Harry's part, a time during which Ron appears to take over as the hero meditates on the best strategy to follow, Harry, once decided on a course of action, immediately retakes the reins and releases a series of "I-message" directives: "I need to speak to Griphook and Ollivander." "I'll speak to Griphook first." "I need you two as well." (VII, 484-5) No one need doubt who is in command.

As a leader, Harry does not predictably solve every problem and meet every challenge like a standard comic-book hero. Still, in the majority of cases, he is adept and skillful in meeting his goals. One of the most outstanding proofs of his competency can be seen in *The Order of the Phoenix*, when he instructs his peers in Defense Against the Dark Arts. Harry performs admirably in the role of teacher. As their leader, despite some heel dragging on the part of some students, he follows his own plan:

1. He insists on starting with the basics for a solid ground to build on.
2. He divides the class into pairs, while he, himself works with an unpaired student.
3. He goes among the students, supervising and giving hands-on help to all who need it.
4. Toward the end of the "term," at Christmas break, he congratulates them on their progress and devotes their last session to review.
5. He announces that the next time they meet he will work with them on one of the most important, exciting charms they can look forward to: conjuring the anti-dementor Patronus charm.

But Harry's intelligence and superior skills will not and cannot be limited to teaching others in a classroom setting. As leader, Seeker and hero of his story, he must act. He must abandon the institution of learning and set out on a quest, until all the pieces fit together and he finally arrives at the truth he has been pursuing. Until he can, at last, rid the world of Voldemort.

An Existentialist Hero?

In his journey from ignorance to truth, from befuddlement to knowledge and victory, Harry's actions and outlook hark back in many ways to post-World War II existentialist theory, chiefly to the ideas of Jean-Paul Sartre and Albert Camus.[11] According to Sartre we are free, that is, free to make our own choices and to act upon them. Moreover, we alone must take responsibility for the choices we make and the actions we take. If we live life as existentialists, we cannot depend on anything outside ourselves for answers or for support. For example, we will not call on religion or some philosophical system as a crutch or as an escape—a means of evading our individual responsibility in the name of some higher order or grand design.[12] We are on our own.

Harry Potter qualifies as an existentialist on several levels. Importantly, with no evidence of a religion or code of ethics to guide him, he makes his choices and acts on his own. He takes responsibility for his actions. At times, however, he ascribes victories to someone or something else. That is because he truly believes he is not acting by himself at those moments but receiving outside help. He thinks, for instance, that once, when his protective Patronus charm did not work against dementors, he saw his dead father cast a Patronus spell, in the form of a stag, and that saved him. However, both Lupin and Dumbledore assure Harry that he, not his father, was responsible for the victory, conjuring his own Patronus—a stag like his father's. According to Dumbledore, "How else could you have produced that *particular* Patronus?" (III, 427-8)

Harry may also assume that, in times of danger, his wand automatically performs charms that protect him. "It wasn't me...It was my wand. My wand acted of its own accord." (VII, 83) But no matter how powerful, Harry's wand cannot take full credit when Harry succeeds, any more than it can take full responsibility when he fails. Various adages in the story indicate an affinity between wand

and wizard: "The wand chooses the wizard," "the wizard learns from the wand" and, conversely, "the wand learns from the wizard." But Harry is in charge, and he possesses enough power, agility and will for a thousand wizards—or wands.

In the last analysis, Harry alone is responsible for his actions, successful or not. That becomes more and more evident as he loses the important father figures he depended on in times of stress, his godfather Sirius and his mentor and savior at times, Albus Dumbledore. True, he has close friends who accompany him everywhere, who advise and support him. However, in a major crisis, at the moment of truth, Harry must proceed on his own.

In *The Prisoner of Azkaban*, though initially accompanied by Ron and Hermione, when dementors arrive, he has to face them himself. Conveniently, Ron is wounded, Hermione faints, and a breath away from the enemy, Harry remains "alone...completely alone..." (III, 383) Harry's face-to-face encounters with Voldemort never occur with a friend at his side. In *The Chamber of Secrets*, when he meets Voldemort in the person of his younger self, Tom Riddle, Hermione lies flat out in the school's hospital wing, while Ron is cut off from Harry by an impenetrable wall. Although surrounded by cohorts toward the end of *The Order of the Phoenix*, Harry Encounters Voldemort alone, in a room apart. The one time Harry approaches Voldemort accompanied by an ally, Cedric Diggory (*Goblet of Fire*), Voldemort quickly murders Cedric. And ultimately, in spite of his loyal friends, he knows he will have to take his journey and make his choices by himself, unassisted.[13]

The fact that he *can* choose his actions, that he possesses the freedom to do so, is undoubtedly Harry's most existential quality. Even when he decides not to act, it is by conscious choice. In the final volume, *The Deathly Hallows*, Harry knows Voldemort is tracking down the Elder Wand, an unbeatable wand, capable of conquering anyone. Harry could try to race Voldemort to it, but he consciously elects not to. Most of the time, however, he chooses positive action. Especially toward the end of the story, when he decides to continue Dumbledore's search for the pieces of

Voldemort's soul contained in the bewitched Horcruxes. Despite all his doubts about the wisdom of such a course, he makes up his mind to carry on Dumbledore's quest. "He had chosen his path." (p. 503) Even after Aberforth Dumbledore reveals details that would stop most young men from trusting his brother Albus, Harry still opts to embark on Dumbledore's perilous mission. "He had made his choice...he had decided to continue along the winding, dangerous path indicated for him by Albus Dumbledore." (p. 563)

Harry's ability to make choices, his conscious exercise of free will would appear to fly in the face of a fatalistic prophecy, a leit-motif of the story. According to a prediction taken seriously by all who know of it, including Voldemort, either Harry or Voldemort must die at the hand of the other for "neither can live while the other survives." (V, 841) Harry, aware of the prophecy, tells Dumbledore that he knows he will have to try and kill Voldemort. However, the Headmaster answers "Of course you've got to. But not because of the prophecy. Because you yourself will never rest until you've tried." Harry doesn't *have* to do anything, Dumbledore adds, "You are free to choose your way, quite free to turn your back on the prophecy." But he knows Harry will choose action, and Harry himself understands it will be "the difference between being dragged into the arena...and walking into the arena with your head held high." (VI, 511-512) No thinking could be more in keeping with an existentialist point of view.

Unfortunately for Harry, toward the end of the story, the fatalism of the story intensifies; doom appears inevitable and threatens to negate the protagonist's free will. For Harry discovers that because he carries within himself a fragment of Voldemort's soul,[14] Voldemort cannot die unless Harry does. Only Harry's death at the hands of Voldemort himself will eradicate that fragment of soul keeping the enemy alive. So Harry—knowing that he cannot allow the monster's evil to prevail—is, in essence, condemned to death.

Destiny does not win. At the last moment, Harry discovers he has, after all, freedom of choice. After he has allowed Voldemort to aim the *Avada Kedavra!* death curse at him, he winds up in a strange sort of dream state in which the dead Dumbledore speaks to him. Dumbledore explains that Voldemort's *Avada Kedavra!* did not work (for reasons too involved to render here). But happily, the curse eradicated the fragment of Voldemort's soul that Harry was carrying within himself. He is now entirely free of that burden, Dumbledore explains: "Your soul is whole, and completely your own." (VII, 708) Finally, when Harry suggests that he must go back and finish the fight with Voldemort, Dumbledore tells him, once again, that he is free to choose. He can hop a train and avoid a final encounter in enemy territory or he can "choose to return" there. (p. 722) Of course Harry takes the latter option.

It would be foolish to imagine that J. K. Rowling wanted to fashion her hero as a paradigm of existentialist thought. Yet he follows a path that could have been programmed by Jean-Paul Sartre. And at times, especially in the final pages of the story, he evokes the absurdist views of Sartre's contemporary, Albert Camus.

In *The Myth of Sisyphus*, Camus uses an example from Greek mythology to illustrate his perspective. Sisyphus, a villainous king, was punished by the gods by having to roll a huge boulder up a hill, only to see it fall all the way down again. Although he knew it would roll down every time, he was condemned to repeat the task throughout eternity. For Camus, we are all like Sisyphus. As mortals we are all condemned to die at some point. While alive we work, make plans and carry on; yet our plans, actions and strivings will, in a sense, be negated by death. The important point for Camus is that although we, like Sisyphus, are condemned, we should not surrender passively to the inevitable, but passionately, living life fully in the face of its absurdity.

And there is Harry, undoubtedly the only teenage hero of a popular adventure story to mull over and come to grips with his own mortality. Other young fictional protagonists courageously meet and defend themselves from the enemy as readers expect them to. But Harry walks toward his fate thinking and feeling "*I must die. It must end.*" Terrified, he asks himself if dying will hurt. And like Meursault of Camus' novel, *The Stranger,* he becomes strongly aware of life, in the face of death. "...he felt more alive and more aware of his own living body than ever before. Why had he never appreciated what a miracle he was, brain and nerve and bounding heart?" (VII, 692) Convinced he is condemned to die, Harry will still do what he has to do, and with passion, head held high and living life to the very end.

Although Harry's behavior strongly reflects Sartre's principles, his character and outlook are far more akin to those of Albert Camus. Sartre presents his views starkly, judgmentally, dogmatically. Camus' writings, on the other hand, are more human and humane, reflecting his passion for life and his capacity for love.[15] It is obvious that the hero of *Harry Potter* belongs in the second camp. His humanity and humaneness are evident throughout his story. His passion manifests itself in his loyalty to friends, in the joy of Quidditch, in his desire to do the right thing and in his quest to rid the world of evil personified.

Above all, he has love. Love of his dead parents and their love for him are his motivating force and perpetual source of salvation. He applies the word "love" to his bonds with his closest friends. True, his romantic attachment to Ginny stays largely on the back burner while he goes off on his adventures, but we cannot discount it. Not when we come to a passage describing Harry invisible behind her just before leaving to fight Voldemort. "He wanted to shout out to the night. He wanted Ginny to know he was there. He wanted to be stopped, to be dragged back..." (VII, 697)

Ultimately, however, the most powerful expression of love in Harry's story is found not in joy and fulfillment but in the loss of, and longing for, people and creatures who loved Harry and whom he loved. His deep and poignant yearning for his dead parents haunts him—and us—throughout the story. The brutal deprivation of two father figures, Sirius and Dumbledore, compound the pain. And all of that is followed by the death and moving burial of the loyal house-elf, Dobby. Harry does not cry on such occasions but many have shed tears in the reading.

In Search of Harry

A hero to be taken seriously, Harry is never made to look ridiculous. His pal Ron may spend hours coughing up slugs, Hermione may look bizarre when her face and body get covered in cat fur. But even when Voldemort repeatedly tosses Harry in the air like a limp rag doll toward the end of *The Deathly Hallows*, a reader is concerned rather than amused. And Harry is never portrayed as a caricature. Those around him have their tics and obsessions, their exaggerated personality traits and recognizable modes of expression. The same does not hold true for Harry. For he is far more than his recognizable physical image—the Harry Potter glasses, the shock of untamable black hair and the scar on his forehead. He is Everyboy, fashioned for universal appeal.

With that said, it is difficult, if not impossible, to offer a neat and complete portrait of Harry Potter. For one thing, being the hero of a *Bildingsroman*, his character develops and transforms as the book progresses. Starting out as an unknown factor, an eleven-year-old suddenly uprooted from an oppressive, stifling environment and plunged into an exciting new world, he learns the ropes, acquires friends and enemies, undergoes joys and dangers, successes and failures and finds a mission in life, or, rather, has it thrust upon him. Such are his experiences; it is how he reacts to them that he reveals himself. But of course he reacts differently as he matures, finding his way at school, going through his painful fifteen-year-old stage and arriving at a very mature age seventeen. Such a state of flux would oblige any portrait of him to be as unpredictable and mobile as the magic pictures on the walls of Hogwarts Academy.

A more important difficulty in summing him up with precision is that Harry behaves as an ordinary human being; in fact, one of the most believably human protagonists to be found in an adventure story. It necessarily follows that he is changeable and contradictory. At one moment amiable and respectful, at another, lashing out or restraining himself from doing so. One day determined to do a job by himself; the next, taking along his best friends. For a long time, mistrusting Dumbledore; suddenly, irrationally, deciding to trust him...

But although we can't deliver a pat description of Harry, we can arrive at some general conclusions.

Despite—or because of—his faults and weaknesses, he is an admirable and engaging personality. He makes mistakes but meets his major goals. He is courageous, but not blindly, unbelievably so, for he has misgivings and undergoes terror. Although hardly a star student, once outside of class he is alert and, when necessary, quick on his feet. Without planning his course, he is a natural leader, often proceeding by instinct. Though not always tolerant of his friends or pleasant in their company, he is completely loyal to them. Straightforward and mainly understated, he tries to be honest with himself and is rarely dishonest with others. (On the few occasions he has to fudge, he does not justify it to himself.) He takes responsibility for his acts. While not demonstrative, he is deeply caring. He shows decency not only to his friends but to his enemies as well. His good behavior is never accompanied by moralizing, boasting, or expectation of gratitude or reward.

The above list—at first glance a string of fortune cookie slogans—more or less adds up to our hero, the incomparable Harry Potter.

* * *

J. K. Rowling has often mentioned the personal connection she feels with Hermione, but her strongest bond is naturally with the hero of her story. Conceived on a train, the whole idea of Harry, his character, his past, his adventures as a boy wizard, came to her like an epiphany on a four-hour trip from Manchester to London.[16] "Harry came into my head almost completely formed—I saw him very, very clearly; I could see this skinny little boy with black hair, this weird scar on his forehead, I knew instantly that he was a wizard, but he didn't know that yet..."[17]

Once inspired, when Rowling took pen to paper and actually breathed life into Harry, it would seem that, like Voldemort, she left part of her own soul in the boy and wound up with some of his.

Because in writing she was clearly with her protagonist every inch of the way, understanding him, feeling as one with him at every moment of his journey. This empathy, this strong connection between Rowling and her brainchild goes a long way in giving Harry's character credibility and contributing to the quality and impact of the *Harry Potter* cycle.

---

[1] See Chapter 4, "Trio Dynamics."

[2] Mary Pharr. "Harry Potter as Hero-in-Progress," *The Ivory Tower and Harry Potter*, 57.

[3] Danielle M. Provezano and Emily C. Rosengren, "Harry Potter and the Resilience to Adversity," *The Psychology of Harry Potter*, 109.

[4] Wind Goodfriend. "Attachment Styles at Hogwarts," *ibid.*, 84-88.

[5] Abused children have been known to suffer from "dissociative identity disorder," at times developing multiple personalities, a phenomenon brilliantly demonstrated by Sally Field in the 1976 film *Sybil*.

[6] Quite a few critics have used the word "Cinderfella" in alluding to Harry.

[7] From Wylaina Hildreth, of the Fort Worth, Texas Public Library, in answer to a questionnaire I sent to librarians and public school teachers throughout the country.

[8] A faceless creature who emanates a freezing wind and sucks the souls out of people, leaving them without hope.

[9] A Seeker in Quidditch has the task of flying on a broom to sight the Snitch, a small golden, winged magic ball. If he captures it, he earns his team 150 points, ending the game (but not necessarily winning it).

Quidditch is played in the air on broomsticks. There are two teams of seven players each: three Chasers, two Beaters, a Keeper and a Seeker. The Chasers try to throw a ball called Quaffle through the rival team's goalpost hoops for a score of ten points each time. The Beaters bat heavy iron balls, called Bludgers, at their opponents to make them drop the Quaffle, so their Chasers can retrieve it, and they try to defend their own teammates from Bludger attacks. The Keeper guards his or her team's goalposts to prevent scoring by the other team.

[10] Ordinary Wizarding Level, taken in June of the fifth year.

[11] The two philosophers differ greatly in approach, as do most thinkers who are considered "existentialist." In fact, there is no actual "school" of existentialism. And Camus, himself, refused the existentialist label, preferring to think of himself as a writer of "the absurd." In the above description, I simplify (without misrepresenting) Sartre's thinking and focus on the aspects most relevant to Harry.

[12] For Sartre, marriage, too, is an escape, since it permits "I" to become "we," diminishing the individual's responsibility for his or her acts.

[13] In *The Half-Blood Prince*, Rowling mentions "the path that he and Dumbledore had set out upon together, and which he knew he would have to journey alone." (635-6)

[14] Voldemort unintentionally transferred a piece of his soul to Harry when he murdered Harry's parents by using the killing curse.

[15] The contrast between the two writers may be attributed at least in part to a difference in their personal histories. Sartre, aware of his physical unattractiveness and resentful of his bourgeois Parisian upbringing, could appear mercilessly sardonic. Camus, who was born and reared in Algiers and loved the sun, the sea, sports and women, had a far more optimistic attitude.

[16] Philosophers and scientists have often had their most notable inspirations in ordinary circumstances. Descartes came up with his *cogito ergo sum* warming himself by a stove in Holland. More famously, Newton simply watched an apple fall from a tree (*voilà*—gravity!).

[17] Interview with Christoper Lydon, WBUR, Oct. 12, 1999.

2

HERMIONE

———◆◆◆———

"Woman must not accept. She must
challenge."
—Margaret Sanger

"A woman with a voice is by definition a
strong woman."
—Melinda Gates

Hermione: the hope and despair of many a critic. Some have viewed her as an activist groomed to inspire young readers to fight injustice and strike a blow for liberty, equality and female empowerment. Others have lamented her stereotypical girlish portrayal: her shrewish shrieking, sobbing in the bathroom and—nearly as bad—getting all dolled up to impress a date.[1] Both sides of the contradiction hold true for Hermione. But in the course of the story, many other dimensions to her character and personality come to light.

First Impressions

On first meeting Hermione, a reader might well be tempted to write her off. Rowling introduces her summarily thus: "She had a bossy sort of voice, lots of bushy brown hair, and rather large front teeth." (I, 105) Her early conversation consists of rapid non-stop monologues that invariably center on how bright she is. And her bossiness surfaces immediately: she no sooner meets Harry and Ron when she admonishes them to change into school clothes before their train arrives at Hogwarts. Then in the first days of school she disapproves heartily and very vocally of the boys' rule breaking. Small wonder they consider her someone to avoid at all costs.

But we soon see a chink in the armor of Miss Superiority. When Hermione overhears Ron telling Harry how no one can stand her, she holes up in the bathroom and cries her heart out. Aside from this unexpected sensitivity on her part, her prim-and-proper, seemingly two-dimensional character offers other surprises. As witness the following scene:

Harry and Ron, faced with a dangerous troll, lock the creature up in the girl's bathroom. Suddenly remembering that Hermione is in that very room, they run in, kill the troll and save her. A livid Professor McGonagall discovers them out of their dorm against regulations and sees the dead troll at their feet. They could be expelled. But then, to everyone's astonishment, Hermione insists that it was all her fault. According to her improvised story, she herself had gone looking for the troll to try to subdue it through magic but could not, and when she shouted the boys came and saved her from certain disaster.

So here we have **1)** the usually self-assured Hermione admitting failure; **2)** the morally righteous Hermione telling an out-and-out lie. And most significantly, **3)** the seemingly self-centered Hermione incriminating herself for the sake of her peers. Besides representing a breakthrough (leading to Harry and Ron's accepting Hermione as a friend), this is the first indication that she is capable of a generous and self-denying loyalty.

While these incidents reveal Hermione's sensitivity and capacity for friendship, they do little to mitigate her bossy-know-it-all behavior, especially early on, when, at age eleven, she is given to phrases such as "You *mustn't*" and "I *told* you." As she matures, she never loses her penchant for lecturing judgmentally. However, in the course of time, she expresses her caveats and her disapproval of Harry's or Ron's actions less and less vehemently. Eventually, toward the end of the series, she conveys her frequent displeasure with them largely through stony facial expressions and pregnant silences.

After the publication of Book IV, *The Goblet of Fire*, J. K. Rowling announced that Hermione would become "less insufferable" in the later books. This is certainly the case. Even in *The Goblet of Fire*, if she tells Harry he "ought to" prepare for the Triwizard Tournament, she does so out of a real concern for him. Then, when he sloughs her off, she doesn't persist but sits down and watches him play chess. In subsequent books she is more likely to suggest rather than demand and to bite her lip when she knows she's going too far, or simply lie low for a while.

In a number of online interviews, Rowling has said that Hermione was a caricature of herself as a young girl. She, like Hermione, had to show she knew it all, had to be the first to raise her hand in class, to impress everyone. She may intentionally have created an exaggerated image of herself in Hermione, but the prissy caricature introduced in Book One soon reveals herself as a multi-dimensional character, capable—despite her apparent rigidity—of evolving during the story.

A Clever Girl

Acing every exam, meeting every intellectual challenge, always quickest with the correct answer, her brain cells brimming with relevant data, Hermione is arguably the top student at Hogwarts. An inveterate bookworm, she haunts the school library night and day. In *The Chamber of Secrets*, Hermione, trying to solve a mystery, suddenly announces she has to go to the library. When Harry asks Ron why, he answers, "Because that's what Hermione does…When in doubt, go to the library." (II, 255)

She stores away details with the avidity of a packrat, for each and any may serve a purpose. When she, Harry and Ron attempt to break into the Ministry of Magic and Ron mentions that the Magical Maintenance crew wear blue robes, Hermione is horrified that the fact escaped her completely. Ron asks if it really matters, and she exclaims: "Ron, it *all* matters!…every little detail matters." (VII, 229) More than Harry and far more than Ron, Hermione can be counted on for specifics.

When it comes to organizational skills, no one matches Hermione. In *The Sorcerer's Stone*, even with exams over two months away, she draws up her study schedules and color-codes all her notes. With an adventure in the offing, Harry and Ron will tend to play it by ear, but—right or wrong—Hermione can be counted on to devise a plan of action.

Hermione's seemingly laborious cleverness may appear prosaic when compared to Harry's almost mystical speedy and intuitive brand of intelligence. In fact, Xenophilius Lovegood makes this disparaging assessment of her: "You are, I gather, not unintelligent, but painfully limited. Narrow. Close-minded." (VII, 410) And at one point, Harry agrees with Xenophilius. Disappointed at Hermione's reluctance to seek the Deathly Hallows, he muses rather meanly, "Xenophilius had been right in a way...*Limited. Narrow. Close-minded.*" (VII, 434)

Despite such deprecation, Hermione's appreciable talents contribute greatly to the success of the trio's adventures and very often save the day. Her boning up on magic spells pays off in opening doors, stunning foes and shunting Harry and Ron out of harm's way. She draws on her positive classroom experience to concoct Snape's polyjuice potion so the three of them can spy invisibly on their enemies. Thanks to her studies, she knows that the Ministry of Magic has access to wills and that, in Book Seven, the Ministry is surveying their hiding place at the house Sirius bequeathed to Harry. Repeatedly, her limitless supply of information provides valuable help, at least in the short run.

Her organizational skills bear fruit as well in the course of their adventures. This is nowhere so apparent as in the final book, *The Deathly Hallows*. Days before leaving the safety of Ron's home she carefully packs all their essential belongings in a small beaded bag that can magically hold, among other things, jeans, sweatshirts, socks, a portrait, Harry's Invisibility Cloak and a stack of books arranged by subject. Before they set off to find the Horcruxes, she tells Harry that they must think the whole thing out carefully "We'll need to practice Disapparating[2] together under the Invisibility Cloak for a start, and perhaps Disillusionment charms would be sensible too…" (p. 320) Although, in this case, her planning strategy falls on deaf ears, it most often proves to be a valuable asset, at times, a life-saving one.

It might be tempting to put Hermione's cleverness down to mere book learning and a talent for organization. But her character has more depth and more dimensions than we might expect. With her factual knowledge as a base, she is able to draw associations, and she has a keen sense of observation. Take the case of the eminently dislikable Rita Skeeter. No one can understand how she could acquire the inside information she publishes concerning Hogwarts. Hermione alone makes the connection: after watching a pesky beetle hovering around them, she realizes that Rita is an "Animagus," capable of turning herself into an animal, in her case, a beetle. Armed with her discovery, she is able to put a wrench in Rita's operations.

Even more impressive, her ability to put two and two together speedily makes her a most effective strategist in action. When the Death Eaters come to get Harry at Xenophilius' house, she asks Harry if he trusts her. He nods and she asks for his Invisibility Cloak. Rather than put it over Harry she covers Ron in it, then casts a spell on Xenophilius to erase his memory, blasts a hole in the floor with her wand and flies off successfully with her two friends. Why did she make Ron invisible rather than Harry? Because if the Ministry knew Ron was on the loose rather than at home, his whole family would be in danger. On the other hand, her own family was safe, somewhere in Australia. She didn't cover Harry up, in order for the Death Eaters to get a glimpse of him and not punish Xenophilius for telling them Harry was there. With such clever quick thinking, Ron calls Hermione a genius and Harry says fervently, "I don't know what we'd do without you." (VII, 425)

A most unexpected aspect of Hermione's thinking—especially in the context of an action story—is her psychological insight. A reader may be surprised by her incisive off-the-cuff comments in Book Five on Harry's behavior with his first crush, Cho Chang. On Harry's first date with her Cho bursts into tears thinking of her boyfriend, Cedric, murdered by Voldemort. Hermione asks Harry if he was nice to her when that happened. When he explains that he "sort of patted her on the back," she has all she can do to refrain from rolling her eyes. Later he tells Hermione that on their next date Cho got upset, began talking about her Cedric, and walked out on him soon after he asked her to go with him to a pre-arranged meeting with Hermione. Hermione patiently explains that he should have been more tactful, that he should have said he really didn't *want* to go to meet Hemione but unfortunately had to, "and would she please, please come along with you, and hopefully you'd be able to get away more quickly? And it might have been a good idea to mention how ugly you think I am too."

A bit dazed by it all, Harry only says "But I don't think you're ugly." Then, as if talking to an eight-year-old, Hermione spells it out. She explains, "Look—you upset Cho when you said you were going to meet me, so she tried to make you jealous. It was her way of trying to find out how much you liked her." Then when Harry objects to the way Cho behaved, Hermione replies, "I'm not saying what she did was sensible...I'm just trying to make you see how she was feeling at the time." (V, 572-3) Certainly, in the realm of analyzing feelings, fifteen-year-old Hermione is light years away from Harry Potter and Ron Weasley.

Independent Actions

In spite of Hermione's dutiful respect for authority, she does not hesitate to break the rules when it comes to accompanying and abetting Harry and Ron. By Book Three, this former paragon is committing acts that astound her cohorts. Infuriated when Malfoy calls Hagrid "pathetic," she slaps him soundly across the face and pulls out her wand menacingly. Ron is both stunned and impressed by her action. And shortly afterwards on that same day she asserts herself in an equally surprising way. In Divination class Professor Trelawney, as is her wont, dramatically predicts a horrible death for Harry. Hermione voices her disgust out loud. When the mystical professor comments on Hermione's "mundane" reactions, the girl simply stomps out of class, to return no more. Later, knowing that Harry will risk all if he tries to retrieve his Invisibility Cloak where he has hidden it, she goes and gets it herself.

This does not mean that Hermione has suddenly become Wonder Woman, totally in charge of herself and the world around her. For shortly earlier, after some needling from Ron, she was running in tears to the girls' dormitory. Even in the final book, she still behaves emotionally and still loses control. She sobs herself to sleep at night after Ron leaves in a huff. She panics in moments of danger. Pursued by Death Eaters, she shakes so much she cannot correctly use her wand or pronounce the magic word that would help Ron. Somewhat hysterical, she asks "How did they find us? What are we going to do?" (VII, 166) In such situations, in the face of her terror, Harry takes over. However, in the course of the series, she becomes increasingly proactive and at times even takes the lead.

That happens as early as Book Three when Dumbledore, knowing that Hermione is secretly wearing a Time-Turner enabling her to go hours back in time, puts her in charge of reversing the events of the previous three hours. That way, she and Harry can save Harry's godfather Sirius from a horrible imprisonment and Hagrid's Hippogriff, Buckbeak, from execution. Since Harry himself is at a loss about the situation, Hermione, terrified as she is, leads him through the adventure.

Her control of situations is nowhere so apparent as in the final book, *The Deathly Hallows.* There she takes charge repeatedly of moving the three of them from one hiding place to another. At one point, just as they are about to enter Sirius' house at Twelve Grimmauld Place, to avoid capture by an enemy she magically whisks her friends into the woods. When that site becomes unsafe she transports them elsewhere. And she uses her magic to spread protective rings around their habitats or to erect invisible shields between them when one of the threesome appears a threat to another.

Hermione may not qualify as an Iron Maiden, but her actions and behavior add up to one strong and capable young woman.

The Activist

In Book IV, *The Goblet of Fire*, Hermione starts a campaign to liberate house-elves, creatures bound for life in the service of wealthy wizards. She is not deterred by the fact that with only one exception (Dobby[3]), not one of these elves cherishes any desire for freedom. For they feel undying loyalty toward their masters and are intensely proud to serve them. But transposing the elves' condition to that of human slaves, Hermione will not rest until they are all out of bondage. In fact, she is so sensitized to what she considers discrimination against the oppressed that when Ron says "We've been working like house-elves here." she glares at him as if he's uttered a racial slur, until he adds "It's just an expression." (IV, 223)

So she starts her idealistic organization S.P.E.W., an acronym for "Society for the Protection of Elvish Welfare." If we had any illusions that Rowling—an activist herself—took Hermione's venture seriously, they would be dispelled immediately. First of all, the author came up with a less-than-dignified acronym that enables Ron to hector Hermione by calling her society "spew." If that were not enough, Hermione explains that she actually wanted to name the organization "Stop the Outrageous Abuse of Our Fellow Magical Creatures and Campaign for Change in Their Legal Status," but it wouldn't fit on the badges she made. And when Ron asks her how many members she has, she answers "Well—if you two join—three." Then she blithely recites details of her projected socio-political campaign, ending with the comment, "Harry, you're secretary, so you might want to write down everything I'm saying now, as a record of our first meeting." And she beams at them. Harry is exasperated and Ron simply amused. (IV, 225)

In a most unpromising beginning to her campaign, Hermione, noting that the Hogwarts house-elves cook all their meals, decides to go on a hunger strike; in sympathy with them she will not eat a morsel of food. The next day, however, Ron sees her buttering her toast liberally.

> "You're eating again, I notice," said Ron, watching
> Hermione adding liberal amounts of jam to her toast too.

"I've decided there are better ways of making a stand about elf rights," said Hermione haughtily.

"Yeah...and you were hungry," said Ron, grinning. (IV, 194)

It should come as no surprise that Hermione's grand scheme comes to naught when the Hogwarts elves won't cooperate in her campaign to liberate them and, on the contrary, bitterly resent her for it.

In spite of her failed crusade, it happens that Hermione's social activism occasionally pays off in unexpected ways. In *The Deathly Hallows*, Harry badly needs help from the Sirius' house-elf, Kreacher. But in his heart, Kreacher remains loyal to his former master, Sirius' brother, Regulus Black, who was once a follower of Voldemort. Hermione explains that, unlike Sirius, Regulus had treated Kreacher kindly, and that more could be gained from the elf by doing just that. So Harry adopts a polite tone of voice and even gives Kreacher a locket which, although fake, passes as a Black family heirloom. Thanks to Harry's decent treatment, the elf serves him loyally and well from that moment on.

Ron, too, profits from Hermione's stance on social justice. Toward the end, during the horrendous battle of Hogwarts, he remembers the house-elves down in the school kitchen and tells Hermione they must be told to get out of danger—which earns him a big hug and his first kiss from Hermione. These may be cases of enlightened self-interest, but they work.

Judging Hermione

Although a number of critics and bloggers pinned their hopes on Hermione as a force for the betterment of society, many were disappointed at her lack of success in bringing her dream to fruition. Understandable as that reaction may be, it is important to see this young woman as Rowling created her: a fictional character in a story meant first and foremost to entertain. Hermione is not an ideal but, in fact, a misguided idealist. Her determination to change the world with the fervor of a missionary eager to impose

Christianity on Islam is meant to elicit not dewy-eyed admiration but understanding and a wry smile.

The examples cited above should convince readers that her S.P.E.W. activism is not to be taken seriously. But Rowling herself has made that point in interviews. In her own words:

> My sister and I both, we were that kind of teenager (dripping with drama). "I'm the only one who really feels these injustices. No one else understands the way I feel." I think a lot of teenagers go through that. Hermione, with the best of intentions, becomes quite self-righteous...my heart is completely with her. But my brain tells me...that in fact she blunders toward the very people she's trying to help. She offends them. She's not very sensitive to their [cut off by interviewer]. Hermione thinks she's going to lead them to glorious rebellion in one afternoon.

Her last word on the subject: "But that was fun to write."[4] For like any author with a penchant for humor, she thoroughly enjoys her packaging and presentation of Hermione, the would-be activist. And making Hermione all the more amusing, Rowling deprives her entirely of the sense of humor she herself possesses. Shopping in Diagon Alley, the thirteen-year-old study addict tells Ron she still has ten galleons left to spend. "How about a nice *book?*" he offers with a straight face. Without getting it, she simply answers, "No, I don't think so." (III, 57) And when a sobbing Winky explains that she and other elves have no right to bewail their plight when there is work to be done for their masters, Hermione is totally unaware of the irony in her reply: "Oh for heaven's sake...You've got just as much right as wizards to be unhappy." (IV, 538) Though capable of understanding others, she has little self-knowledge and totally lacks the ability to laugh at herself.

Far from personifying an ideal, Hermione the activist comes across as an all-too-human, at times winsome, source of amusement.

The "Her" in Hermione

With all the strong qualities she displays, Hermione remains very much a traditional female. As objectionable as that may seem to some feminists,[5] Rowling would not have had it otherwise. Besides drawing on memories of herself as a teenager, she also had experience teaching and observing young girls, and her grasp of their psychology would naturally inform her writing as well.

She would have noticed a number of marked behavioral differences between boys and girls, since differences, and not merely physical ones, do exist. We see it in the playground, where at the earliest ages, girls smile much more than boys. It is apparent at the pre-school level, where a little girl would be far more likely than her male counterpart to run to an adult and complain dramatically "She (or he) hurt my feelings!" And although many females grow up as tomboys, young girls in general are more apt to be clothes conscious than boys.

According to Matt Ridley, who wrote *Genome* as the Human Genome Project came to completion in 2000, much of the male/female difference is genetic. While not discounting the role of nurture in the disparity, he writes "Boys and girls have systematically different interests from the very beginning of autonomous behavior. Boys are more competitive, more interested in machines, weapons and deeds. Girls are more interested in people, clothes and words…it is no thanks to upbringing that men like maps and women like novels."[6]

Whether nature or nurture, the reality of "la différence" becomes eminently clear in Book IV, *The Goblet of Fire*. The fourth-year students learn they all have to attend the upcoming Yule Ball—with the boys inviting partners. Fourteen-year-old Ron and Harry are appalled. How could they possibly get up nerve enough to ask a girl…and then to *dance* with her? Only at the eleventh hour do they manage to do the asking, and they somehow muddle through the event. Meanwhile, the girls, who have, of course, matured earlier, are waiting impatiently to be invited, gossiping and giggling about the boys and possibilities for partners. Though parodied for comic effect, the sexual differences portrayed here are nonetheless real.

And in the same book, Ron, notices the "difference" in Hermione for the first time. Having no date for the Yule Ball, it suddenly dawns on him that he could invite her, and he exclaims, "Hermione, Neville's right—you *are* a girl." (P. 400) If there were any doubt, the author makes it clear in the following passage in which Hermione appears at the Yule Ball in all her feminine glory. Here is how Rowling describes her entrance into the Great Hall:

> She had done something with her hair; it was no longer bushy but sleek and shiny, and twisted up into an elegant knot at the back of her head. She was wearing robes of a floaty, periwinkle-blue material, and she was holding herself differently, somehow... (IV, 414)

And she could smile broadly, since her protuberant teeth had been magically reduced in size. In short, a girl's dream of Cinderella at the ball. Or the classic Hollywood gimmick of boss to dowdy secretary-turned-sex-object: "Why Miss Jones, I've never seen you before without your glasses!"

Hermione's femininity is multi-layered and ever-present. She is the sensitive girl who cries when her feelings are hurt; the vocal girl with high verbal skills; the girl who knits details together as neatly and speedily as she knits clothing for elves; the girl who knows how to analyze and articulate feelings of others (if not of herself). She bosses in the manner of that Great Earth Mother, Molly Weasley, and is in a sense a younger version of Molly, virtually clucking like a mother hen as she tells Ron, Harry and others what they should and should not do.[7] Most significantly, as the story moves toward its climax in *The Deathly Hallows*, Hermione becomes the Protectress, solicitous of Ron and Harry, as they suffer hard times. in hiding from their enemies and isolated from their friends. In fact, the magic she performs most consistently is that of casting a protective circle around whatever hiding place she brings them to.

Hermione's unmistakable feminine component does not equate to weakness. Throughout the series she exhibits proof after proof of her forcefulness, speed and bravery in action. Except for Harry's encounters with Voldemort, which must take place in a one-on-

one contest, readers will not find her cowering behind the scenes while the boys do the dangerous work. She is there, fighting in the front lines whenever she gets the chance. But for the "m," her name would be an anagram of "heroine." Rowling could not make her "the heroine," since Harry is the star and must remain so throughout the series.

But her actions are nothing less than heroic. She is a powerful witch indeed.

A seeming caricature at first glance, Hermione has more complexity to her than first meets the eye. Despite her apparent rigidity, she surprises us by constantly evolving and breaking new ground. The second most developed character in *Harry Potter*, Hermione is understandably, a favorite of young female readers, who identify with her throughout the story.

---

[1] For an optimistic assessment of Hermione as an activist, see "Brycchan Carey, "Hermione and the House Elves: The Literary and Historical Context of J. K. Rowling's Anti-Slavery Campaign," in *Reading Harry Potter*. A more ambivalent view is expressed by Eliza T. Dresang, "Hermione Granger and the Heritage of Gender," *Ivory Tower*. Farah Mendlesohn holds little hope for Hermione as a force for change in "Crowning the King: Harry Potter and the Construction of Authority," *Ibid*.

[2] A difficult form of magic transportation without a broom or other equipment.

[3] Already freed by Harry.

[4] www.accio-quote.org/articles/2000/0700-hottype-solomon.htm

[5] One example of such criticism is in Eliza Dresang's writing, cited in note one of this chapter. Other criticism may be found online in the many *Harry Potter* blogs.

[6] 217-218. Ridley cites, in particular, M. Diamond and H. K. Sigmundson "Sex Assignment at Birth."

[7] In *The Order of the Phoenix*, Ron, agreeing with Sirius, tells her "You *do* sound just like my mother." P. 378.

3

RON

———◆◆◆———

"I'm a loser
And I'm not what I appear to be."
—The Beatles

It would be hard to imagine a more suitable or more appealing member of Rowling's triumvirate than Ron Weasley. He shares some admirable traits with Harry and Hermione, for all three are housed in Gryffindor ("where dwell the brave at heart"). Yet his colorful, original personality stands in utter contrast to theirs.

At first glance, Ron might appear a weak link in the triangle. His character has less variety, fewer dimensions than theirs, and unlike the other two, he does not evolve throughout the story but undergoes noticeable change only in the final volume. However, there is much more to him than the caricature presented in films, and he is far more than a mere foil for the other two. On the contrary, in Ron, Rowling has created an engagingly human character, possessing qualities one would not suspect.

A Born Loser?

Ron is lucky enough to be Harry's best friend and, eventually, Hermione's beloved. But through much of the story he sees himself as hopeless, unable to measure up. His is a severe and chronic case of insecurity, daily nurtured by the belief that he is, and always will be, inferior.

Rowling's thumbnail sketch of Ron in *The Sorcerer's Stone* pictures him as "tall, thin, and gangling, with freckles, big hands and feet, and a long nose." (I, 93) But it is not his appearance that makes him insecure. He reveals the real reasons in his first conversation with Harry as they go off to their first year at Hogwarts. Speaking of his older brothers and their accomplishments, he explains that they were all achievers, hard acts to follow:

> "Bill was Head Boy and Charlie was captain of Quidditch. Now Percy's a prefect…Everyone expects me to do as well as the others, but if I do, it's no big deal, because they did it first. You never get anything new, either, with five brothers. I've got Bill's old robes, Charlie's old wand, and Percy's old rat." (pp. 99-100)

Add to that Ron's awareness that his father cannot support his large family in style and we can understand the boy's embarrassment when Harry visits his cluttered old house during their second summer vacation. Or his mortification and anger when Draco Malfoy twits him mercilessly about his family's lack of funds.

How does he cope with all that? Partly with his steady stream of sarcastic remarks. When he is impatient to eat during the Hogwarts sorting ceremony and the ghost, Nick, tells him that the ceremony is more important than food, Ron replies, "'Course it is if you're dead." (IV, 180) When the students are naming horrors they most dread, Ron asks Hermione, whether her worst fear imaginable would be "a piece of homework that only got nine out of ten." (III, 140) And most often his sarcasm takes the form of a flat put-down. Almost all the characters he mentions, deserving or not— Dumbledore, Sirius, Lupin, Lockhart. Kreacher, Hagrid and others—he refers to as "nutter," "git," "crazy," "idiot" or "mental" at some point in the story.

Note that Ron's middle name is Bilius—just one letter short of that cranky adjective "bilious."

His Own Worst Enemy

Unfortunately, dishing out sarcasm and jibes can only go so far in helping someone so thoroughly convinced of his inadequacy to cope with it. For no hope is available to him as long as he holds that low opinion of himself. In fact, throughout the whole series, Ron's insecurity and his low self-esteem work entirely against him. In Book Six, he is so rattled about his lack of expertise in Quidditch that he loses a match for his team unnecessarily. He tells Harry "I resign. I'm pathetic." (p. 291) And Harry proves later that Ron's conviction that he's "pathetic" is the very cause of his failure. (Harry pretends to pour a luck-inducing liquid into Ron's drink; as a result, Ron, convinced of his invincibility, wins the next game.)

Ron's basic insecurities undermine him in other, more important ways, for at times they threaten to destroy his close bonds with Harry and Hermione. That happens most notably in Books Four, *The Goblet of Fire*, and Seven, *The Deathly Hallows*. Before the fourth book, Ron supported Harry in all his endeavors. But as soon as Harry's name magically appears out of the Goblet of Fire as a Hogwarts champion, eligible to compete in the big Triwizard tournament, Ron becomes moody and deeply resentful. Although Harry had nothing to do with being chosen, Ron is sure he rigged it without letting him in on the secret. Now, for the first time, his sarcasm targets his best friend.

> **Harry:** "I didn't put my name in that goblet!"
> **Ron:** "Yeah, okay...I'm not stupid, you know."
> **Harry:** "You're doing a really good impression of it."
> **Ron:** "Yeah?...You want to go to bed, Harry. I expect you'll need to be up early tomorrow for a photo-call or something." (IV, 287)

Given Ron's deep sense of inferiority, one can imagine his resentment toward Harry whom he deeply cherishes but who suddenly, spectacularly, becomes the star of the show, getting the attention of the entire school. In this instance, Ron's negative side wins out completely, throwing a wrench into his friendship.

There are times in Book Four when fourteen-year-old Ron has happy experiences that bolster his ego: winning, at last, at Quidditch and hearing the cheers of his schoolmates, having success with the opposite sex and gaining Hermione's affection. But even all that does not add up to a cure-all, for the young man's insecurity is chronic.

Three years later, it will cause him to strike out at his closest friends in a more serious, damaging way.

In *The Deathly Hallows*, he, Hermione and Harry are hiding out in the woods. Ron has several things going against him. First of all, he never gets enough decent food to eat and blames Hermione for that. He is also aware that, most often, Harry and Hermione work together to plot out the trio's course, so of course he feels left out and unwanted. Further, by this time he is in love with Hermione, and a question badgers him: why wouldn't she prefer clever, heroic Harry to a loser like himself? But worst of all is the fact that when it is Ron's turn to guard the magic Horcrux locket by wearing it around his neck, the evil instrument works on his insecurities, exacerbating them many times over. In thrall to the Horcrux, Ron hits bottom.

It is interesting that, unlike Ron, neither Harry nor Hermione despairs when it's their turn to wear the Horcrux. Harry does feel scar pains and some unpleasantness, but he and Hermione are clearly strong enough to withstand the locket's powerful magic. On the other hand, when Ron wears it—especially if he is hungry—it seems to sense his weaknesses and intensifies them brutally. So much so that at one point he blows up at his friends, leaves them and is not able to make his way back to them for ages.

Brain Power

Given his low self-esteem, we would not expect Ron to shine intellectually. Of course we can't blame him for his inadequate performance in school, because nobody except Hermione aces all her assignments, and even Harry struggles unhappily with his. However, he never appears to match the other two. Hermione learned how to "Apparate" in Book Six, that is, transport herself in a flash from one place to another. And even though Harry was underage and not allowed to perform the feat he managed to do it. Yet Ron, although old enough, could not. And as bad as Harry was in their classroom experiments in magic, Ron was far worse.

When mysterious events occur, Ron is quick to come up with an explanation—nearly always the wrong one. Harry receives an anonymous gift, a Firebolt, the newest and finest broom to fly in Quidditch. Who sent it to him? "Dumbledore," says Ron, although the Headmaster would never have given a student such a valuable present. Then "I know...I know who it could've been—Lupin!" Harry has to remind Ron that Lupin couldn't even afford decent robes for himself. (III, 223-224) When a hospital patient is strangled by a lethal potted plant someone sent him as a "gift," it doesn't occur to Ron that the sender had murder in mind. He says, "Whoever sent it to the bloke...must be a real prat, why didn't they check what they were buying?" (V, 547) And in Book Four the Triwizard contestant, Viktor Krum, is found knocked out from a stunning spell after being with Mr. Crouch of the Ministry of Magic, who is nowhere to be seen. Naturally Ron comes up with a (wrong) hypothesis.

> **Ron:** "It must've been Crouch. That's why he was gone when Harry and Dumbledore got there. He'd done a runner."
> **Harry:** "I don't think so. He seemed really weak..."
> **Ron:** "Okay...How's this for a theory...Krum attacked Crouch—no, wait for it—and then Stunned himself!"
> **Hermione:** "And Mr. Crouch evaporated, did he?"
> **Ron:** "Oh yeah..." (IV, 564)

One would think that the law of averages would give Ron a shot at being correct a decent percentage of the time. On occasion he can provide details about the magic world that Harry and Hermione, both brought up by Muggles, are unaware of, but in most situations his answers only muddy the waters. Then when he does get it right, more often than not, his success is due to luck or serendipity. In Book One, face-to-face with a dangerous troll, he pulls out his wand and yells the first spell that comes into his head. To his utter astonishment, it floors the troll. Elsewhere, a word pronounced by Harry can trigger something helpful in Ron. In Book Six, Harry has tried unsuccessfully to get important information from Professor

Slughorn. When Hermione tells him to keep at it, Harry, pessimistic, answers bitterly, "Fifty-seventh time lucky, you think?" and Ron says,

> "Lucky...Harry, that's it—get lucky!"
> **Harry:** "What d'you mean?"
> **Ron:** "Use your lucky potion!" (VI, 471)

Thanks to the lucky mention of "lucky," Ron is able to steer Harry in the right direction. And earlier, in Book Two, when the trio are trying unsuccessfully to discover the entrance to the Chamber of Secrets, Harry's mention of "pipes" and "plumbing" makes Ron think of the girls' bathroom as a conduit (although Harry undoubtedly already figured that out).

Exceptionally, in the very first book, Ron has a scene in which he masterfully works out strategy, from start to finish, and even assigns roles to Harry and Hermione.

Trying to reach the Sorcerer's Stone, the three of them find themselves in a room with towering black and white chessmen, apparently made of stone but capable of coming to life. Harry is dumfounded and, for once, asks the others "Now what do we do?" As it happens, Ron's forte is playing magic chess, so he takes over completely. He answers Harry:

> "It's obvious, isn't it?...We've got to play our way across the room."
> **Hermione:** "How?"
> **Ron:** "I think we're going to have to be chessmen." (p. 281)

He tells Harry to take the place of a bishop and has Hermione replace a castle while he himself becomes a knight. He instructs them on all their moves, and when they get near the end, Ron lets himself be taken by the queen, leaving Harry free to checkmate the king, win the game and escape with Hermione. As Ron himself would say, "Brilliant."

And Ron has another brainstorm early in the next book. Harry and he are prevented from taking the Hogwarts Express to school for the start of their second year. Ron remembers his father's magic car, and it transports them, albeit with several mishaps, to school.

But these positive examples surprise us; they are atypical. For afterwards, in chapter after chapter, if we wish answers or decisions, we can mainly discount Ron's hapless ones and must turn instead to Harry and/or Hermione for more likely readings of situations. Sadly, Ron does appear to be a loser. That is, until the very last book, *The Deathly Hallows*.

Getting it Right, Eventually

When Adam-Troy Castro wrote his study, *The Unauthorized Harry Potter*, Rowling's final volume had not yet been published, but Castro suggested that it would show Ron finally coming into his own, even having his heroic moment. His supposition was correct, because that does happen in *The Deathly Hallows*.

Before that, Ron commonly deferred to Harry, asking "Where are we going now?" "What are we going to do?" And early in Book VII, he still takes a back seat: "You're the boss," he says, sounding "profoundly relieved." (p. 167) But he soon shows signs of a greater maturity. Even though Harry and Hermione continue to make most of the major decisions, as the *The Deathly Hallows* progresses, Ron Weasley himself makes progress.

For one thing, he no longer suggests off-the-wall theories but speaks sensibly, contributing cogent explanations. In fact, in Chapter Ten, he surprises us with an unaccustomed astuteness. He is the only one of his peers who can explain how the elf, Kreacher, escaped from a seemingly inescapable cave through "elf magic." (p. 195) Later, when he grills Mundungus Fletcher about the locket he stole from Sirius' house, Mundungus asks why: "Is it valuable?" Hermione says "You've still got it!" but Ron contradicts her. "No he hasn't," said Ron shrewdly. "He's wondering whether he should have asked more for it." (VII, 222) "Shrewdly" is hardly an adjective Rowling or her readers would have used to describe Ron's previous way of explaining things. Later, at one point, Hermione suggests that Xenophilius Lovegood made up the story of the Deathly Hallows in order to keep the three of them talking and listening until the Death Eaters arrived. But Ron disagrees, convincingly telling her:

"It's a damn sight harder making stuff up when you're under stress than you think. I found that out when the Snatchers caught me. It was much easier pretending to be Stan, because I knew a bit about him, than inventing a whole new person." (VII, 426)

Although it appears to have taken forever, mid-way into this final volume, Ron finally grows up. The main events that turn the tide and impel him from hapless boyhood to confident maturity are his retrieval of the Sword of Griffindor and his destruction of the Horcrux locket. To summarize briefly: Harry plunges into an icy pool to fish out the Sword of Gryffindor, and he nearly chokes because of the Horcrux locket squeezing his throat. Ron, who has just returned after his angry departure weeks before, rescues him. Here we find Ron totally in command of the situation. He grabs the sword and pulls the locket off Harry's neck. His first words to Harry are not those of an incompetent inferior but of someone in charge. "Are—you—*mental?*" he shouts*?*" "Why the *hell*...didn't you take [the Horcrux] off before you dived?" (VII, 371)

Ron's subsequent destruction of the Horcux locket is a crucial turning point in his evolution. Since it was he who retrieved the Sword of Griffindor, Harry insists that he use it to inactivate the locket. But Ron must struggle to manage the task, for the Horcrux works on his insecurities—telling him that Hermione naturally prefers a vastly superior Harry to him. Only after intense anguish, grappling with the locket in a trial of fire, does Ron finally inactivate the charm, falling to his knees, weak and shaking.

Ron's struggle with the Horcrux and his victory over it act as a sort of exorcism, ridding him, painfully, of his demons. From that moment on, he appears to come into his own. His insecurities and self-doubt disappear, or at least they no longer surface as issues. From that point to the end of the story, we find the young man thoroughly caught up in the action and acting just as maturely and effectively as Harry or Hermione.

Now, whenever a situation warrants it, he does not hesitate to take over. For the first time, he offers suggestions about where to go and how to proceed. Harry registers his friend's newfound assertiveness, musing that:

> Ron seemed to be taking charge. Perhaps because he was determined to make up for having walked out on them, perhaps because Harry's descent into listlessness galvanized his dormant leadership qualities. Ron was the one now encouraging and exhorting the other two into action. (p. 436-7)[1]

And Ron furnishes proof of an unexpected cleverness as well. The most striking example: how he inactivates another of Voldemort's Horcruxes, the Hufflepuff cup. He manages to enter the Chamber of Secrets the only possible way, by speaking Parseltongue, the language of snakes. How does he do that when he doesn't know Parseltongue? He vaguely remembers the sound Harry made in uttering Parseltongue words, and he fakes it with a strange, strangled hissing noise that finally works. Then he has Hermione destroy the cup with a basilisk fang. According to Hermione, "He was *amazing!* Amazing!" (p. 623) This is our classic underachiever, Ron, that Hermione is describing. And the young man maintains that high level to the end of the story.

And, as it turns out, Ron's telling Harry not to pronounce Voldemort's name is entirely justified, since Harry's insistence on using it provides the Death Eaters a way to track the three of them down. This young man may, at last, be taken seriously.

What's to Like?

Insecure, sarcastic, moody through most of the series, Ron may strike some readers as someone to be written off, with his theories that miss the mark, his hormonal angst, gripes, and self-hatred. Of course, Potterphiles his age, adolescents and pre-adolescents, may well understand him, identify closely with him and fancy him as a friend. Still, until the final part of the story, compared to Harry, he is bound to look more than a bit inadequate.

On the negative side of the ledger, Ron is beset by mishaps and catastrophes at every turn. He breaks his wand, patches it, then tries to use it on Malfoy and it backfires, hitting him in the stomach and toppling him over. Immediately he begins vomiting slugs, and they keep popping out of his mouth for what seems an eternity. He is bitten by Hagrid's baby dragon and by his own rat Scabbers, hurt when his father's magic car is attacked by the Whomping Willow, forced to deal with a giant spider, although he suffers from arachnophobia, is physically attacked twice by Sirius, gets "splinched," losing flesh in his upper arm, after he transforms himself into a Ministry of Magic employee and back to himself again, is hexed into a laughing fit by magic brains, is buried under rubble at Lovegood's house—the list is endless.

Of course it makes sense for Rowling to have Ron incapacitated, out of commission, when Harry must face Voldemort on his own. But most often that happens only at the very end of a book, whereas Ron is frequently hurt and out of commission at other times as well. One might point out that Harry and Hermione have their own ample share of physical damage and time spent in the school infirmary. However, Ron's casualties are legion, and his medical record far outstrips theirs. To put it mildly, the fellow is downright accident prone.

But a loser? No, not at all. First of all, there is something appealing about his weaknesses and his sporadic attempts to cope with them. His transparent ploys for attention can be amusing, even endearing. At one point in Book Six, Hermione is trying to convince Harry that he is in good shape, that he has become popular at Hogwarts and that the students now understand he was persecuted by Dolores Umbridge for sticking to his guns.

> **Hermione:** "You can still see the marks on your hand where that evil woman made you write with your own blood."
> **Ron (rolling up his sleeves):** "You can still see where those brains got hold of me in the Ministry, look."
> **Hermione (to Harry, ignoring Ron):** "And it doesn't hurt that you've grown a foot over the summer either."
> **Ron (inconsequentially):** "I'm tall." (VI, 219)

Adding to Ron's appeal is his humorous awkwardness and naiveté in his dealings with the opposite sex, his embarrassment when Ginny teases him about never having kissed a girl or his grudging attitude toward Hermione when he suffers his first pangs of jealousy. And there is also the fact that no one expects Ron to succeed at anything, so that when he does excel at Quidditch or become a Prefect, we, as readers, are not only surprised but gratified by his "Cinderfella" triumph.

In the final analysis Ron comes out a winner. Primarily because of two important qualities: his courage and his loyalty to his friends. And, with Ron, the two qualities are often intertwined.

The word "courage" here might surprise those who only know the story through the films, which often portray him as a wide-eyed and whining trembler in the face of danger.[2] But Ron is, indeed, courageous. And his bravery, unlike his decision making and leadership, does not evolve slowly, to emerge only at the end of the story. His mettle is tested from day one, and he rises dauntlessly to the challenge. Early in the first volume, taunted by Malfoy, he is ready to fight him immediately. Although that might be ascribed to a hurt ego and a short fuse, there are countless other cases when Ron risks his own safety for the sake of his friends. If ever he hears Hermione called "Mudblood" (an insulting label for a person descended from Muggles), he is on his feet, ready to attack. And he rises to heroic heights when needed by Harry or Hermione. Although it takes Harry a long while to force himself into the frigid pond to retrieve the Sword of Gryffindor, Ron unhesitatingly plunges in, fully clothed, to save his drowning friend. In the dangerous chess game of *The Sorcerer's Stone*, Ron doesn't think twice before sacrificing himself to the queen, so Harry can go on with his mission. And although spiders are the worst fear of his life, when Harry needs to deal with those creatures deep in the Forbidden Forest and asks Ron, "What d'you reckon? Should we go in or not?" he answers simply, "We've come this far." (II, 273)

Ron's heroism is a direct result of the fact that he is not one individual but part of a closely knit trio. The force of their bond endows him with a strength he undoubtedly would never have possessed on his own. In *The Prisoner of Azkaban*, the three friends are disarmed, without wands, and at one point it looks like Sirius is about to murder Harry. Ron, although in severe pain from a broken leg, tries to stand and shouts at Sirius: "If you want to kill Harry, you'll have to kill us too!" Sirius orders him to lie down, but Ron says, "Did you hear me? You'll have to kill all three of us." (III, 339) Note that Ron does not say, "You'll have to kill me too," but "all three of us." That, of course, would include Hermione.

Now Ron is in love with Hermione and could never stand to see any harm done to her. But his use of "all three" here is not just a ploy, a way of getting Sirius to spare Harry unless he wants to commit a triple murder. He rightly believes that the three of them are one, a solid union, their goals and loyalties identical and inseparable. They would walk through fire for each other—without wands—if necessary.

Harry's Friend

If Harry treasures Ron, it is not for his bravery, his ability to grow and take charge or any other fine and admirable quality he might develop. It's simply because Harry feels close to Ron and loves having him as his best friend. Moreover, with rare exceptions, it is clear that Ron is there for him, ready to help and looking out for his interests and peace of mind. Knowing that Harry is worried about the prophecy that threatens his future, Ron encourages him, saying,

> "[Dumbledore] wouldn't be giving you lessons if he thought you were a goner—wouldn't waste his time. He must think you've got a chance!" (VI, 98)

Later, when Harry's nose looks out of kilter (Draco Malfoy stamped on it after flooring Harry), Ron uses his best effort not to react: "It was a mark of their friendship that Ron didn't laugh." (VI, 169)

Equally important, if not more so, outside of the occasional foul mood or temporary rift, each can be totally, naturally, himself with the other. And Ron is fun to be with. In *The Goblet of Fire*, during the period when the two aren't speaking to each other, Hermione tries to reconcile them, telling Harry that he misses Ron. Here is how Rowling describes Harry's reaction:

> *"Miss him?'* said Harry, *'I don't miss him…"*
> But this was a downright lie. Harry liked Hermione very much, but she just wasn't the same as Ron. There was much less laughter and a lot more hanging around in the library when Hermione was your best friend. (IV, 316-7)

Even without that explanation, we are clear about Ron's being Harry's first choice as a friend when, in the same book, Harry is faced with the second task of the Triwizard Tournament. Dobby tells him at the last moment that he will be expected to find someone at the bottom of a lake and to rescue that person from the "merpeople." He refers to that someone as Harry's "Wheezy." It is Ron Weasley that Harry must pull out of the lake, because his assignment is to save "the thing that Harry Potter will miss most." (IV, 491) Whoever assigned that tournament task to Harry had to be fully aware that Ron was uniquely important to him.

Original, engaging Ron Weasley is the perfect third in Rowling's unforgettable threesome, counterbalancing the other two with his ever-present wry humor, his self-doubt and mood swings and his gratifying, albeit belated, development into maturity. Prized by Harry Potter, eventually loved by Hermione Granger, this young man, so unpromising at first glance, becomes, in the course of the story, greater than the sum of his parts.

---

[1] Prior to that, Ron's taking charge happened only rarely, as in Book Three when he took on responsibility for working on Buckbeak's appeal, knowing that Harry and Hermione were unable to do so (p. 300).

[2] The young actor, Rupert Grint, expertly conveys a fearful Ron in much of the film series.

4

TRIO DYNAMICS

———◆◆◆———

"Those friends thou hast, and their adoption tried,
Grapple them to your soul with hoops of steel."
—William Shakespeare

The Bonding

Judging from their personalities, three individuals could not be more different than Harry, Ron and Hermione. Yet they form a solid, unbreakable unit from age eleven throughout the seven years spanned in *Harry Potter*.

The two boys hit it off in no time, from the first chug of the train to Hogwarts Academy. Mutual insecurities help cement the bond. A sharing of confidences, a sharing of food, a similar antipathy for the bully, Malfoy, and they are well on their way to a permanent friendship.

And Hermione? It would be unrealistic if Harry and Ron accepted her immediately. For what would two eleven-year-old boys want to do with a bushy-haired, bossy, Miss Know-It-All? Pictured as someone to avoid like the plague, her acceptance must be gradual, logical and neatly maneuvered in stages by the author.

Here is how it happens. Ron says to Harry, à propos of Hermione, "It's no wonder no one can stand her…She's a nightmare, honestly." Harry tells Ron that Hermione has overheard him and is in tears. Ron's answer is "So?" (I, 172) But he looks a bit uncomfortable. Moments later they hear that she's crying inconsolably in the girls' bathroom. Ron looks "still more awkward at this" but in no time they have both put Hermione out of their minds.

This boys-will-be-boys attitude might have prevailed if Harry and Ron hadn't mistakenly locked Hermione up with a violent troll. As explained above,[1] they realize their mistake and save her by killing the troll but are discovered out of bounds by Professor McGonagall. Upon which, Hermione quickly invents and blandly recites a cock-and-bull story incriminating herself to get her two saviors off the hook. From that moment, Hermione is one of them. Rowling concludes the episode with an upbeat explanation:

> There are some things you can't share without ending up liking each other, and knocking out a ten-foot mountain troll is one of them. (p. 179)

Although that is a neat, even cute, ending, in keeping with the sprightly atmosphere of Book One, it does not explain the true groundwork Rowling has laid for cementing the friendship. That is, the apparently super-moral Hermione has astounded and impressed the boys by lying to protect them.

> Hermione was the last person to do anything against the rules, and here she was, pretending she had, to get them out of trouble. It was as if Snape had started handing out sweets. (p. 178)

In subsequent episodes Hermione provides many other examples of "uncharacteristic" behavior—sassing Professor Trelawney, slapping Malfoy, dissimulating and breaking a whole series of rules—behavior that solidifies and legitimizes her place in the trio.

Now a team, the three eleven-year-olds are primed to embark—from their first school year on to maturity—on a long series of adventures. Ordinary kids, they will have challenges to meet and mysteries to solve as they find themselves pitted against the dark forces of evil.

Interacting

Think of three allied nations, Britain, France and the United States, for example. They faced a common enemy in two world wars,[2] and if one of them were seriously threatened now, the other two would be outraged. Yet among the three, there occur disagreements, resentments and misunderstandings, at times with two of them ganging up against the third.

Similarly, throughout the seven years of their time together, Harry, Ron and Hermione undergo periods of conflict, complicity and shifting alliances. Of course, the three friends would do anything and everything for each other, but, as Rowling obviously knows, regular infighting is characteristic not only of nations but of ordinary teenagers as well.

If we think of the three friends as three sides of a triangle, H^P for Harry Potter, R^W for Ron Weasley and H^G for Hermione Granger, those shifting alliances form recurring patterns. Here is the most common one: Hermione and Ron are on the outs and, consequently, each maintains good relations only with Harry:

R^W☹H^G☹ →→ H^P☺ (the tenable relationships here are $R^W H^P$ and $H^G H^P$)

In *Harry Potter*, Ron and Hermione perpetually indulge in chronic bickering. Much of that has to do with the oil and water of their personalities. Righteous Hermione tends to speak judgmentally and often reads the riot act to Ron and Harry when they break important rules, endanger themselves or, to her mind, behave wrongly. But it is Ron who takes the bait, striking back with his customary sarcasm. Naturally, his needling infuriates Hermione, thereby creating a vicious circle.

Serious arguments between the two don't really occur until Book Three, *The Prisoner of Azkaban*, when they are both thirteen. Before that Hermione might express disapproval and Ron might enjoy teasing her, but from the third book on, they lock horns repeatedly. A major blow-up between them occurs in *The Prisoner of Azkaban*, when Hermione's cat, Crookshanks, keeps attacking Ron's feeble rat, Scabbers. In reality, those attacks are a set-up by the author who intends to show ultimately that Crookshanks has recognized Scabbers as a vile murderer in animal form. But meanwhile, the situation provides a constant source of quarreling between the two friends. And that is only one example; almost anything can—and does—ignite a fight where Ron and Hermione are concerned.

Resentment and ill will come to the fore where Ron's ego is involved. In *The Goblet of Fire*, infuriated when he sees Hermione pairing off with Victor Krum (rather than Ron himself) he camouflages his jealousy by shouting that Victor is an outsider competing against Harry in the tournament, so Hermione is *"fraternizing with the enemy!"* (IV, 421) And because of jealousy and a hurt ego, he later storms out on Harry and Hermione. Of course Hermione, too, is capable of resentment, and after attacking Ron physically when he returns she takes quite a while before deigning to speak civilly to him again. (Happily, that physical abuse did not compare with the attacking canaries she unleashed upon him in Book Six, when he fell into the clutches of a female classmate.)

Not all the battling is confined to Ron and Hermione, however, for Harry, much as he would like peace, is not above the fray and occasionally becomes part of the stormy equation. This happens notably in *The Goblet of Fire* when Ron's fragile ego makes him resentful of Harry. As noted above,[3] Ron is livid when Harry's name appears in the Goblet of Fire, making him a contender in the Tri-Wizard Tournament. Convinced that his best friend, eager for the spotlight, sneaked his name in without even telling him, he refuses to speak to Harry for a long time. Harry is furious with Ron for not believing he never volunteered as a candidate[4] and for his spiteful behavior. So each of them communicates only with Hermione.

R^W☹H^P☹ →→ H^G☺ (the tenable relationships being R^WH^G or H^PH^G)

Harry is hardly a passive victim; at times he acts up himself, venting his rage on the other two. This is certainly the case in *The Order of the Phoenix* when he rejoins his friends after a summer at the Dursleys and lets all his anger splash over them in a screaming tantrum. And in *The Deathly Hallows*, when he becomes suspicious and resentful of them. At this stage, the three have been together continuously and mired in an impasse, with no visible course of action, like seamen stuck in a stifling submarine. "Harry felt sure they were looking at each other behind his back, communicating silently." (VII, 215) And: "As the days stretched into weeks, Harry began to suspect that Ron and Hermione were having conversations without, and about, him." (p. 291) His suspicions were undoubtedly true. At that point, his friends were in agreement and criticizing him behind his back. To put it graphically,

(R^W☺H^G☺) ← → H^P☹ (Obviously, the tenable relationship here is R^{W}H^G)

Other patterns could be mentioned, for example, Harry blowing up at Hermione or Hermione getting upset with Ron and Harry— and they at her. But generally, where Harry and Hermione alone are concerned, a falling-out doesn't last long. For one thing, Harry is not in love with Hermione, nor she with him, whereas love does exacerbate problems between Ron and Hermione. Besides that, neither Harry nor Hermione harbors insecurities as deep as those that plague Ron, contributing to his leaving in a huff in *The Deathly Hallows*. So generally, Harry and Hemione can work together and get along without a host of messy emotional complications.

Interestingly, although it takes a bit of time for the trio's fights to blow over, what often brings peace is their mutual hostility toward an outsider (again, think of geopolitics). In one case, it is only after hearing that ambitious Percy has coldly walked out on his family that Harry finally recovers, forgets his resentment of his friends and engages with them. Later on, when Hermione is furious with Xenophilius Lovegood, the author comments, "The one good thing about her exasperation with Xenophilius was that it seemed to have made her forget that she was annoyed at Ron." (VII, 414)

As for Ron and Hermione, it would seem as though their scrapping would never stop unless some turn of events forced it to. In *The Prisoner of Azkaban*, they stopped fighting about Crookshanks as soon as they became aware of Harry's unhappiness in not being able to join them at Hogsmeade. Later in the book their arguing is forgotten in the light of Buckbeak's impending execution.

But at the height of an angry set-to, with absolutely nothing to diffuse anger, the only remedy is having the third of the trio intervene, if necessary using magic as a deterrent. During the first half of *The Deathly Hallows*, when Hermione and Harry have a shouting disagreement, Ron breaks their stand-off by telling Hermione to "drop it." (p. 235) Not long after that, Hermione prevents the two boys from attacking each other by magically erecting an invisible shield between them. And when Hermione, furious with Ron for having deserted them, starts covering him with physical blows, Harry uses his wand to create an invisible shield to separate the two of them. In such cases, a threesome has obvious advantages over a duo.

Love and Friendship

As Harry, Ron and Hermione approach their teens, falling in love can appear to pose a threat to their friendship. This is the case in Book Six, when Harry hears Ron and Hermione engaged in a quarrel that ends on a romantic note. Harry must have been aware, at least since *The Goblet of Fire*, that the two squabblers had more than a passing interest in each other. But now, at age sixteen, he registers the romance as a problem for him and a threat to the stability of the threesome.

In the midst of one of their fights a jealous Ron sneers that Hermione should hook up with McLaggen at Professor Slughorn's party. Hermione blurts out that she had intended to invite Ron himself to the party.

> "You were going to ask me?" asked Ron, in a completely different voice.
> "Yes," said Hermione angrily. But obviously if you'd rather I *hooked up with McLaggen...*"

There was a pause while Harry continued to pound the resilient pod with a trowel.

> "No, I wouldn't," said Ron, in a very quiet voice.

Harry missed the pod, hit the bowl, and shattered it.
(VI, 282)

At this point our only indication of a reaction on Harry's part is his pounding the pod and shattering the bowl. Then Rowling gives us a glimpse of his mind and heart.

> He had had an inkling that this might happen sooner or later. But he was not sure how he felt about it...what if Ron and Hermione started going out together, then split up? Could their friendship survive it? Harry remembered the few weeks when they had not been talking to each other in the third year; he had not enjoyed trying to bridge the distance between them. And then, what if they didn't split up? What if they became like Bill and Fleur, and it became excruciatingly embarrassing to be in their presence, so that he was shut out for good? (p. 283)

And it happens that the Ron-Hermione romance does cause some awkward moments as the story progresses. When Ron is wounded in the final book, there is such tenderness in Hermione's expression as she looks at him "that Harry felt almost as if he had surprised her in the act of kissing him." So he quickly asks her if she has the locket they need, "partly to remind her that he was there." (p. 275)

Harry's own strong feelings for Ginny also strike him as a potential threat: would Ron hate him for running after his sister? As it turns out, however, Harry's falling in love and the intimacy of Ron and Hermione provide only temporary stumbling blocks in the way of the trio's close connection. For one thing, to preserve the formula of a threesome on an adventure, Harry's love for Ginny is conveniently put on hold. Rowling has him break up with her, at least temporarily, in Book Six so that the trio's quest for the Horcruxes in the final book can proceed without romantic complications for Harry. And throughout that quest Ron and Hermione helpfully keep their own relationship non-sexual (or "off-camera") and limit sentimentality to a few fleeting moments.

As a result, the individual love lives of these friends have no great impact on their closeness and their mission. A far greater threat to them is the contentiousness described here, the moods, resentments, surly silences and outbursts of anger. At one moment in the story, Hermione pauses in the midst of one of Harry's verbal attacks to point out the great danger that loomed in their infighting: potential weakness and vulnerability in the face of the enemy. After all, didn't Dumbledore warn them that unity was their only defense against Voldemort? In Dumbledore's words,

> *"His gift for spreading discord and enmity is very great. We can fight it only by showing an equally strong bond of friendship and trust."* (V, 223)

But in the last analysis, that reminder can be seen as superfluous, for however often the three of them bicker, the bond between them remains too strong and too immutable to shatter. No matter what happens, no matter what they do to themselves and each other, these sometime squabblers are friends forever.

Each of the three places enormous value on friendship, but Harry's take on it is most evident to us, since, as always, Rowling makes us privy to his thoughts and reactions. Consider the scene in *The Deathly Hallows* when Harry sees a painting on the wall of Luna Lovegood's bedroom. Until that moment he knew she was an ally but had no idea of the depth of her feelings for him and his friends.

> Luna had decorated her bedroom ceiling with five beautifully painted faces: Harry, Ron, Hermione, Ginny, and Neville…What appeared to be fine golden chains wove around the pictures, linking them together…were actually one word, repeated a thousand times in golden ink: *"friends…friends…friends…"* (p. 417)

Taking all that in, Harry feels a great rush of affection for Luna.

Naturally, his feelings for Ron and Hermione run even deeper, although he finds it impossible to express them openly. When they tell him they have arranged everything so they can accompany him on his dangerous mission to find the Horcruxes, "he wanted to tell them what that meant to him, but he simply could not find the words important enough." (VII, 99) And every one of the seven books in the series ends with the three of them together, usually with Harry wondering when—or if—he will see them that summer. At the end of Book Five, when they see him off, along with Ron's family, Lupin, Tonks and Moody, they assure him they'll meet again soon, Harry just nods.

> He somehow could not find words to tell them what it meant to him, to see them all ranged there, on his side. Instead he smiled, raised a hand in farewell, turned around, and led the way out of the station to the sunlit street... (p. 870)

And the last line of Book Six:

> He felt his heart lift at the thought that there was still one last golden day of peace left to enjoy with Ron and Hermione. (p. 652)

And for Ron and Hermione, as for Harry, it is a friendship forged of iron and synonymous with love.

The Magic Number Three

Although Harry is indisputably the hero of the story, he is joined at the hip to his two friends, who accompany him from the first day of his adventure to the last. J. K. Rowling might have had Harry go it alone, like Ged in LeGuin's *Earthsea*, as a duo like the Hardy boys or as one member of a foursome like the children of *Narnia*. Or she might have had a slew of characters accompany him, as with Tolkien's Frodo. But her choice of a threesome is neat and effective.

For one thing, a threesome—so common in classic children's stories—is a very practical choice for working relationships. As with Harry, Ron and Hermione, a third member can serve as an escape hatch, someone to communicate with when two of the three are on the outs, someone to break an impasse when an agreement can't be reached, someone to swing a vote. More specifically, in the context of *Harry Potter*, the interplay of Rowling's three completely different personalities helps keep the plot alive and interesting.

Most important, in her conception of this triad, Rowling broke entirely new ground. For in no other adventure story for children or young adults to date do we find such a realistic portrayal of relationships between pre-teens or teenagers, one so true and convincing in its nuanced psychological complexities. Within the framework of the fantastic, three characters, maturing from age eleven to seventeen, interrelate in an authentic, completely natural way. The characters may be fictitious, a product of Rowling's imagination, but their interplay is real, a product of her understanding. And therein lies one of *Harry Potter's* most original qualities.

---

[1] See the first section of Chapter Two.

[2] Although the U.S. did not enter either until late in the game.

[3] See Chapter III, p. 47.

[4] In fact it was Barty Crouch, Jr., a Voldemort supporter, who secretly put Harry's name into the Goblet of Fire, in order to lead him into danger.

5

DUMBLEDORE

"A superior man is modest in his
speech but exceeds in his actions."
—Confucius

In *If Harry Potter Ran General Electric*, Tom Morris describes
Albus Dumbledore as "the embodiment of nobility, goodness,
prowess, wisdom, intelligence, and sound perspective."[1] He
considers the man an ideal role model, incorporating all the virtues
admired by Aristotle: rational moderation and self-restraint,
liberality, a capacity for acting on a grand scale, a sense of honor,
good temper, friendliness, truthfulness, wit and justice.

Other critics have likened Dumbledore to Tolkien's Gandalf,
friend of Bilbo Baggins and mentor to Frodo in the *Ring* cycle. For
Hogwart's Headmaster, like Gandalf, is portrayed as a mentor and
venerable figure with his sweeping silver hair, his flowing silver beard,
his half-moon spectacles and long, thin fingers.

Such comparisons are useful in giving us a sense of the man but
cannot convey his uniqueness. Because Albus Dumbledore, unlike
Gandalf and unlike the Aristotelian ideal, is a personality: complex,
contradictory and ambiguous. He is a great wizard, and at the same
time, a human being.

Oddly, when he first appears on the scene at the opening school
ceremony, he exhibits extremely bizarre, even clownish behavior.
Opening his arms wide and beaming at the new and returning
students, he blithely utters a bit of gibberish and sits down. Harry,
bewildered, asks Percy, "Is he—a bit mad?" And Percy answers, "He's

a genius!...But he is a bit mad, yes." Dumbledore ends the festivities by conducting students and teachers in the school "song" (an embarrassing attempt at verse) after instructing everyone to sing it to any tune that appeals to them. When they finally finish—each at a different time—visibly moved, he wipes tears from his eyes and says, "Ah music...A magic beyond all we do here! And now, bedtime. Off you trot!" (I, 127-8)

But except for wearing a floral paper hat from a snap cracker favor at Christmas dinner—and, later, choking on an earwax-flavored candy—his clownishness and ludicrousness evaporate, and he emerges as the Dumbledore we are most familiar with, Harry's wise and powerful advisor and protector. One might wonder whether Rowling intended the Headmaster's initial buffoonery to suit the more lighthearted ambience of Book One before having him develop into the grand old sage.

The Mentor

Only near the end of Book One does Dumbledore adopt the role of advisor to Harry, speaking seriously for the first time. Harry has been irresistibly drawn to the magic Mirror of Erised,[2] in which his dead parents appear to him, waving and smiling at him. The seemingly all-knowing Dumbledore, secretly aware of Harry's nightly visits to the mirror, shows up unexpectedly. He explains the dangers of such an obsession to Harry, cautioning him,

> "This mirror will give us neither knowledge [nor] truth. Men have wasted away before it, entranced by what they have seen, or been driven mad, not knowing if what it shows is real or even possible." (p. 213)

Clearly, the mirror, a vehicle of fantasy, is perilously counter-productive. It is the triumph of dream and obsession over life and action. And it is inimical to the knowledge and truth that Harry must search for. Dumbledore not only advises against using the mirror but takes measures to keep Harry out of temptation's way by hiding it elsewhere. Yet, surprisingly, the wise old Headmaster ends this solemn episode on a light note, with a bit of ironic drollery. When

Harry asks him what he himself sees when he looks in the mirror, Dumbledore answers, "I see myself holding a pair of thick, wool socks." Harry stares at him dumfounded, but Dumbledore continues,

> "One can never have enough socks...Another Christmas has come and gone and I didn't get a single pair. People will insist on giving me books." (I, 214)

Obviously Dumbledore would not trade gifts of books for socks, but his flippancy is a way of passing off an all-too-personal question asked by an eleven-year-old. Only in the last book of the series will Harry come up with a more likely answer: Dumbledore's dead sister.

Almost always Dumbledore has answers at his fingertips. But he tends to be slow, even recalcitrant, in releasing them to Harry. When eleven-year-old Harry asks Dumbledore for "things I want to know the truth about," his guru replies oracularly, "The truth...It is a beautiful and terrible thing, and should therefore be treated with great caution." If that seems designed to leave Harry out on a limb, the man inspires a certain trust by adding, "However, I shall answer your questions unless I have a very good reason not to, in which case I beg you'll forgive me. I shall not, of course, lie." (I, 298) Still, throughout the story Dumbledore provides precious few answers. Finally, at the end of Book Six, he apologizes to Harry for having kept him in the dark for years about the harsh realities looming before him. His explanation? He kept thinking the boy was too young to face such realities. Somehow, that justification doesn't seem to make up for Harry's pain and frustration in not knowing the truth.

Dumbledore, however sparing with facts, is liberal with his philosophical insights. We see this most often toward the end of a book, after Harry has had some horrific encounter with Voldemort and is sitting safely in Dumbledore's office, with the Headmaster offering explanations and words of wisdom.

Among the kindly lectures he dispenses to Harry, the importance of free will ranks high. Witness Dumbledore's oft-quoted comment, "It is our choices, Harry, that show what we truly are, far more than our abilities." According to Dumbledore, Harry was placed in

Gryffindor House not because of the Sorting Hat but because he himself chose not to be put in Slytherin. And throughout the series he will continue to offer variations on that same Sartrean theme: Harry is free to make his own choices.

During their one-on-one sessions, Dumbledore continually emphasizes the power of love. He explains that Harry's mother's love for him, her offer to sacrifice of her own life to spare him from Voldemort and, especially, Harry's own capacity to love, have saved him from death at Voldemort's hands. At one point the Headmaster's insistence on the protective power of love bores an unreceptive Harry. In Book Six, when Dumbledore tells him, "You have a power that Voldemort never had. You can—" Harry interrupts impatiently with: "I know! I can love!" And the author comments, "It was only with difficulty that he stopped himself adding, 'Big deal!'" (VI, 509) But Dumbledore, though aware of Harry's skepticism, reiterates the point and stresses it again in the course of the story.

Dumbledore's themes are varied and his comments on them often pithy. On tyranny: "Have you any idea how much tyrants fear the people they oppress?" (VI, 510) On death: "To the well-organized mind, death is but the next adventure." (I, 297) "You think the dead we love ever truly leave us?" (III, 427) "The true master of death...understands that there are far, far worse things in the living world than dying." (VII, 720) On friendship: "It takes a great deal of bravery to stand up to our enemies, but just as much to stand up to our friends." (I, 306) Dumbledore is not intended as a groundbreaking philosopher, but the precepts and maxims uttered by this seasoned old man, often quotable, are suited to his character, to the context of the story and appropriate to its readers.

Human Flaws

Dumbledore enjoys the reputation of being the greatest wizard alive, but, as Adam Troy-Castro has noted, he is neither all-knowing nor all-powerful. As Headmaster, he makes a whole series of mistakes, hiring unqualified faculty, putting Harry, Cedric and others in the path of mortal danger in the Triwizard Tournament and, worst of all for the whole magic community, wounding himself fatally by keeping and wearing the Resurrection Stone ring.

Moreover, despite Dumbledore's judicious manner and sage advice, his laissez-faire policy toward Harry and his friends might strike us as reckless and irresponsible. From start to finish, he not only allows the trio to break important school rules but at times actively abets them. He anonymously sends Harry his deceased father's Invisibility Cloak, fully aware that the boy will use it to leave the premises without permission, safely unseen by the authorities. Knowing that Hermione is in possession of a Time Turner that permits her to take several classes in the same period, he encourages her to use it to break a whole series of rules. He subtly suggests that she back up the clock three hours, so that she, Harry and Ron can rescue both Hagrid's pet hippogriff, "Buckbeak," and Sirius Black from dire punishments And generally, in a pinch, he covers up for Harry.

Obviously, Dumbledore is no model of perfection, consistency and good judgment.[3] He does not give evidence of due caution and moderation, He fails to rise above human frailties. In fact, he can be a prey to his emotions. Although he rarely shows anger, more than once he sheds tears when touched by Harry or by his own failings. On a far more negative note, he can become avidly obsessed at times: at one point he is drawn to the Invisibility Cloak. And even after he counsels Harry to put obsessions aside and forget the Mirror of Erised, he himself covets and holds onto the Resurrection Stone in order to resuscitate his dead family. But with Dumbledore, such weaknesses or lapses are temporary and his good judgment eventually prevails.

With all of his foibles and contradictory behavior, Albus Dumbledore's character is shrouded in ambiguity. Harry, from age fifteen on, constantly wants to know, "What is Dumbledore intending?" "Where is he?" "Why haven't I heard from him?" "Why doesn't he tell me what's going on?" "Doesn't he trust me?" "Care about me?" But no clear messages come his way. Finally, in the last book, Harry concludes that Dumbledore, ever the teacher, wouldn't like to hand him answers and solutions on a silver platter but prefers that he try his own strength, take risks and work things out for himself.

When Dumbledore does provide messages, his words often mystify rather than enlighten. For instance, he bequeathed Harry a tightly locked golden Snitch on which he inscribed the words, "I open at the close." Harry, completely puzzled, has no way of knowing what the oracular phrase means; the Snitch only opens near the end of the story (at the "close") when Harry, going off to duel with Voldemort, says, "I am about to die."[4] (VII, 698) Later, when Harry, unconscious after Voldemort's final attack, speaks with the dead Dumbledore, he asks, "Is this real? Or is this happening inside my head?" and Dumbledore replies paradoxically, "Of course it's happening inside your head, Harry, but why on earth should that mean that it is not real?" (p. 723)

His Shadowy Past

If Dumbledore's words and behavior are befogged by ambiguity and contradiction, the story of his youth, a source of conjecture and scandal, is veiled in the murkiest of mysteries. In *The Deathly Hallows*, the last volume of the series, Rita Skeeter hints darkly about a scandal in Dumbledore's youth; later, Dumbledore's brother Aberforth gives Harry a summary version of the story from his point of view. Finally, toward the end of the book Dumbledore himself tries to explain his past to Harry. The operative word is "tries," because even he cannot be sure of all the facts. Here is how he describes the major events of his early life:

Consumed with ambition, young Albus sought glory in the world, but after his mother's death, he was forced to stay at home to care for an incapacitated sister, Ariana. He resented it bitterly. Then Gellert Grindelwald entered his life. The boy enchanted him, enlisting him in his scheme to triumph over the Muggle world and make Muggles subservient to wizards. The two of them would reach that goal through the discovery and possession of the magic "Deathly Hallows" which would grant them not only omnipotence but immortality as well. They prepared to set off on their quest, when Albus's younger brother Aberforth interfered, fiercely opposing their plan. Their argument led to a fight, with Albus, Aberforth and Gellert Grindelwald dueling with wands. In the mêlée, his sister was killed. Dumbledore states merely: "And Ariana...after all my mother's care and caution...lay dead upon the floor." (VII, 717) Grindelwald fled.

That vague explanation leaves behind a trail of unanswered questions. For instance, how did Albus, a decent young man, become lured into Grindelwald's suspect plot despite his qualms? What were his feelings when battling his own brother? How did he react when Grindelwald ran off? And most vital, which of the three killed Ariana?

Bits and pieces of this early history of Albus Dumbledore surface in the course of the story. Although such isolated facts never add up to a complete, coherent chronicle, they provide us with some background vis-à-vis this important, formative period of his life. Here are the principal facts:

When Albus's sister Ariana was only six, three Muggle boys spied her performing magic in her back yard. As Aberforth told it,

> "She was a kid, she couldn't control it, no witch or wizard can at that age. What they saw scared them. They forced their way through the hedge, and when she couldn't show them the trick, they got a bit carried away trying to stop the little freak doing it...It destroyed her, what they did. She was never right again. She wouldn't use magic, but she couldn't get rid of it; it turned inward and drove her mad, it exploded out of her when she couldn't control it, and at times she was strange and dangerous. But mostly she was sweet and scared and harmless." (VII, 564)

"What they did" to Ariana is never spelled out, but it so incensed her father that he attacked the boys and, as a result, ended his life in Azkaban prison. The rest of the family had to keep the girl sequestered lest the wizarding authorities lock her up in the insane asylum. When she was fourteen, in one of her rages, Ariana accidentally killed her mother. Albus took care of her, insisting his younger brother finish school, and he managed to live with the situation, that is, until Grindelwald appeared on the scene. Clearly, when it comes to dysfunctional families, the Dumbledores outclass even the Dursleys.

As for Albus Dumbledore's short-lived and intense friendship with Grindelwald, it too is clouded in mystery, with much of the puzzle missing or hidden from view. To try understand it, let us begin with chronology based on Rowling's own information.[5]

Dumbledore was born in July or August of 1881 (making him around a hundred and ten at the start of the book). He met Grindelwald Gellert at age eighteen, just after graduating from Hogwarts in 1899. Later, in his fifties, he became transfiguration professor at Hogwarts. The year: 1938. That very same year, Dumbledore came in contact with Tom Riddle, the future Lord Voldemort. The timing here is significant. For by 1938, in world history, Adolph Hitler had come into power. Rowling has pointed to Voldemort's likeness to Hitler in his insistence on a pure-blooded race, his obsessive, cold-blooded ambition and tyranny.[6]

In the story, Grindelwald Gellert, like Voldemort, holds exactly the same belief in totalitarianism and a "master race" as Hitler in the thirties. For Grindelwald's ambition is to conquer the whole Muggle world in order to forge a race of pure-blooded wizards.

That Dumbledore himself could be attracted by such an idea would shock people years later, for the mature Dumbledore came to be known as a champion for justice and a fierce opponent of tyranny. One might explain his temporary adopting of Grindelwald's totalitarian beliefs as teenage political idealism, the common attraction of youth to the extreme right or left—to communism, fascism or fanatical jihad warfare. And if young Dumbledore felt any discomfort about the questionable aspects of his friend's policies, he could bury it in the high-minded belief that it was all for the "greater good." But Rowling herself shed light on the question, explaining that the eighteen-year-old Albus had simply come under the spell of his new friend, magnetized by the brilliance of his mind, and by love.[7]

In any case, the fascination, or passion, lasted only two months. Dumbledore would become aware of Grindelwald's emergence as a "dark wizard," a brutal despot and a serious danger to the world. In 1945 (the year World War II ended)[8] he fought and defeated Grindelwald, thus becoming, at age 64, "the greatest wizard of modern times." (I, 102-3) Eventually, during Harry's years at Hogwarts, rumors about Dumbledore's past would surface; they would fail to mar or undermine his greatness.

J. K. Rowling has maintained on several occasions that "Dumbledore is gay," and there is no reason to disbelieve her. For she created a backstory for each of her main characters as a frame of reference, and in profiling Dumbledore, she saw him as homosexual. However, readers of *Harry Potter* would have no visible proof of that orientation. For instance, outside of the Grindelwald episode, there is no indication of any close relationship with a person of his own sex.

Searching meticulously for clues, bloggers have come up with the fact that in his younger days Dumbledore was seen sporting a "flamboyantly cut suit of plum velvet." (VI, 263) Some have also noted that he enjoys knitting patterns (not that either example would prove the case). But on the latter score we can say more accurately that he only *claims* at one point—undoubtedly in jest—to enjoy the patterns. Here is the context. Dumbledore goes to the bathroom in Horace Slughorn's house and stays there a long time, to give Slughorn the chance to meet—and be impressed with—Harry. When Dumbledore finally emerges, Slughorn mentions his lengthy stay in the loo and asks if he has stomach problems. He answers,

> "No, I was reading the Muggles magazines…I do love knitting patterns. Well, Harry, I think it is time for us to leave." (VI, 73)

Obviously, Dumbledore's claim to like knitting patterns, far from serious, is merely one of his glib responses to questions he prefers to evade. It is in keeping with his flippant words to Harry, "wool socks," when the boy asks him what he would most want to see in the Mirror of Erised.

As for the Albus-Grindelwald relationship, in the course of the story, no one—not the author, not even the snidely vicious scandalmonger, Rita Skeeter in her *Life and Lies of Albus Dumbledore*—characterizes it as more than a very close friendship. In Dumbledore's case, by and large it would appear that he is gay in the mind of his creator but not in her fictional creation. That contradiction was more or less explained by Rowling in an interview of March 8, 2008, in which she stated that after Grindelwald, Dumbledore "became quite asexual. He led a celibate, bookish life."[9]

Rowling was undoubtedly wise to play it safe. Outing Dumbledore in the book could have risked befuddling very young *Harry Potter* fans and possibly offending some parents.

A Man Of Style

"I disagree with Dumbledore on many counts...but you cannot deny he's got style." (V, 623)

Thus speaks Phineas Nigellus, long dead but commenting from his portrait in the Headmaster's office. He has just witnessed Dumbledore's escape from disaster at the hands of Cornelius Fudge, Director of the Ministry of Magic. Nigellus is referring not to Dumbledore's victory, not *what* he achieved but *how* he achieved it. For Dumbledore impresses us, here as elsewhere, with his poise, his composure and unshakeable equanimity. Along with his generosity, intelligence and skill as a great wizard, such qualities make the man superior to those who would take him down.

In this instance, to protect Harry, Dumbledore claims to Fudge that it was he, not Harry, who organized the subversive "Dumbledore's Army." Harry protests, but Fudge is livid. As punishment, the Headmaster is to be sent to Azkaban prison—a ghastly fate. In this scene, Dumbledore, uniformly casual, even pleasant, could be simply discussing the day's events over a glass of wine. Fudge yells at him, "Then you *have* been plotting against me!" and Dumbledore answers calmly, cheerfully, "That's right." Then, when Fudge tells him he will be sent to Azkaban to await trial, he answers gently, even apologetically,

"Yes, I thought we might hit that little snag."

"Snag...?"

"Well—it's just that you seem to be laboring under the delusion that I am going to—what is the phrase? 'Come quietly.' I am afraid I am not going to come quietly at all, Cornelius. Consequently, I have absolutely no intention of being sent to Azkaban. I could break out, of course—but what a waste of time, and frankly, I can think of a whole host of things I would rather be doing."

And when Fudge asks him whether he imagines he can defend himself against all the Ministry officials there, Dumbledore, unflappable, replies with a smile, "Merlin's beard, no. Not unless you are foolish enough to force me to." And after a bit he disappears into thin air. (V, 618-22)

Dumbledore's composure is ever enhanced by wit and good manners. He displays both these qualities when, earlier in Book Five, Fudge changes the time and location of Harry's hearing at the Ministry so Dumbledore would be too late to support the boy. But Dumbledore arrives on time and finds the correct room. Fudge, surprised and rattled, says, "You—er—got our—er-message that the time and—er—place of the hearing had been changed then?" Dumbledore answers cheerfully, with wry tact,

> "I must have missed it. However, due to a lucky mistake I arrived at the Ministry three hours early, so no harm done."

And when Fudge, highly flustered, looks around for an extra chair, Dumbledore tells him not to worry. He casually gives his wand a flick, and a chintz armchair materializes next to Harry. Then Dumbledore sits down on it, puts his fingertips together and looks over them at Fudge "with an expression of polite interest." (V, 139)

In *The Half Blood Prince*, when Dumbledore makes a necessary visit to Harry's uncle and aunt, the Dursleys, behave boorishly, as expected, while the Headmaster himself maintains his unfailing sense of style. Standing at the threshold while Uncle Vernon glares at him in silence, he announces pleasantly,

"Judging by your look of stunned disbelief, Harry did *not* warn you that I was coming...However, let us assume that you have invited me warmly into your house. It is unwise to linger overlong on doorsteps in these troubled times."

At one point Vernon is clearly going to come out with something nasty and begins by grumbling, "I don't mean to be rude..." And Dumbledore finishes the sentence:

"—Yet sadly, accidental rudeness occurs alarmingly often. Best to say nothing at all, my dear man. Ah, and this must be Petunia."

Since neither Vernon nor Petunia invites him to sit down, he has his wand make their sofa zoom up to them, forcing them to plop down on it. He then conjures four glasses of oak-matured mead, which the Dursleys try to ignore although their two glasses keep nudging them. Harry suspects that Dumbledore is enjoying himself enormously. Vernon screams when the glasses literally attack them, and Dumbledore says politely, "Oh, I'm so sorry," as he makes the glasses vanish, "But it would have been better manners to drink it, you know." (VI, 45-51)

It might seem strange that such a powerful wizard, a threat even to the fearsome, tyrannical Lord Voldemort, should be concerned with manners. Or that he has such a propensity for wit— a quality one might find somewhat frivolous in a man larger than life. Yet these two things, manners and wit, contribute greatly to his superiority, raising him far above the level of his demeanors and adversaries. And possessing them gives him a handy *modus operandi*, a way of dealing with sell-outs like Fudge or oafs such as Vernon Dursley.

Those qualities never desert Dumbledore. Even at the end, when he knows he is cornered, wandless, about to meet his death, he greets one of his enemies calmly, as Rowling puts it, "as though welcoming him to a tea party," saying, "Good evening, Amycus... And you've brought Alecto too...Charming." Alecto gives an angry titter and jeers, "Think your little jokes'll help you on your deathbed

then?" Dumbledore answers, "Jokes? No no, these are manners."
(VI, 592-3)

There is no doubting it: the man has class.

* * *

Dumbledore's character, admirable though it may be, leaves one vital question unresolved: If he is as omniscient and omnipotent as he appears, why does he let, even encourage, Harry to get into so much danger on his own? Although he prompts Harry to search for Voldemort's perilous Horcruxes he provides him with only a few—opaque—clues. If he loves the boy, why not give him more help? The answer Harry comes up with (He wants me to find out by myself) does not explain the huge burden Dumbledore lets Harry carry and the traps he allows him to fall into throughout the series.

At the end of the story, Harry poses the question to Dumbledore. During a comatose or semi-conscious state, he speaks with the dead Headmaster and asks, "Why did you have to make it so difficult?" Dumbledore replies that he wanted to slow Harry down. He feared that Harry, in searching for the Horcruxes, might have become carried away—like himself—by a desire for the Deathly Hallows, reputed to grant immortality to their possessor. But in the light of all the sufferings Harry and his two friends had to endure, that is a lame excuse.

The real answer is quite simple. If Dumbledore had given Harry the answers up front or had helped him solve the problems facing him along the way, the plot would have no suspense. And suspenseful plotting, as we shall see, is a hugely important part of *Harry Potter* and a key to its success.

---

[1] P. 1.

[2] "Desire" spelled backwards.

[3] To Dumbledore's credit, he recognizes that he doesn't have all the answers, and he is not afraid to reveal his imperfections to others. Generally, such modesty can be dangerous, since people tend to rate others by their self-

image. But Dumbledore has enough confidence to admit mistakes, as he does in his comments on "The Tale of the Three Brothers:" "Even I, Albus Dumbledore, would find it easiest to refuse the Invisibility Cloak, which only goes to show that, clever as I am, I remain just as big a fool as anyone else." *Tales of Beedle the Bard*, p. 107.

[4] When the Snitch opens, Harry finds the Resurrection Stone inside. It enables him to have his dead parents with him for support before coming face to face with Voldemort. (VII, 698)

[5] See *hp-lexicon.org/timelines/timeline-dumbledore.html*

[6] *E.g.*, in an interview of July 18, 2000, *CBSNewsWorld: Hot Type*.

[7] Carnegie Hall interview, October, 19, 2007. Rowling amazed the audience by announcing that Dumbledore was gay, had been in love with Grindelwald and was "horrible, terribly let down by him."

[8] Rowling has said that it was no coincidence that Grindelwald was defeated in that historic year. Interview, July 16, 2005 in www.accio-quote.org/article/2005/0705-tic_mugglenet-anelli-3.htm.

[9] Interview published in an Edinburgh student newspaper. See www.the-leaky-cauldron.org/2008/3/8/new-j-k-rowling.

Part II

Plotting
The Course

6

THE SHAPE OF THE JOURNEY: FORM AND FORMULAS

"If you don't know the story before you begin
the story, what kind of a storyteller are you?"
—John Irving

Clearly, it pays to be well organized. Before starting to pour the stuff of *Harry Potter* into her literary cauldron, J. K. Rowling had her recipe in hand and her ingredients lined up before her. She had created past histories of the characters, structured her whole system of magic and carefully devised grids of the plots and sub-plots of every volume in the cycle.

Given *Harry Potter's* breadth and complexity, such preliminary work had great advantages. Armed with her notes and grids, knowing precisely where she was going, Rowling had in mind solutions to a plethora of mysteries, explanations of the characters' hidden motivations and, most importantly, the ultimate fate of Harry Potter.

That fate is played out over the course of seven volumes, each book corresponding to one school year, with Harry progressing from age eleven to seventeen. As in other *Bildungsromans*, Rowling's hero, young and uninitiated at the start, embarks on a voyage of discovery and self-discovery, ending up more mature and enlightened by his experience.

Harry's journey does not follow a simple, linear path or curve. Instead, as Rowling charted it, it resembles the jagged vertical waves of an arrhythmic electrocardiogram. For in each chapter Harry has his ups and downs, a perpetual see-sawing between tension and relief. Any period of rest and recovery lasts but a moment, for something immediately interrupts it: a mystery, conflict, or unexpected occurrence. Nearly every page of any individual book contains some attention grabber that affects Harry and engages readers, drawing them along in the relentless tide of events.

To take just one illustration, this is what happens in only eight pages of Book One, *The Sorcerer's Stone*. When Harry, Ron and Hermione try sneaking out after hours on a highly dangerous mission, they encounter obstacle after obstacle.

> **1.** Their friend Neville tries to stop them and Hermione petrifies him with her wand. **2.** Although they are wearing Harry's invisibility cloak, an enemy, Peeves, suspects their presence. Harry comes up with a ruse that lets them continue their secret mission. **3.** They encounter a vicious three-headed dog but manage to neutralize him by playing music. **4.** They go through a trap door and fall to a lower level where they are immediately attacked by the Devil's Snare, a plant that attempts to bind them with its tendrils. **5.** Hermione remembers a charm that nullifies the plant's power. **6.** They come to a chamber filled with what looks like flying birds but are really keys. They must capture the one that will open a locked door. **7.** Using his skill as a Quidditch Seeker,[1] Harry nabs the right one. **8.** Their way is obstructed by a set of dangerous chessmen.

Such an accumulation of barricades and breakthroughs is typical of almost any of Harry's adventures. Yet all the ups and downs and the turbulent cascade of events eventually lead somewhere. Each of the seven books ends with a kind of resolution, with a number of perplexing questions answered. Then finally, in Book Seven, Rowling provides us with the grand resolution, the final explanations of mysteries as yet unsolved and with the loose ends tied up at last. So Harry's story, though convoluted, is not haphazard, since Rowling knows where he is going and how he will get there.

But in order to keep readers accompanying him on his journey, Rowling, consciously or not, resorted to some tried-and-true formulas guaranteed to hold their interest.

A Familiar Recipe

In *Harry Potter*, readers will recognize many devices exploited by writers of detective stories and crime novels. To name a few: a protagonist is strongly motivated to search for clues; obstacles impede the search; clues wind up as red herrings; a good person sneaks into a dangerous place looking for clues and is trapped by the enemy; suspense; the chase; a seemingly decent character is really a foe, or vice versa; the protagonist is suspected of being guilty of a crime; shocks and surprises are common currency; danger looms everywhere.

Consciously or not, in targeting young readers, J. K. Rowling incorporated all the techniques used by Agatha Christie, Raymond Chandler and commonly found in television mysteries today. Of course, other adventure stories geared to children and young adults— the *Nancy Drew* series, for instance—have used such techniques. But Rowling, gearing her work to a modern audience, filled her story with fireworks. Readers are frequently bombarded with a fast-paced volley of shock effects such as those found in Thomas Harris' *Silence of the Lambs* or Tom Brown's *Da Vinci Code*.

As in such novels, the greatest shocks often occur at the end of chapters. To take *The Prisoner of Azkaban* as one illustration, at the end of Chapter Seventeen Ron, defending his pet rat from suspicious accusations, says protectively,

> "What's my rat got to do with it?"
>
> "That's not a rat," croaked Sirius Black suddenly.
>
> "What do you mean—of course he's a rat."
>
> "No he's not," said Lupin quietly. "He's a wizard."
>
> "An Animagus,"[2] said Black. "By the name of Peter Pettigrew." (p. 348)

As Chapter Eighteen closes, just when a big mystery is solved and tension and conflict give way to calm and understanding, peace suddenly shatters in the closing lines of the chapter. Harry, speaking with Sirius, asks,

> "So that's why Snape doesn't like you..."
> "That's right," sneered a cold voice from the wall behind Lupin.
> Severus Snape was pulling off the Invisibility Cloak, his wand pointed directly at Lupin. (p. 357)

A chapter of *The Deathly Hallows* ends with these words:

> And then he saw the door of number twelve, Grimmauld Place, with its serpent door knocker, but before he could draw breath, there was a scream and a flash of purple light; Hermione's hand was suddenly upon his and everything went dark again. (p. 267)

Although, as we have seen, the pages of the plot have more than enough to hold the reader, such end-of-chapter zappings are guaranteed page-turners.

As for danger, there is no dearth of it in *Harry Potter*. In fact, dangers surround Harry like fruit flies on a tomato. To begin with, Hogwarts is not a school you would want to send your kids to without an armed guard. Consider the Forbidden Forest, where students are not allowed to go but where Harry and his friends inevitably venture. It holds the scariest of creatures, such as the giant spider, Aragog, who would have Harry and his friends on his children's dinner menu. Or the human-hating centaur, Magorian. Luckily, Harry gets saved from their clutches by more kindly "creatures" like the centaur Firenze or Mr. Weasley's flying car. And there are human threats aplenty, such as Voldemort's Death Eaters or despicable Professor Umbridge, who tortures Harry mentally and physically.

Still any good detective or crime story needs one truly formidable antagonist, someone over whom the protagonist must triumph one way or another. These days, the more monstrous the villain, the better. As monsters go, it would be hard to match terrifying Hannibal Lechter in *The Silence of the Lambs*, a fiend who dines on humans, or, in the same novel, Jame Gumb, who skins women to make a vest for himself. But Rowling's villain, Voldemort, measures up on a grand scale.

Villain, Hero and *Deus ex Machina*

The epitome of cruelty, Voldemort commits murder at the drop of a hat or commands his venomous snake Nagini to do the killing. He has a horde of followers, the Death Eaters, ready to carry out his evil bidding, for they all bear a black insignia on the skin of one arm, linking them to their master. But he is so frightening and awesome they dare not mention him by name but refer to him as "the Dark Lord," while others use expressions like "You-Know-Who" or "He-Who-Must-Not-Be-Named."

Unfortunately for Harry, Voldemort's top priority is to murder him. Over a decade earlier, a prophecy led the tyrant to believe Harry was the only person with the power to vanquish him. But when Voldemort tried to kill the child, Lily Potter gave her son the magic protection of her love, and he survived. Although Voldemort murdered Lily and James Potter, because of Lily's love, he failed to kill Harry. Instead, when he aimed the death curse against the boy, it rebounded against himself, and he lost almost all of his human form, becoming a tiny, shapeless monstrosity. For thirteen years he stayed in hiding, while his followers attempted to whitewash or deny their previous connection with him.

As the story begins, Voldemort has started to make a comeback. By the end of Book Four he has regained a vaguely human form: thin, "whiter than a skull, with wide, livid scarlet eyes and a nose [as] flat as a snake's with slits for nostrils." (p. 643) Looking a bit more human, however, does nothing to humanize Voldemort. As villains go, he can still match or top the vilest of them.

Who will rid the world of Voldemort and his tyranny? Harry, naturally. Our young hero comes to realize that the dangerous job has landed on his shoulders; he is the "Chosen One," marked by

Voldemort and famous for having survived his attack. And it is eminently clear that he himself is targeted as a victim—the first order of business on Voldemort's evil agenda. So throughout the cycle, Harry must try to cope with the pain and anguish of his foe's sadistic persecution, running great risks and enduring those periods when the villain infiltrates into his mind and takes over. But worst of all, he must try to escape annihilation when Voldemort confronts him face to face, in surprise appearances, prepared to annihilate Harry with the death curse, *Avada Kedavra!*

Those Voldemort-Harry face-offs occur in the *dénouement* of every book except Volumes Three, *The Prisoner of Azkaban*, and Six, *The Half Blood Prince*. At the end of Book One, *The Sorcerer's Stone*, Voldemort, still formless, threatens Harry from the back of Professor Quirrell's head. In the next-to-last chapter of Book Two, The *Chamber of Secrets*, he lures Harry into his clutches in the guise of his young self, Tom Riddle. As Book Four, *The Goblet of Fire*, nears its end, having regained a physical form, he traps Harry on his own home ground, has his blood drawn, inflicts the agonizing Cruciatus curse on him and nearly succeeds in finishing him off in a duel. At the close of Book Five, *The Order of the Phoenix*, he once again invents a ruse to draw Harry into mortal danger and this time uses the killing curse on him. (Of course, Harry escapes each time or the volumes in the cycle would not reach the magic number of seven.)

Finally, as the last book, *The Deathly Hallows*, closes, we come to the grand confrontation. After a long fight between the students of Hogwarts and Voldemort's odious allies, Harry walks with heavy heart to meet Voldemort and an almost certain death. Miraculously he gets away and even winds up triumphant. Of course, he had to survive at the end. Although Rowling killed off some important and likable—even lovable—characters, she clearly wouldn't do that to Harry. She has explained in interviews that she spared him so he could continue fighting for justice. One would also think that she cared too much for him to let him die. But had she made a casualty of him, imagine the outcry from Harry Potter fans!

Now in every instance that Harry is trapped by Voldemort, the cards are stacked against him. He is alone,[4] helpless, in a snare, and there appears to be no means of escape. That must have presented a challenge to his creator. After all, Rowling got him into such troubles in the first place. So how could she best get him out? In less dire situations a friend might come to the rescue. But Harry's friends would never have the power to save him in his battles with Voldemort; in fact, they would just be in the way.

So occasionally, when all seems lost, Rowling makes use of that time-honored device, the *deus ex machina*, a technique at least as old as ancient Greek theater: a God suddenly appears at the very last moment, descending to the stage mechanically on a big crane and saves the hero from a dire fate.[5]

In *Harry Potter*, the obvious candidate for the great eleventh hour savior is, of course, Dumbledore. The great wizard does come to Harry's aid in *The Prisoner of Azkaban* and saves him from Barty Crouch Junior in *The Goblet of Fire*. But the only time he intervenes in a face-off between Harry and Voldemort is in the last pages of *The Order of the Phoenix*. No sooner does Voldemort reach Harry, when Dumbledore appears by magic in the Department of Mysteries atrium to take the villain on himself. The one other occasion on which Dumbledore makes a personal appearance in a Harry-Voldemort encounter is in Book Two, *The Chamber of Secrets*. But there he only arrives after Harry has already done the major work of fighting off his nemesis (with the help, admittedly, of Dumbledore's phoenix).

Rowling knows better than to give Dumbledore the role of *deus ex machina* more frequently. Too competent to resort to exploiting a trick that would become repetitive and boring, she offers other solutions to Harry's encounters with Voldemort. For example, on occasion, when he is completely on his own, no allies present, trapped with no means of escape, his dead mother or father gives him encouragement or advice.

Such is the case in the climax of Book Four, *The Goblet of Fire*, where an injured Harry is drawn unwittingly into Voldemort's net, gagged and bound from neck to feet to a tombstone, while his companion, Cedric, lies dead on the ground, killed on Voldemort's orders. Harry is forced to witness terrible scenes: the treacherous lowlife, Pettigrew, is obliged by Voldemort to cut his own hand off. After some of Harry's blood is drawn and emptied into a huge cauldron, a shapeless Voldemort gets lowered into the receptacle where he is transformed into a quasi-human with a snake-like face. Then a crowd of his Death Eaters arrive at his command.

At that point both Harry and the reader yearn for some help to arrive, something on the order of that handy figure, the *deus ex machina*. "*Let the police come...anyone...anything...*" (IV, 648) But this time, no one arrives. Instead, Rowling has him saved by a strange phenomenon: in dueling with his enemy, his wand neutralizes Voldemort's and conjures up the shades of the fiend's murder victims. They include Harry's father, who tells the boy to run for it.

After that episode, Harry has outside help only once in dealing with Voldemort.[5]

And in every encounter with him he shows courage and astuteness. By the end of the story, Harry, whether he realizes it or not, has become powerful and capable enough to go it alone and to take on his archenemy by himself.

Harry Against the Dementors

Harry's ability to grow and strengthen through the course of the story, to contend with foes with no outside help, is dramatically apparent in his encounters with the dementors, creatures that suck all hope out of a person's soul. The fact that Harry fears them more than anything, even more than he does Voldemort, is a good thing, according to Professor Lupin, since it shows that what he fears most of all is not his foe but fear itself.[6] At the start of the story, when Harry is only thirteen, he is not yet capable of battling the monsters. Attacked by them while high in the air in a Quidditch match, he has no way of defending himself, and he falls to earth. Dumbledore, a spectator at the game, magically deflects Harry's fall so he is not severely wounded.

But Harry does not want to depend on others; he needs to be able to fend off such horrors as dementors on his own. So at his request, Professor Lupin shows him how to conjure up a "Patronus," a protective charm that takes the form of an animal. He must concentrate on his happiest thought, then, raising his wand, cry out "Expecto Patronum!" and his Patronus will materialize to shield him. Throughout the cycle Harry becomes increasingly effective in calling up his personal Patronus which, like his father's, materializes as a silver stag. Harry's subsequent experiences with the dementors never become easy, but at least he has learned to cope with them by himself.

* * *

Harry's journey from youth to maturity, from inexperience to understanding, from dependence on others to self-sufficiency and capability takes a timeworn literary path, in the tradition of Dickens' *David Copperfield* or Horatio Alger's *Ragged Dick*. Yet Rowling makes the story of that journey completely original, not only by setting the plot of her *Bildungsroman* in a magic world but by applying to it techniques of other well-worn genres—notably the detective or mystery story.

As the next chapter will illustrate, in *Harry Potter* she demonstrates her command of a good crime writer's best asset in building suspense: a sense of timing.

----

[1] See Chapter I, note #7.

[2] Meaning he can transform himself into an animal.

[3] Even in *The Order of the Phoenix*, although a number of friends accompanied him to the Ministry of Magic, he encounters Voldemort, without them in the nearby atrium.

[4] Bertolt Brecht used the device humorously in *The Threepenny Opera*, having a god-like messenger arrive at the last moment to announce that Mack the Knife, condemned to execution, has been pardoned by the Queen.

[5] In the previously cited episode where Dumbledore saves the day in the Department of Mysteries.

[6] III, 155. "All we have to fear is fear itself," a phrase used by Franklin D. Roosevelt in the Second World War.

7

A TIME FOR EVERYTHING

———•◆•———

"There are very few human beings who receive
the truth, complete and staggering, by instant
illumination. Most of them acquire it fragment by
fragment...by successive developments, cellularly,
like a laborious mosaic."

—Anaïs Nin

Any self-respecting crime novelist knows enough to keep characters and readers in the dark—to reveal information only sparingly, drop by drop, much as a gardener enriches a flower bed with time-release fertilizer. Rather than hit upon satisfactory answers early in the game, a protagonist will meet obstacle after obstacle, taking the wrong paths, chasing red herrings and seldom correct about which of the suspects to suspect. Enlightenment filters in gradually, in bits and pieces. Only toward the end will the hero or heroine be able to connect all the dots and finally arrive at the truth.

In *Harry Potter*, Rowling incorporated the crime novel's time-release device smoothly and adroitly. Unsolved mysteries appear from the start of the cycle and surround Harry like scattered segments of a cardboard puzzle. Even before his entry into Hogwarts Academy, a break-in occurs at Gringott's Bank, a place so secure that illegal entry seemed impossible. Who could have done it? And at school, more mysteries arise: Who sent Harry his father's Invisibility Cloak? Why does Snape hate him? Who is trying to steal the

Sorcerer's Stone? Every book of the cycle contains a whole series of baffling questions. Taking Book Six at random, here are only a few of them: Who is the Half Blood Prince? What happened to Dumbledore's hand? Who gave Katie Bell the package with the cursed necklace? For whom was it really intended? Where does Dumbledore go during his absences? The list goes on.

One of the greatest of unsolved mysteries is Hogwarts Professor Snape. He hated Harry's father and obviously despises Harry; he has great disdain for Muggles; he was a long-time follower of vicious Voldemort and currently appears to be spying for him. Yet Dumbledore, who is hardly a fool, trusts the man completely. Is Snape loyal to Dumbledore? To Voldemort? A double agent, and, if so, for which side? When he actually kills Dumbledore at the end of Book Six and runs over to Voldemort, there is no question about his loyalties...or is there?

Things Are Seldom What They Seem

Of course, solutions to such mysteries must stay out of reach until the timing is exactly right. Meanwhile, Rowling further muddies the waters with the classic technique of having innocent characters act suspiciously and portraying guilty ones as very convincing allies.

So Harry, Ron and Hermione continually come up with wrong answers and make false assumptions. In Book One, when Harry's broom goes out of control in a Quidditch game, Hermione is convinced that Snape is uttering a curse to make him fall off. It turns out only later that it is innocuous appearing Quirrell—actually Voldemort's servant—who jinxed Harry's broom, and that Snape had been mouthing words of a charm to keep Harry from falling. In Book Two, Harry suspects Malfoy of wounding him in Quidditch, when the culprit is really the well-meaning elf, Dobby, And through almost all of Book Three, everyone, including Harry, considers Sirius a traitor, a criminal and a constant threat. Naturally, he turns out to be the exact opposite: a faithful ally (and, incidentally, Harry's godfather).

Even Harry's close friends can surprise us by seeming the opposite of what they really are. We learn early on that kindly Hagrid was expelled from Hogwarts for allegedly causing the death of a female student in the Chamber of Secrets. Then later he is found to be completely innocent of the crime. On the other hand, in Book Two, the person who opened the door to the Chamber of Secrets, causing mayhem and putting Harry, Ginny and others in mortal peril, turns out to be sweet Ginny herself (who did it under the spell of Voldemort's diary, written in his youth).

Besides such examples, there are so many characters who give the impression that they could be either enemies or allies that a reader might well wonder, "What about the Ministry's Mr. Crouch—friend or foe? What about Bulgarian Viktor Krum and his suspicious mentor Karkaroff? Or Dumbledore's surly brother Aberforth? Or ambitious Percy Weasley? With ambiguities sending up smoke screens everywhere, small wonder that Harry and his crew so often wind up completely off the mark.

Clues are supposed to help, and there is no dearth of them, for Rowling scatters them abundantly throughout every book. Harry, Ron and Hermione eagerly follow them, but all too often they prove to be red herrings, leading the trio astray. One example: in Book Two, convinced that Draco Malfoy is the culprit who opened the Chamber of Secrets, they take great pains to spy on him, manage to infiltrate into his territory and discover…exactly nothing.

Far worse than that, following false clues can lead to sheer calamity. In *The Order of the Phoenix*, Harry, who, through his mental connection with Voldemort, visualizes Sirius being tortured in the Department of Mysteries, and he immediately rushes there with his friends. But after undergoing danger after danger, they wind up in a trap, caught and surrounded by Death Eaters. Harry's vision was actually "planted" by Voldemort, who knew all along it would motivate Harry to save his godfather and would deliver the boy into his clutches. Disastrously, Sirius—who was not undergoing torture at all—comes to rescue Harry from Voldemort and is killed.

But even the most unlikely clues have their use. They often point the way to discoveries that propel the story onwards. As in crime novels, in *Harry Potter*, following up on one clue may appear futile, but it may well lead to another one that provides a bit more knowledge, and yet another, until everything begins to add up. Here is an illustration from Book Two of such cumulative, time-release clues that will eventually provide answers:

1. Hagrid, suspected of attacking students in the Chamber of Secrets, is about to be imprisoned. Before they take him away he tells Harry to "follow the spiders."

2. Harry and Ron see spiders creeping toward the Forbidden Forest and follow their trail.

3. They wind up faced by the giant spider, Aragog, who nearly has them killed. But the spider also reveals that Hagrid is innocent of the charges against him.

4. They visit Hermione, who is out cold in the school infirmary, and find, clutched in her hand, a paper on which she has written, "Pipes."

5. That clue leads them to the bathroom inhabited by the ghost, Moaning Myrtle.

6. Myrtle reveals how the toilet pipes can take them to the Chamber of Secrets. They follow the prescribed route.

So here the trail does lead somewhere. Even when Harry's attempt to follow up on a clue or a hunch seems completely counter-productive, a wild goose chase, it can provide useful information, clarifying a piece of the mystery and serving as a guide for future action. In Book Seven, for instance, Harry regretted making the trip to Godric's Hollow with Ron and Hermione, because they were found and attacked by Voldemort there. But their trip to the Godric's Hollow cemetery provided them with important background about the Deathly Hallows. And in the same book, Hermione was sorry she convinced Harry and Ron to visit Xenophilius Lovegood's home, for there they were drawn into a trap there and attacked. However, it was at Lovegood's that they learned the key story of the three brothers who possessed the Deathly Hallows.

As Leibniz held in his *Theodicy*, we mortals get only a tiny glimpse of what is going on, while God sees the whole picture. In *Harry Potter*, the protagonist and his friends can't be expected to know where the road is leading, but, happily for the reader, their omniscient maker, Rowling, has their fate all mapped out.

Unraveling the Mysteries

Until Dumbledore's death, there is a scene near the end of every volume where Harry is sitting in the Headmaster's office listening to his explanations.[1] In those sessions Dumbledore occasionally sheds light on some of the mysteries. But generally, these end-of-the-year meetings are not designed to tie up the loose ends. They give Dumbledore the opportunity to offer Harry moral comfort, to discuss what is bothering the boy, to explain the ways in which love protects him, to compliment him on his bravery. These are primarily soothing or bolstering moments, a salve or tonic for Harry after he has undergone traumatic experiences.

Mysteries do get cleared up during each book but the bulk of them not by Dumbledore. Friends and allies sometimes provide bits and pieces of the puzzle. However, the most informative person, the one with the answers, is most often the villain himself. At the end of Book One, Voldemort's agent, Quirrell, informs Harry that it was he who broke into Gringotts Bank and that it was he, not Snape, who tried to curse him off his broom at Quidditch. Then Voldemort himself describes to Harry how he has kept himself alive, waiting to get his hands on the Sorcerer's Stone with which he can make the elixir of life and regain his human form. Just before Book Two comes to a close, young Voldemort, Tom Riddle, reveals how he framed Hagrid and caused his expulsion from Hogwarts, and he tells of his strategy in getting Ginny to open the Chamber of Secrets. As Book Four ends, the traitor, Barty Crouch Jr., under the influence of a truth serum, explains all the evil he wreaked throughout the year.

Although at the end of Book Two, young Voldemort asks Harry questions and tells him that the longer he talks, the longer he stays alive, in actuality, it is Voldemort himself who prefers to do the talking². And so much the better, since what he has to say about his past, his motives, his plans and actions is most enlightening. Throughout ten whole pages near the end of *The Goblet of Fire*, voluble Voldemort delivers a long monologue to the Death Eaters, explaining his fall and rise and his *modus operandi*. It is far from boring; we hang on his every word.

But Rowling does not depend overly on end-of-the book explanations from Voldemort or anyone else to solve mysteries. For her releasing of information must continue to be a gradual, cumulative process. In every volume characters embark on a follow-the-spiders type of quest. The nuts and bolts of the story—the questions, the clues, obstacles and breakthroughs—turn up partial answers, answers that come from a variety of sources, to be amplified and fully explained later, when the time is ripe.

A prime example of Rowling's calibrated, gradual release of information is the Pensieve, the stone urn containing memories of the Headmaster. In *The Goblet of Fire*, Harry immerses himself in it and witnesses a trial of Death Eaters. In later books he will discover other scenes from the past. With the Pensieve, Rowling has modified the standard flash-back technique, filling the reader in by way of Harry Potter's real-time experience, as he submerges himself in other people's memories.

The scenes Harry witnesses in the Pensieve may appear to be isolated, disconnected episodes, but they gradually add up to a larger picture. Harry first sees Voldemort as his younger self, Tom Riddle, before he starts at Hogwarts. Then a later look at the Pensieve reveals a somewhat older Riddle, a self-assured, ambitious young man. Importantly, he will view Snape as a young man and be privy to the dynamics between him, Lily Potter, James Potter and James' friends. Such fragmented memories, parts of the puzzle that must ultimately be pieced together, are slow in revealing final answers but eventually do so.

That is certainly true of Professor Slughorn's memory of his conversation with his student, young Voldemort. Dumbledore shows Harry that memory in his Pensieve, but an important piece of it is missing, since Professor Slughorn withheld it out of shame. (That is, the part in which Riddle asks Slughorn if it is possible to split his soul into seven pieces and hide the pieces in Horcruxes.)[3] Harry knows that Dumbledore wants him to retrieve the piece of memory from Slughorn, but he must expend a lot of time and effort to get the professor to hand it over to him. Only with great persistence, patience and a good dose of luck does he obtain the missing segment of the memory.

If Harry had not been forced to spend time trying to get the missing part of the memory, if he had had that information up front, there would, of course, have been no suspense and far less interest in the story. So the quest had to be stalled temporarily. Good things come to those who wait. And for purposes of the narrative, the wait is all to the good.

Although sometimes the wait for time-release answers lasts only a few chapters or until the next volume, in some cases nothing is clarified until the seventh and last book. That holds true for Snape and the question, "which side is he on?" At times, he appears to do Dumbledore's bidding. At others, he feeds information to Voldemort. Of course he is so detestable—the character you love to hate—that one naturally has the feeling he just couldn't be on the right side of things, that he has somehow deluded Dumbledore, a man too kind and/or naive to mistrust anyone. How could Snape be decent when he clearly detests and cruelly harasses Harry? When he actually kills the Headmaster in Book Six and runs off to Voldemort's camp, a reader can no longer doubt that vile man's guilt.

Only in the last pages of the final book, when Harry immerses himself in Snape's memory through the Pensieve, do we discover the truth. Only then is it clear that his murder of Dumbledore was forced on him by Dumbledore himself. That when Snape points his wand at him a the end of Book Six and the Headmaster pleads, "Severus...please..." he is not begging Snape to spare him but to kill him.

In *Harry Potter,* Rowling does not use time release by rote. As with her incorporation of other crime story devices, a reader does not have the sense she is tritely repeating gimmicks or following a set pattern. For she integrates the technique adeptly, with naturalness and variety. And her pages build dynamically as she injects in them a heavy dose of suspense.

The Page Turner

How does Rowling create suspense? Often by means of classic crime novel techniques. Take, for instance, the race against time, a race usually impeded by obstacles and delays. At the start of Harry's second school year, he and Ron can't get through the invisible entrance leading to the express train for Hogwarts Academy. The train is about to leave: "Three seconds...two seconds...one second..." (II, 68) They missed it! How can they make it in time for the opening ceremony? They fly there in Mr. Weasley's magic car, which nearly breaks down on the way. Then, on arrival, they are delayed even more when the car falls into the clutches of a violent tree, the Whomping Willow.

The race against time provides even more suspense in *The Prisoner of Azkaban.* Toward the end of the book Dumbledore permits Harry, Ron and Hermione to leave the premises for three hours to save Sirius and Hagrid's hippogriff, Buckbeak—both of them condemned by the Ministry of Magic. The Headmaster subtly suggests that Hermione use her magic Time Turner to back up three hours, so she and Harry can change the preceding events and let Sirius and Buckbeak escape together. But they must return to the dormitory exactly within three hours. Of course they meet with delays and catastrophes: enemies sighted, the Whomping Willow on the attack, even dementors threatening Harry. They manage to rescue Sirius and Buckbeak and then, at the very second of their deadline, they make it back.

In Book Four, Sirius plans to appear in the fireplace of the Gryffindor House lounge, and Harry must be there to speak with him at exactly 1:00 a.m. It is a long awaited moment for Harry.

However, at the last minute Hagrid insists on seeing him in his cabin. Harry goes there, then, fearful of missing his appointment, he rushes back. But on the way, he bumps (literally) into Karkaroff, the headmaster of a visiting school. In spite of it all, he makes the appointment in time. Then just as Sirius is about to give Harry some eagerly awaited advice, the interview is interrupted by the sound of footsteps. Someone has entered the lounge. Harry tells Sirius to leave lest he be discovered. It turns out to be only Ron, but Sirius has already disappeared.

In Harry Potter, this formula of an urgent contest with time is effective but not overused. For Rowling has many other means of gripping the reader, and she does so diversely throughout the cycle. Her pages are rife with suspense whenever Harry and his friends are menaced by foes (will they get away?), when they sneak unseen into enemy territory (will they be found out?) or when they strive against the odds for victory (will they make it?). Even where there is no ostensible action or movement, Rowling creates suspense in a number of gripping scenes. There are the times, for instance, when Harry has to endure taunts by Professor Snape, Or when he forces himself not to scream as Dolores Umbridge slowly has the words *"I must not tell lies."* magically cut into the back of his hand with his own blood. (V, 267)

This darker type of suspense holds and absorbs readers concerned for Harry. A painful example is seen in Book Six. Harry, who reveres Dumbledore and cares deeply for him, must keep his promise to him and make the Headmaster drink a large amount of liquid that will cause him intense anguish and bring him close to death. Half way through the fourth goblet, Dumbledore can take no more. He says, weakly,

> "I don't want...Don't make me..."
>
> Harry stared into the whitened face he knew so well, at the crooked nose and half-moon spectacles, and did not know what to do.

"You...you can't stop, Professor...You've got to keep drinking, remember? You told me you had to keep drinking. Here."

Hating himself, repulsed by what he was doing, Harry forced the goblet back toward Dumbledore's mouth.

The force-feeding continues until Dumbledore moans,

"Make it stop. Make it stop."

"Yes...yes, this'll make it stop" lied Harry. He tipped the contents of the goblet into Dumbledore's open mouth. (VI, 571-2)

Harry's hands are shaking so badly he can hardly hold the goblet, while he loudly assures Dumbledore that the liquid will quench his thirst (he knows it will do exactly the opposite). When Dumbledore begs to be killed and released from the dire pain, Harry claims that drinking it all up will do just that. The scene is excruciating. We feel Harry's suffering as much as Dumbledore's. But we can't stop reading.

To end this section on a lighter note, a Quidditch match in Book Three provides a far more entertaining brand of suspense. It is the final game of the year, and Harry's team from Gryffindor House is up against players from hateful Slytherin, including despicable Draco Malfoy. Harry is flying his new, impressive Firebolt broom, and, as Seeker, he must capture the winged golden Snitch. Excitement builds in a series of short or fragmentary sentences, while the action is interspersed with the shouts of the sports commentator, carried away by emotion.

"Angelina Johnson gets the Quaffle for Gryffindor, come on, Angelina, COME ON!"

...Harry wheeled the Firebolt around, bent so low he was lying flat across the handle, and kicked it forward. Like a bullet, he shot toward the Slytherins.

"AAAAAAARRGH!"

They scattered as the Firebolt zoomed toward them; Angelina's way was clear.

"SHE SCORES! SHE SCORES! Gryffindor leads by eighty points to twenty!"

Harry, who had almost pelted headlong into the stands, skidded to a halt in mid-air, reversed, and zoomed back into the middle of the field.

And then he saw something to make his heart stand still. Malfoy was diving, a look of triumph on his face—there, a few feet above the grass below—was a tiny golden glimmer—

Harry urged the Firebolt downward, but Malfoy was miles ahead—

"Go! Go! Go!" Harry urged his broom. He was gaining on Malfoy—Harry flattened himself to the broom handle as Bole sent a Bludger at him—he was at Malfoy's ankles—he was level—

Harry threw himself forward, took both hands off his broom. He knocked Malfoy's arm out of the way and—

"YES!"

He pulled out of his dive, his hand in the air, and the stadium exploded. Harry soared above the crowd, an odd ringing in his ears. The tiny golden ball was held tight in his fist, beating its wings hopelessly against his fingers. (pp. 311-12)

The Grand Finale

Since suspense in each book builds up to an exciting climax, the final one naturally has to top them all. Where there were previously fireworks, inevitably, Book Seven ends with sheer dynamite. When the great Battle of Hogwarts gets under way, Rowling pulls out all the stops: flames that attack in the form of serpents, chimaeras, raptors and dragons, dementors, Death Eaters, giants, spiders, ghosts, blood-thirsty dragons, not to mention Malfoy and his buddies Crabbe and Goyle aiming curses at Harry, Ron and Hermione.

But that is only a prelude to the crucial battle, when Voldemort arrives at Hogwarts with the presumably dead Harry in tow.

> Chaos reigned. The charging centaurs were scattering the Death Eaters, everyone was fleeing the giants' stamping feet, and nearer and nearer thundered the reinforcements that had come from who knew where; Harry saw great winged creatures soaring around the heads of Voldemort's giants, thestrals and Buckbeak, the hippogriff, scratching their eyes while Grawp punched and pummeled them...
> (VII, 733-4)

And so it continues. The momentum builds to such an extent that a reader is not shocked when Ginny's sweet and matronly mother, Molly, seeing the dastardly Bellatrix aim her wand to kill Ginny, shouts: "NOT MY DAUGHTER, YOU BITCH!" (p. 736) Previously the word would have been taboo, but at that point one can only think, "Go, Molly!"

If Rowling pulls out all the stops in *The Deathly Hallows*, she also ties up all the threads. Gradually, in the course of the book, after many twists and turns, the Horcruxes are found and dealt with and the unsolved mysteries are cleared up at last. And, of course, Harry has the necessary final confrontation with Voldemort.

It is the moment of truth. During this gripping scene, Harry uses the ploy of engaging his enemy in dialogue. But interestingly, Harry speaks as a man, and not just as Voldemort's equal but as his superior. Significantly, he demeans Voldemort by calling him constantly by his real, prosaic name, "Riddle." In a sense, he breaks the charm, exploding the mystique by reducing the tyrant to a deflated old wizard. In this case, it is Harry himself who explains everything, speaking to Voldemort/Riddle as to a child. And there is a poetic justice here. At the end of the episode, Harry, no murderer, only disarms Voldemort while the latter utters the death curse at him. But thanks to Harry's wand—and quick thinking—Voldemort's curse rebounds and kills the monster himself.

Although Rowling wrapped up the cycle effectively with Harry's victory and his relinquishing of the Elder Wand, she decided to do more, and she added an epilogue. In it she explained what happened to Harry and company nineteen years after the close of the story. They were alive, married to the ones they loved and sending their children off to Hogwarts. The parents even included Draco Malfoy and his wife. And—as a yet bigger surprise—one of Harry's children was called "Severus," after the formerly reviled Snape.

A goodly number of *Harry Potter* fans have protested on blogs and elsewhere that this epilogue has no place in the cycle. Evidently Rowling's quick everyone-lived-happily-ever-after ending strikes them as out of keeping with the whole Harry Potter adventure. Granted, the epilogue does amount to a rapid wrapping up (only a scant seven pages) with a simple idealism that contrasts with the rest of the work. But this writer considers it a fitting addition to the cycle. Although Rowling tied up all the loose threads of the story in the final book, she left her hero tired and drained from his dangerous exploits, in a final chapter with no closure.[4] And she must have known that many fans who followed Harry and his friends for seven years—especially the very young ones—would want to know what happened to them and, "How did it all turn out?"

So why not give them a happy ending?

The Story Teller

Given the fast pacing and momentum of the cycle, it might seem surprising that Rowling periodically stops the action to have a character tell a story. Yet she does, indeed, intercalate stories that interrupt the main tale to provide background material: stories within the story.

That is an age-old device. In adventure tales of centuries past, for example, characters are shipwrecked, marooned with no prospect of getting out, and to bide the time, each tells the story of his or her life. Cervantes makes ample use of the intercalated story in *Don Quijote*. But his inserted romances of lovelorn shepherds and shepherdesses can go on for chapters, and the reader begins to miss the droll doings of ill-fated Don Quijote.

In *Harry Potter*, the stories within the story all relate to the main action. They provide explanatory material shedding light on the adventures at hand. And they do not slow the action, because these narratives are designed both to pique and to satisfy our curiosity. They have their own momentum and cannot fail to hold the reader's interest.

The Order of the Phoenix contains a chapter entitled "Hagrid's Tale." After much prodding by Harry, Ron and Hermione, Hagrid finally consents to satisfy their curiosity and tell them where he went and what he experienced when he recently disappeared from the area on a mysterious adventure. The "tale" does not slow the narration a bit because it is not a monologue but a lively exchange between Hagrid and his young friends. Here is a typical part:

> **Hagrid**: "We had to go slow, 'cause I'm not really s'posed ter use magic an' we knew the Ministry'd be lookin' fer a reason ter run us in. But we managed ter give the berk tailin' us the slip round abou' Dee-John—"
>
> **Hermione** (excitedly): "Ooooh, Dijon? ...I've been there on holiday, did you see—?"
>
> She falls silent at the look on Ron's face. Hagrid continues his story and pauses for a long draft of tea.
>
> **Harry** (urgently): "Go on!"
>
> **Hagrid**: "Found 'em [giants]...It was like watchin' bits o' the mountain movin.'"
>
> **Ron** (in a hushed voice): "How big are they?" (pp. 425-6)

A good many of the stories introduced fill us in about the former life of key characters. Sometimes Harry witnesses scenes of the past in the Pensieve where he sees and hears his mother as a child conversing with an equally young Snape. Or where he discovers his father and Sirius performing cruel practical jokes on Snape during their student days at Hogwarts. Characters also describe their own past to Harry. He learns the story of Dumbledore's role in the fate of his unfortunate sister Ariana only gradually, in fragments. His first source of information is a sympathetic eulogy written by Elphias Doge. Next, supposed facts are divulged in a snide and slanted book by Rita Skeeter. Later, Aberforth and, finally, Albus Dumbledore fill Harry in with the truth as they experienced it.

Since Rowling had at her disposal back stories of so many of her characters, there is little wonder that she introduced chapters entitled "Kreacher's Tale" or "The Prince's Tale," much as Dumbledore and Snape siphon off their extra memories into a Pensieve. But also, as Rowling has said, even as a child she loved inventing stories and telling them to her sister and other children. So it is natural that rather than content herself with one plot, she would let her imagination take her down a whole variety of fictional paths.

In fact, some stories introduced in *Harry Potter* would seem at first glance to have no bearing at all on the characters. Of course, nothing in the cycle is arbitrary, and every part eventually does connect with the entirety. But on the surface, these episodes appear as simply intriguing vignettes, making their cameo appearances in the form of mini-romances or fairy tales.

Two of these tales are especially worth highlighting here. One is the story of the ghost, Helena Ravenclaw, daughter of one of the four founders of Hogwarts Academy, Rowena Ravenclaw. In the last volume, during all the hectic action of the Battle of Hogwarts, Harry makes a mad dash to follow a lead and capture one of the Horcruxes containing part of Voldemort's soul. It is the diadem once worn by Rowena Ravenclaw. After the usual frustrating delays he manages to speak with the shade of Rowena's daughter Helena. Where is the tiara? When she finally consents to give him information, it comes in the form of a story, beginning with these words:

> "I stole the diadem from my mother."
> "You—you did what?"
> "*I stole the diadem*…I sought to make myself cleverer, more important than my mother. I ran away with it…My mother, they say, never admitted that the diadem was gone, but

pretended that she had it still. She concealed her loss, my dreadful betrayal, even from the other founders of Hogwarts."

Interrupted occasionally by Harry's reactions, this is the rest of her story. It is narrated in the style of an old-fashioned romantic novel.

"Then my mother fell ill—fatally ill. In spite of my perfidy, she was desperate to see me one more time. She sent a man who had long loved me, though I spurned his advances, to find me. She knew that he would not rest until he had done so.

...He tracked me to the forest where I was hiding. When I refused to return with him, he became violent. The Baron was always a hot-tempered man. Furious at my refusal, jealous of my freedom, he stabbed me."

Harry: "The Baron? You mean—"
Helena: "The Bloody Baron, yes..." (VII, 616)

What could be a finer twist than to have her violent lover turn out to be the surly, unlikable ghost dragging his chains through the corridors of Slytherin House? After murdering his adored one, he "took the weapon that had claimed my life," and he stabbed himself to death, wearing chains forever after as an act of penance.

Listening to Helena's story may have meant using up some of Harry's precious time, but speaking with her, he did wind up with a clue about where to find the tiara. And heard a cracking good story to boot.

"The Tale of the Three Brothers" is a classic children's fairy tale of the once-upon-a-time variety. It is found in a volume bequeathed to Hermione by Dumbledore: *The Tales of Beedle the Bard*, a collection of children's stories known only to the magic community.[5] What is its relevance to *Harry Potter?* It has great significance in Book Seven, *The Deathly Hallows*, because, as Xenophilius Lovegood suggests to Harry, "The Tale of the Three Brothers" explains what the mysterious Hallows are truly about.

To summarize the plot: three brothers, traveling on a lonely road, meet Death, but through magic they manage to escape him. Death, although disappointed, cunningly congratulates them and offers each a gift. The eldest, a combative man, chooses an unbeatable wand (the Elder Wand, Hallow #1); the second, an arrogant type, opts for a charm to bring back the dead (the Resurrection Stone, Hallow #2); the third asks more modestly for something to enable him to move about unseen (the Invisibility Cloak, Hallow #3). As it turns out, the charms granted to the first two brothers work against them, and they meet an early demise. The third and youngest brother managed to delay his death through invisibility but when he lived long enough, *"...he greeted Death as an old friend, and went with him gladly, and, equals, they departed this life."* (409)[6]

Of all the intercalated stories found in the cycle—even those such as the last two that stand on their own—not one delays the action or saps the reader's interest. And every one of them relates significantly to the main plot, impelling it forward and adding to, rather than subtracting from, the rhythm and timing of the work.

---

[1] In *The Goblet of Fire*, Dumbledore interrogates Harry at length before offering clarifications.

[2] In fact, in *Harry Potter*, as in a Sue Grafton whodunnit, the longer the enemy talks, the better the protagonist's chances of learning the truth and staying alive. So Harry asks questions and keeps Quirrell talking at the end of *The Sorcerer's Stone* and uses the same ploy with Bellatrix at the close of *The Order of the Phoenix*. In *The Half Blood Prince*. Dumbledore asks questions of Malfoy while the young man is trying to get up the courage to kill him.

[3] To do so he would have to murder seven people, but that would allow him to live forever.

[4] As one reader said, "the happy ending was earned."

[5] Rowling incorporated "The Tale of Three Brothers" into her own *Tales of Beedle the Bard*, published in 2007. It is the final and most impressive story in the short collection.

[6] Rowling is not the only author to have used the figure of Death in a story. Other examples: Grimm's *Godfather Death*, and folk tales such as *Death and the Maiden* or the one known as *Appointment in Damascus*. Rowling herself has said she may have based her story partly on Chaucer's "The Pardoner's Tale," in which three brothers meet Death. *www. mugglenet.com/app/news/full_story/1156.*

8

THE WHOLE PICTURE

"It is good to have an end to journey toward, but
it is the journey that matters, in the end."
—Ursula LeGuin

Charting the Course

Harry's seven-year odyssey from boyhood to manhood, as adventuresome as Odysseus' decade-long journey, comes to a close in the final pages of *The Deathly Hallows*. If we go back to square one and retrace his story from dismal childhood to victorious finale, we can distinguish an overall pattern in his trajectory. Most notably, Harry's personal evolution is mirrored in the increasingly serious and mature quality of the narration as the plot unfolds.

A number of readers could see that already happening on reading the fourth volume, *The Goblet of Fire*. Aware that Rowling had introduced a sinister quality in the work, some wrote to her online, asking if the cycle was becoming "darker." She answered that it was, indeed, and would become even more so. Rowling gave her reasons: Voldemort was becoming stronger, and, meanwhile, the characters were getting older and had to cope with the real world.[1] Such developments would not necessarily oblige an author to alter the tone and ambience of a narrative. But that was clearly part of Rowling's grand design.

The first two books are each a light-hearted romp, full of exciting scenes and irresistible humor. Book Three, *The Prisoner of Azkaban*, is entertaining, despite some ominous moments. Near the beginning, a rather frightening dog stares piercingly at Harry from the shadows. Still, that is not enough to send chills to readers who have just been regaled with a farcical scene in which Harry magically inflates his despicable aunt. And the inflation episode is followed almost immediately by Harry's madcap trip on the Knight Bus with the comical cockney conductor, Stan Shunpike.

Later in the book, some alarming events do take place: A dementor stalks Harry on the Hogwarts Express. Sirius Black, an alleged killer who escaped from Azkaban prison, is said to be on the prowl and looking for Harry. And at one point, the escapee comes to threaten Harry and his friends in a most violent way. But in the end, all is resolved. Book Three finishes on an up-note, with the seemingly monstrous Sirius proven innocent and really on Harry's side. Finally, at the close of the school year Harry leaves, grinning broadly, anticipating a liberating stay at the Weasley household and "a much better summer than the last." (p. 435)

Book Four, *The Goblet of Fire*, while as entertaining and adventurous as the first three volumes, begins to draw readers into deeper waters. The very first chapter startles and horrifies us. Instead of beginning, like the previous books, with Harry bored but safe at the Dursley's, Rowling takes us to a creepy, deserted house in a far-off village, where an ugly and terrifying Voldemort puts the fear of death into his servant, Peter Pettigrew (a.k.a. "Wormtail"), and brutally murders an innocent bystander, the owner of the property. The chapter ends with the words, "Two hundred miles away, the boy called Harry Potter woke with a start." (p. 15)

In his sleep Harry has just observed that whole terrible scene, although he thinks it was only a dream. But after witnessing Voldemort's act of murder, his scar suddenly hurts him intensely. He can't understand why. In the past it ached whenever Voldemort was nearby, but at present the man is far away. What Harry does not understand, is that the game has changed; it has become far more lethal. Because the piece of Voldemort's soul lodged in Harry's mind when he was one year old[2], is making their connection stronger and more painful. From this point in the cycle on, Harry will witness other scenes featuring Voldemort, scenes causing scar pains that become more and more anguishing as the story progresses.

The Goblet of Fire is the pivotal book in which Voldemort finally regains a human form and calls forth his army of Death Eaters (acolytes previously imprisoned, in hiding or feigning innocence). It is the book where Voldemort's sign—the "dark mark" in the form of a skull with a serpent hanging from its lips—is ominously emblazoned in the sky.[3] It is the first book where a decent likable character, Cedric Diggory, is killed. And where serious emotion comes into play, as Dumbledore, in a moving speech, urges Hogwarts students to "remember Cedric Diggory." (724) Finally, it is the first book to end on a solemn, uneasy note, as Harry muses:

> There was no point worrying yet...As Hagrid had said, what would come, would come...and he would have to meet it when it did. (734)

From Book Four on, as Harry matures and develops and as he tries to come to grips with danger, his inner life and moods take on a greater complexity and he becomes more and more introspective. Reflecting this, the books become longer, the tone more mature, the atmosphere more serious than the first three volumes. This trend is especially remarkable in Book Five, *The Order of the Phoenix*, the most somber book of the cycle.

Unlike all the other volumes, *The Order of the Phoenix* includes very few breathers—for example, no exhilarating Quidditch victory for Harry and precious little comic relief. It does contain a few cheerful happenings: Harry regains the trust of his classmates and trains them in his underground "Dumbledore's Army." Fred and George Weasley cause mayhem in Hogwarts, leaving the tyrannical Dolores Umbridge covered in soot and at her wit's end. But beyond such high points, in the main, the book is colored by gloominess and a dismal outlook.

Small wonder, because ugly things happen from start to finish. In the very first chapter, when Harry is supposedly safe near the Dursley home, a dementor appears out of nowhere, aiming to suck all hope out his soul. Although Harry escapes, that episode sets the tone for the following pages. Harry must face a trial and possible expulsion from Hogwarts; the obscenely evil Bellatrix Lestrange and other Death Eaters have escaped from Azkaban prison; Hagrid is in trouble and on probation; Sirius is in hiding and later killed in battle by Bellatrix; Mr. Weasley is tortured and nearly killed; sadistic Dolores Umbridge becomes High Inquisitor at Hogwarts and inflicts excruciating pain on Harry. Disaster looms at every corner.

Misfortunes accumulate. Harry's headaches become so intense that at times he winds up screaming or writhing on the floor. Worse, night after night his mind is possessed by Voldemort. In fact, at times, Harry actually *becomes* Voldemort. Whenever he sees Dumbledore, irrationally, he wants to kill him. And because Dumbledore senses what is happening in Harry's mind, he averts his eyes when they are together. It makes Harry even more furious that Dumbledore won't look at him. With all he is going through he winds up behaving nastily, even smashing the Headmaster's belongings, and never apologizes.

With this abundance of calamities and comedowns, one could not expect Harry to be pleasant company, and he most certainly is not. In the throes of ennui, anxiety and dread, he is often edgy, resentful and angry and lashes out at his closest friends. He finds himself generally unable to connect with those around him. In Rowling's words, "…an invisible barrier separated him from the rest of the world." (p. 855) This sentence goes far in summing up his angst:

> "As a dull March blurred into a squally April, his life seemed to have become one long series of worries and problems…" (p. 605)

What is going on here? We cannot blame the gloominess pervading *The Order of the Phoenix* on the author's clinical depression. For one thing, as Rowling has said on several occasions, that occurred in 1994.[4] In discussing her writing of the book, she did say that she thought it could have been shorter but that she had run out of energy toward the end and didn't have time to do anything about it.[5] But that does not address the matter of the tone of the book. Could the descent into bleakness be a way of plunging Harry—and the plot—into darkness before opening the way to light at the end of the tunnel? Whatever the case, the somberness of *The Order of the Phoenix* certainly mirrors Harry's emotional state in that period of his adolescence,[6] a time when the problems tormenting him loom larger than life.

One might expect that the persistent grimness of this volume would discourage readers and possibly destroy the momentum of the whole cycle. Fortunately, despite the book's somberness, it works. For it is rescued not only by its occasional moments of respite and fun but by Rowling's continuing ability to engage readers through suspenseful scenes and lead them to identify with Harry and his fate.

The last two volumes lift us out of the mire. In the sixth, Harry appears to have outgrown his feelings of depression and oppression. Despite his awareness that he is fated to kill Voldemort or be killed by him, he is back on track. And so Rowling seems to be, with her lively pacing and her matchless mix of ups and downs, including new mysteries to solve, surprising revelations, frightening events and humorous episodes.

As for the progressive darkening of the series, that is evident in the disfiguring of Bill Weasley, in Snape's increasingly sinister actions, culminating in his shocking murder of Dumbledore, his flight and apparent defection to Voldemort's side. Dumbledore's death itself, surely a heart breaker for admirers, lends pathos to the final pages of the book. Readers, faced with that catastrophe, understand that the final volume will be more than fun and games.

It is much more. Book Seven, *The Deathly Hallows*, is dense, crammed full of adventure and nearly epic in scope. It contains a section where action is delayed, as Harry, Ron and Hermione, stymied, stay in hiding for a good period of time, living in Spartan conditions, hungry, frustrated, quarreling with each other. Still, that long stretch is full of riveting moments and serves as a logical and useful prelude to the ensuing action.

Some critics have felt that Rowling tried to pack too much into this volume and could not handle everything effectively. Writing for the *Atlantic*, Ross Douthat objected to too many magical objects and thought the book was marred by "increasingly incomprehensible" magic, "confusing metaphysics" and "predictable plotting."[7] He would have preferred to have Rowling duplicate the format of preceding books and keep Harry and his friends engaging in their usual activities at Hogwarts rather than have them off on a "meandering quest" around England.

It is true that Rowling is juggling a lot in this volume, for she must have her characters complete a search that will solve all the mysteries, track down the Deathly Hallows, destroy the Horcruxes and sew up all the threads. She must ultimately bring Harry face to face in single combat with Voldemort and subject the hero to the necessary trials of fire before leading him to a difficult, stunning victory. To be exciting, the route must be circuitous. To be perpetually surprising, it must be convoluted. And in the last analysis, Rowling does pull it all off. *The Deathly Hallows* may have its ambiguities and imperfections. But readers of *Harry Potter* would find it difficult, if not impossible, to put the book down before the final page.

As for repeating the old Hogwarts formulas, we can be grateful to Rowling for being inventive enough not to plow the same furrow over again.

Two Worlds

Some young people's fantasy books, such as Tolkien's *Hobbit* or Ursula Le Guin's *Earthsea* series, are set entirely in a mythological, magic world, far from the here and now of modern society. Others, like C. S. Lewis' *Chronicles of Narnia* or Philip Pullman's *His Dark Materials*, have characters who can travel from the real to the magic world and reverse direction.[8] Rowling's *Harry Potter* obviously belongs to the second category. But with this difference: in *Harry Potter* the wizard and non-wizard, or Muggle, worlds intersect, and there is a constant interplay between them. In fact, the magic/Muggle duality lies at the heart of the story. It is clear that although authoring a fantasy, Rowling, wants her feet solidly on the ground and refuses to lose sight of the here and now. She injects reality into every aspect of the fantastic tale—into her psychological portrayal of characters and, as we shall see, into her humor, narration and dialogue.

Throughout the cycle, the magic sphere and Muggledom are joined at the hip. Hogwarts school has its "Muggle studies" course, taken notably by Muggle born Hermione. The Ministry of Magic has its Misuse of Muggle Artifacts Office. Some wizards detest and constantly harass those born of a non-magical family. The Minister of Magic leaves his world to pay a visit to the Muggle Prime Minister of England.

Yet, while cohabitating, the two worlds are very dissimilar. A case in point: their habitats. In the non-magic sphere, Rowling takes readers inside only one Muggle household: 4 Privet Drive, the Dursley residence inhabited by Harry's aunt, uncle and cousin. A cookie-cutter replica of all the other dwellings in its unremarkable neighborhood, it is the only house we find that is neatly kept, with its tidy front garden and manicured hedges and spic-and-span living room. Rowling views this place with humorous disdain, for it obviously reflects the rigidity and conventionality of its very unlikable owners, bent on keeping up appearances at any cost.

That conformity and lack of imagination contrasts sharply with descriptions of wizards' abodes. "The Burrow," home of the Weasley family is pictured as a patched-together, cluttered and untidy house with everything awry.

> It looked as though it had once been a large stone pigpen, but extra rooms had been added here and there until it was several stories high and so crooked it looked as though it were held up by magic (which, Harry reminded himself, it probably was). Four or five chimneys were perched on top of the red roof. A lop-sided sign stuck in the ground near the entrance read, THE BURROW. Around the front door lay a jumble of rubber boots and a very rusty cauldron.

Several fat brown chickens were pecking their way around the yard. (II, 32)

But of course, for Rowling, such a place is a thousand times preferable to 4 Privet Drive. And for Harry, it is a haven, a place to "burrow" in with his friends, mercifully far from the Dursleys. Other wizards' abodes appear even messier than the Burrow and far less inviting. Places like Snape's house or the one inhabited by Voldemort's grandfather are gloomy, dusty or filthy and in need of repair. Bathilda Bagshot's "home" is not only dirty and shabby but it (or Bathilda) smells of unwashed clothes or meat gone bad. To approach Xenophilius Lovegood's front door, Harry goes through a creaking gate and down a zigzagging path, is met by Lovegood wearing a stained nightshirt and enters rooms cluttered with books and papers everywhere. Even Sirius Black's house, which must have been a richly appointed townhouse at one time, has a "battered door," "dirty walls" and "grimy windows" (V, 59), along with shabby, scratched black paint, peeling wallpaper, a threadbare carpet, a long gloomy hall, a cobwebby chandelier. (The one example in the story of a presentable home in the wizard world appears to be the manor of wealthy and powerful Lucius Malfoy.)

So in *Harry Potter*, as elsewhere, the magic world is almost always presented as eerily off kilter, with its oddly shaped houses, creaking gates, dark and dusty interiors and lots of cobwebs. Additionally, the story has its dependable supply of caves, towers, rustic cabins, murky lakes, and a cast of characters that includes witches, ghosts, talking animals, flying humans and all sorts of fantastic beasts.

In this magic setting much of the Muggle apparatus is left behind, forgotten or completely unknown. Ron Weasley has no idea about Muggle money, for rather than pounds or dollars the characters deal in gold Galleons,[9] silver Sickles and Knuts. Except for the Hogwarts Express and the magical Knight Bus, the wizards' means of transportation bears no resemblance to ours. They do quite well, however, with Portkeys, objects that whiz them in seconds from place to place, by Floo Powder taking them sootily through a network of fireplaces, or with brooms and other flying objects, on air-borne beasts and by Apparating, a difficult skill that enables you to disappear from one place and wind up, in a flash, exactly where you want to be.

In Rowling's story, most of the magical phenomena revolve around Hogwarts School of Witchcraft and Wizardry. Hogwarts is housed in a most intriguing castle located at an unnamed site in the highlands of Scotland, and it is undiscoverable by Muggles. As in most tales of witchcraft, this building is not of our century. In fact, the school dates from over a thousand years ago. However, with its rambling construction, its seven floors plus cellar and ground level, topped with a number of towers, it could not have been built in such a style a millennium ago but would have either acquired additions over the centuries or undergone a complete face lifting. Whatever the case, Hogwarts has enough patina to serve as a proper venue for some good old-fashioned sorcery.

But how old-fashioned is it? Harry attends the school not long before our time, in the 1990s. However, his experiences there are set in a décor and ambience of a previous time frame, one without cars. TVs, computers or even electricity—one with narrow cobblestone streets nearby, functional fireplaces, four-poster beds, bed warming pans and water in ewers. The story has its share of nineteenth-century inventions that seem quaint to us today: the steam engine locomotive that transports Hogwarts students to and from school and the camera humorously caricatured in Book Two.[10] The elevator in the Ministry of Magic, with grilles that open and close and chains that rattle as the car ascends and descends—evokes turn-of-the-century lifts hoisted by cables. And Sirius Black's house has an array of gas lamps. Given such props, generally speaking, readers might imagine themselves back in the late 1800s of the Victorian era.

Yet we cannot take the Victorian time frame literally, for at Hogwarts heat is not generated by the customary gas stove but by an old-fashioned fireplace. And students have neither pens nor notebooks for writing but archaic quills and parchment paper of centuries back. And on the other hand, there are more modern touches in the magic setting: tissues for nose blowing and radio (magically powered) which were not common items before the 1920s and 1930s.

Rowling may strike us as even more contemporary in her descriptions of food. For Hogwarts cuisine has everything a hungry teenager of modern times could crave. In Tolkien's cycle, hobbits and elves are content to dine on "yellow cream and honeycomb, and white bread, and butter, milk, cheese, and green herbs and ripe berries gathered."[11] And in other children's fantasy stories, characters often make do with staples like cabbage, potatoes and tea. But at Harry's first dinner at school, the table is laden with "roast beef, roast chicken, pork chops and lamb chops. sausages, bacon and steak, boiled potatoes, roast potatoes, fries, Yorkshire pudding, peas, carrots, gravy, ketchup..." (I, 123) Christmas dinner resembles an American Thanksgiving feast with roast turkey, gravy and cranberry sauce. Then if more ordinary fare is wanted, youngsters can have items such as hamburgers, Jell-O, doughnuts and assorted sandwiches. Favorite drinks are a bit more exotic: pumpkin juice or butterbeer, for instance, and Rosemerta's mead for adults. But sweets of every sort come in abundance, even ice cream sundaes, not to mention comforting chocolates and other assorted candies (some of them practical jokes like Bertie Botts Every Flavor Beans).

Although some other writers of magic stories offer their characters enough decent food to eat,[12] Rowling sets an improbable table but one designed to make twenty-first century readers salivate.

If a present-day Snape were to look at *Harry Potter* with a hyper-critical eye, he might very well want to take points away from Rowling for venturing beyond a set timeline or for apparent chronological contradictions. He might object: how is it that Harry and Hermione, so familiar with the Muggle world of computers, cell phones, TVs, cars and the like, suddenly undergo amnesia upon reaching Hogwarts and blank out about such modern inventions? Instead of spending so many hours searching through ancient books in the library to find out about Nicolas Flamel, why not just Google him?[13] Rowling more or less answered that question in the series by stating that there is too much magic in the Hogwarts atmosphere for such modern devices to work. But since the story has cameras, radios and an automobile made operative through magic, why not computers as well?

Or, more likely, our zealous critic could ask why, in this seemingly Victorian milieu, are students using today's slang and—worse—snogging in public rooms in full view of others? But such carping and hair-splitting have little relevance to *Harry Potter*. For in writing it Rowling was more concerned with fun and fantasy than with a narrowly circumscribed interpretation of time. Moreover, her readers are too engaged in the story to notice or care if she steps over the line.

Like young *Harry Potter* fans, adult readers, once drawn into the story, don't stop to quibble. They may appreciate Rowling's cleverness and her mastery of the genre; they may smile at the visible layer of inside jokes geared to parents and older siblings. Or like younger fans, they may simply go along for the ride and enjoy the adventure.

---

[1] See, for example, Rowling's interview of October 16, 2000, on scholastic.com.

[2] See Chapter II, p. 333.

[3] At the Quidditch World Cup tournament.

[4] Among the many websites in which she discusses that period, see www.accio-quote.org/articles/2000/0700-hottype-solomon.html. More recently, she spoke of a brief period of depression just after having completed the first volume, *The Sorcerer's Stone*. See, for example, Penny Linsenmayer's article: www.hpfgu.org.uk/faq/rowling.html.

[5] *Time Magazine*. July, 17, 2005. A famous author once said, "I would have made this long letter shorter but didn't have enough time to do so."

[6] See Chapter I, p. 13.

[7] *rossdouthat.theatlantic.com/archivs/2007/07/the—deathly—hallows.*

[8] In Pullman's stories characters can enter and leave a whole variety of worlds.

[9] One can estimate, from statements made by Rowling in *Fantastic Beasts and Where to Find Them* (pp. vii-viii) and elsewhere that a Galleon is worth around five English pounds. (At current rate, the U.S. dollar is valued at a little over one-half a pound.) In Book One, Harry pays seven Galleons for his wand—a steal, considering its efficacy. See online Wizarding World Currency Converter: www.hp-lexicon.org/wizworld/galleons.html.

[10] "A short... man was dancing around taking photographs with a large black camera that emitted puffs of purple smoke with every blinding flash." (p. 59) Later in Book Two, Colin Creevey would take pictures with a hand held camera, invented in the late 19th century. In her official website, Rowling explains that in the story radios and cameras work not on batteries but on the magic atmosphere at Hogwarts. (That might strike us as an old-fashioned version of wi-fi.)

[11] *Fellowship of the Ring*, 122.

[12] E.g., Roald Dahl's *Fantastic Mr. Fox* or Jill Murphy's *Worst Witch*.

[13] The internet has a good amount of material on Flamel and his wife.

PART III

HUMOR
AND STYLE

9

LAUGHTER AND SMILES

"Wit without measure is man's greatest treasure."

—Motto engraved on Rowena
Ravenclaw's tiara,
The Deathly Hallows

When asked if her writing had been influenced by J. R. R. Tolkien, Rowling replied, "Tolkien created a whole new mythology, which I would never claim to have done. On the other hand, I think I have better jokes."[1] That self-effacing answer ends in a rank understatement, since Rowling's so-called "jokes" are nothing less than a masterful display of humor and wit, delighting readers of all ages.

To analyze humor is a dangerous enterprise. To explain a joke, break it down into its basic ingredients is serious business, guaranteed to stifle laughter. In any case, Rowling did not use formulas to create funny remarks and humorous incidents. She simply has a keen sense of humor and a wonderful facility for conveying it. Jests and gibes, satire and shenanigans, all manner of drollery flow from her pen as spontaneously as lines from Rita Skeeter's Quick-Quotes Quill.

With that said—and at the risk of blowing a dementor's cold wind over her treasury of humor—let us proceed with the scalpel. What is funny about *Harry Potter* and why does it make us laugh?

Easy Laughter

Harry Potter's most accessible humor, appealing to the youngest of readers, is the sight gag or humiliating pratfall, often magically induced. Hagrid endows nasty Dudley Dursley with a well-deserved pig's tail. A bewitched teapot unexpectedly spouts boiling water over a man who winds up in the hospital with sugar tongs clamped to his nose. Trying to learn switching spells in Charms class, bungling Neville Longbottom somehow transplants his ear onto a cactus. Hearing his Aunt Marge demean his dead parents, Harry inflates her with a charm until she hovers on high like a huge balloon. And when poor Eloise Midgen tries to curse her acne off, her nose has to be tacked on again.

The Dursleys provide fertile ground for the visual gag. Vernon Dursley tries to knock in a nail with his wife's fruitcake. And later, when he snarls, "Do I look stupid?" a bit of fried egg dangling from his bushy mustache provides the answer (II, 1). Other characters and other situations provide ample fodder for the sight gag throughout the story.

Visual or not, much of this farcical humor stems from what philosopher Henri Bergson described as characters behaving mechanically in a living, changing situation.[2] For example, we laugh when a cartoon mouse goes scurrying over a cliff and, although in mid-air, continues mechanically pumping his little feet as though his situation hadn't changed at all. Or when a bespangled diva trilling on stage, continues singing and gesturing grandly without realizing her elaborate wig has fallen half off. Or when Groucho Marx, eyes closed, is caressing the woman of his dreams and, not registering that his inamorata has been replaced by a mule, he continues his lovemaking and romantically caresses the animal.

In *Harry Potter*, examples of not adapting are especially funny when the person who continues to behave mechanically suddenly faces reality and—oops!—comes down to earth with a jolt. Dumbledore, for example, is wary of the candies known as "Bertie Botts Every Flavor Beans" because he once swallowed a vomit-flavored one. But at one point he smilingly pops a bean into his mouth and then—the "oops" moment—he chokes, exclaiming, "Alas—ear wax!" (I, 300-1)[3] In the same vein, when Mr. Weasley, passionate about Muggle contraptions, learns that his sons illegally flew in the Muggle car he had enchanted, he asks eagerly, "Did you really? Did it go all right?" But as soon as he sees the sparks flying from his wife's eyes, he immediately follows that with, "I mean... that—that was very wrong, boys—very wrong indeed." (II, 39)

Perfectly suited to bringing the distracted person back to reality is no-nonsense Professor McGonagall. In a Quidditch match, commentator Lee Jordan is so biased in favor of Harry's team and so carried away by Harry's new flying broom, the "Firebolt," that he forgets he is supposed to describe the game rather than the broom and must be brought back to earth by McGonagall.

> **Jordan:** "Gryffindor leads by eighty points to zero, and look at that Firebolt go!...the Firebolt's precision-balance is really noticeable in these long..."
>
> **McGonagall:** "JORDAN! ARE YOU BEING PAID TO ADVERTISE FIREBOLTS? GET ON WITH THE COMMENTARY!" (III, 260-1)

In short, in a whole variety of comic situations, Rowling's characters behave like automatons stunned when they slip on the banana skin of reality. To find their situation laughable, we must not identify too strongly with them.[4] When magic works havoc on the likable Weasley brothers (depriving George of an ear, disfiguring Charlie), we react, of course, with sympathy rather than mirth. And at the end of *The Deathly Hallows*, when Voldemort tosses Harry in the air three times, and the boy rises and falls flopping like a rag doll, it is breath-holding, nail-biting time, not an occasion for laughter.

However, when we are not particularly concerned with fate of a character, his or her mechanical behavior will continue to entertain us. That is often the case when a proud or vain person is deflated and tumbles to earth with a comic thud.

Exploding the Myth

In *Harry Potter*, Gilderoy Lockhart is a prime example of a pompous character deflated and brought down by humor. Handsome and extravagantly conceited, Lockhart exposes himself to ridicule when unexpected visitors to his room get a glimpse of portraits with his golden hair wrapped in rollers and a hair net.

Percy Weasley is another likely candidate for the humorous comedown. Ambitious and self-important, Percy prides himself on being indispensable to his boss, Mr. Crouch—although Crouch mistakenly calls him "Weatherby." At one point, Percy announces to his family: "Mr. Crouch is really starting to rely on me." Upon which his brother George says seriously: "Yeah, you know what, Percy? I reckon he'll know your name soon." (IV, 161) And when Percy makes a particularly priggish statement, Fred Weasley says, "Oh shut up, Weatherby." (IV, 92)

Joining the ranks of high and mighty pulled down to earth (or as Bergson put it, "the sublime undermined by the mundane") is Sir Cadogan, a short, squat knight in a Hogwarts painting. As it happens in other pictures, this man can speak and move; he can even pop in and out of his frame at will. A sort of Don Quijote with a good dose of Sancho Panza, Sir Cadogan has a comical cameo role in *The Prisoner of Azkaban*. Early in the book Harry, Ron and Hermione, trying to find their way to class, pass in front of Cadogan's painting. At that moment the little knight, who has fallen off his pony, is clanking back into his frame, hoping to remount the animal. Spotting the trio, he shouts in heroic style:

> "Aha! What villains are these, that trespass on my private lands! Come to scorn at my fall, perchance? Draw, you knaves, you dogs!"

He tries to brandish his sword about, but it is too heavy, and it lands deeply embedded in the turf. He makes futile attempts to pull it out but finally gives up and farcically flops down on the grass. Seeing his plight, Harry asks Sir Cadogan if he is all right, but he gets more angry verbosity in return, So, making the best of the situation, Harry inquires how they can get to their class in the North Tower. "A quest!" shouts the knight, having forgotten his rage. "We shall find our goal, or else shall perish bravely in the charge!"

Sir Cadogan tries in vain to get atop his pony, finally gives up and shouts "On foot then, good sirs and gentle lady!" And leading the way by slipping from one portrait to another, he encourages them with a sentence that starts with a high-flown phrase and ends in bubble bursting: "Be of stout heart, the worst is yet to come!" Finally at the end of the "adventure," Sir Cadogan's would-be lofty image is toppled by Ron's cynicism. When the knight offers them future help if ever they have need of "noble heart and steely sinew," Ron mutters, "Yeah, we'll call you...if ever we need someone mental." (III, 99-101)

These are but a few instances in *Harry Potter* of the sublime undermined by the down-to-earth and self-importance laid low by ridicule.

A Strange Perspective

Much of *Harry Potter*'s humor derives from the collision and collusion of two worlds, magic and real. On the one hand we have the Wizards; on the other, ordinary non-magic Muggles. When the two come in contact with each other the situation is rife with comic possibilities. And Rowling does not hesitate to exploit them. Consciously or not, she uses a device found in much of classic satire: a stranger enters our world and sees it through a completely different lens, forcing us to laugh at ourselves, at our society, our politics or religion, our pretensions, prejudices and obsessions.

The perspective of the stranger has been used for satiric effects in Swift's *Gulliver's Travels*, where Lilliputians and Houyhnhnms are used to target behavior and social institutions in England. In Voltaire's works, a naïve Westphalian, Candide, and an interplanetary voyager in the short novel *Micromegas* humorously prick the bubble of belief and custom in eighteenth-century French society. Anthropomorphized animals play a similar role in fables of Aesop or La Fontaine or George Orwell's grimmer *Animal Farm*, just as children do in a cartoon series like *Peanuts*.

That is precisely the case of Ron's father, Arthur Weasley, a stranger to the Muggle world but intensely interested in it. He encounters the telephone and is amazed. Although he himself can communicate with others at a distance, instantly, by Floo Powder or other magic means, his reaction to the phone is: "Fascinating!...Ingenious, really, how many ways Muggles have found getting along without magic." (II, 43) After Mr. Weasley acquired his Muggle automobile, he charmed it to make it accommodate his whole family. His wife, on entering it (with five sitting comfortably in the back seat), declares, "Muggles *do* know more than we give them credit for...You'd never know it was this roomy from the outside." (II, 66) And if you wondered why you can never find your keys, according to Arthur Weasley, it's because pranksters in the magic community charm them occasionally so they shrink to nothing. However, that truth never comes to light since "no Muggle would admit their key keeps shrinking—they'll insist they just keep losing it." (II, 38)

In the framework of this magic/Muggle duality, the tables are turned on us ordinary humans. The magician—whom we would consider the exotic outsider—thinks of us ordinary folk as strange, often inferior, beings. So when Harry asks Ron whether all his family are wizards, Ron answers, "Er—I think Mom's got a second cousin who's an accountant, but we never talk about him." (I, 99) Later, when Muggle born Hermione mentions Cinderella, Ron asks, "What's that, an illness? (VII, 135)

Some of the most amusing effects of this displacement occur when our own contemporary fads and hype invade the universe of magic. Rowling must have thoroughly enjoyed herself composing a jazzy pop song number for witch Molly Weasley. That plump homemaker often listens to the suggestive "Cauldron Full of Hot, Strong Love," rendered by her favorite singer, Celestina Warbeck:

> "Oh, come and stir my cauldron,
> And if you do it right,
> I'll boil you up some hot, strong love
> To keep you warm tonight." (VI, 330)

The humorous crossing over between the Muggle and magic worlds recurs as our modern advertising ploys appear unexpectedly in the most unlikely places. At Hogwarts, the ill-tempered caretaker, Filch, has been hiding the fact he can't perform magic. Harry, alone in the caretaker's office, sneaks a peak at a flyer Filch has sent for. Entitled "Kwikspell, a Correspondence Course in Beginners' Magic," it is a clever send-up, full of testimonials like:

> *"I had no memory for incantations and my potions were a family joke! Now, after a Kwikspell course, I am the center of attention at parties and friends beg for the recipe of my Scintillation Solution!" —Madam Z. Nettles, Topsham*

> *"My wife used to sneer at my feeble charms, but one month into your fabulous Kwikspell course and I succeeded in turning her into a yak! Thank you, Kwikspell!" —Warlock D. J. Prod, Didsbury* (II, 127)

In *The Prisoner of Azkaban*, Harry looks longingly at a sign describing the Firebolt, the latest in Quidditch racing brooms. It reads:

> *This state-of-the art racing broom sports a streamlined, superfine handle of ash, treated with a diamond-hard polish and hand-numbered with its own registration number. Each individually selected birch twig in the broomtail has been honed to aerodynamic perfection, giving the Firebolt unsurpassable balance and pinpoint precision. The Firebolt has an acceleration of 150 miles an hour in ten seconds and incorporates an unbreakable Braking Charm. Price on request.* (III, 51)

As in our own experience, the wizards' big commercial games are underwritten by businesses promoting themselves in conspicuous ads. At the Quidditch World Cup game, advertisements like "Gladrags Wizardwear—London, Paris, Hogsmeade" flash in gold on a gigantic blackboard.

At times, to the reader's amusement, the interaction of Wizardry and Muggledom misses the mark. In the matter of dress, for example. Cornelius Fudge appears within bounds when, befitting his distinguished position as Minister of Magic, he goes to work in a pin-striped robe. But when wizards gather en masse on public ground at the Quidditch World Cup, they try to disguise themselves as Muggles—and fail. A number of them arrive in the most unlikely combinations of mismatched clothes, only to be outdone by an old wizard in a long flowery nightgown. When his friend urges him to exchange the gown for trousers, the Wizard insists, "I bought this in a Muggle shop. Muggles wear them." (IV, 83)

Such lack of adapting can prove explosive. Witness the case of the Weasleys who come to get Harry from his Muggle guardians, the Dursleys. Instead of arriving by car, they enter from their fireplace to the one in the Dursley's living room, by means of Floo powder. But it happens that Aunt Petunia Dursley is an obsessive-compulsive housekeeper with a spic-and-span household, and Arthur Weasley had no idea her fireplace would be neatly boarded up with an electric unit inside. So when the Weasleys emerge, the fireplace explodes with all sorts of rubble blasted into the spotless living room. Aunt Petunia nearly faints. Uncle Vernon is speechless.

> "Well," said Mr. Weasley, swinging his arms slightly, while he tried to find words to break through the very nasty silence. "Very—erm—very nice place you've got here." (IV, 45)

A Cast of Characters

Rowling has created an inexhaustible supply of colorful comic characters. The most amusing ones are not the stars but the supporting roles. Mainly caricatures, they look and behave outrageously, each in a different way. At the most elementary level are the visually grotesque, such as beefy, stupid Vernon Dursley, with a huge mustache and no neck, and his obese, waddling bully of a son, Dudley. Or the lovable but clumsy half-giant, Hagrid, especially ludicrous when he tries to dress up nattily, with disastrous results. Or Mad-Eye Mooney, with one revolving eye that can peer at you from the back of his head.

One of the most developed examples of a humorous character in *Harry Potter* is Hogwarts Professor Gilderoy Lockhart, who hopelessly, and very temporarily, attempts to teach Defense Against the Dark Arts. Even before we meet the man, we know he'll provide comic grist for the mill. Seven of the eight books required for Harry's second year class are written by Lockhart himself, and a large banner on the front of Flourish and Blotts bookshop proclaims that he will be there, signing copies of his autobiography, *Magical Me*. And there he is, his hat set at a jaunty angle on his blond wavy hair, "surrounded by pictures of his own face, all winking and flashing dazzlingly white teeth at the crowd." (II, 59)

The man believes he is engaging, irresistible. At one point he says something he thinks is terribly cute and gives his class a roguish wink. Ron simply stares at him, "an expression of disbelief on his face." (II, 100) Lockhart's good looks can blind women to his ridiculousness, to the fact that he is a fake and a bungler: Molly Weasley and Hermione, among other females, are smitten with him. But Harry, Ron, Lockhart's colleagues and readers themselves can't wait for his inevitable comeuppance. Rowling gives us a foretaste of that when Lockhart is obliged to let Harry and Ron into his room and they discover that despite his bravado he's packing to run away rather than face danger. At the end of the book, when he finally has his comedown and his image crashes completely, our amusement is heightened by a sense of justification and relief ("Aha! take that, you phony!").

And speaking of phonies, meet Professor Sybill Trelawney. Completely different from Lockhart, she amuses us by surrounding herself in an aura of mysticism. Her classroom, high in a tower, looks like "a cross between someone's attic and an old-fashioned teashop." (III, 102) Stifling, heavily perfumed, its lamps are draped in red scarves, the room's shelves crammed with dusty feathers, candle stubs, tattered playing cards, crystal balls and a bevy of teacups. A self-styled seer, Trelawney utters random pronouncements in a soft, misty voice. And to convince students of her supernatural powers, she constantly predicts imminent disaster for them—Harry in particular. Naturally, her acquired persona tends to backfire and, as with Lockhart, her frequent slips and tumbles provide a goldmine of humor.

Beyond the realm of eccentric teachers, there are characters aplenty to raise a laugh or a smile. Molly Weasley, for example. We find wholesome Molly perpetually dishing out tons of comfort food to her children and Harry, "seeing [the boys] off in the morning "after a quick half a dozen bacon sandwiches each." (II, 47) But this mother hen especially evokes laughter when her temper is aroused, for instance, when she lambastes her sons for sneaking out and transporting Harry to their house in Mr. Weasley's magic automobile. Picture the little woman in a flowered apron, arms akimbo, addressing her boys in a "deadly whisper" that builds to a high crescendo.

As Rowling tells it, "All three of Mrs. Weasley's sons were taller than she was, but they cowered as her rage broke over them."

> "Beds empty! No note! Car gone—could have crashed—out of my mind with worry—Did you care?—never, as long as I've lived—you wait until your father gets home..." (II, 33)

And Mrs. Weasley does not hesitate to make Ron a butt of ridicule at school after he misbehaves again, by sending him a "Howler," a bright red envelope that explodes if you don't open it. A surefire means of embarrassing anyone who doesn't toe the line, the opened envelope releases a scolding voice that screams a hundred times louder than normal speech.

> Mrs. Weasley's yells...made the spoons rattle on the table and echoed deafeningly off the stone walls...Ron sank so low in his chair that only his crimson forehead could be seen. (II, 88)

Other humorous characters abound, the house-elf Dobby among them. This little creature has huge tennis ball eyes and, like other house-elves, wears a pillowcase with slits for armholes. Having little dress sense, when he eventually acquires socks, he firmly believes that mismatched ones are a must. But Dobby's most amusing feature is his unusual behavior. By the code of house-elfdom, he must remain loyal to his masters who, in Dobby's case, are villainous enemies of Harry Potter. Still, he deeply admires Harry and wants to help him.

So whenever he tries to do something for his idol he feels guilty and punishes himself by hitting his head against something very hard or sticking it in the oven. But in any case, Dobby's idea of "helping" Harry wreaks havoc every time. At one point, when he tries to save the boy's life, Harry winds up in a hospital bed, having a ruined arm re-grown. When Ron hears about Dobby's doings he comments, "You know what, Harry? If he doesn't stop trying to save your life he's going to kill you." (II, 184)

And there is Hagrid, that well-meaning half giant with a penchant for nurturing ferocious animals. When a baby dragon he's raising, snaps at his fingers and bares its pointy fangs, Hagrid exclaims, "Bless him, he knows his mommy!" (I, 235) But later, when Ron complains that Hermione won't get rid of her annoying cat, we hear Hagrid wisely commenting "Ah, well, people can be a bit stupid abou' their pets." (III, 274)

But even a serious, central character like Hermione serves, at times, as the butt of humor—a humor that dwells precisely on her seriousness. Hermione's staunch commitment to social justice is misplaced. Although she longs to free the Hogwarts house-elves, outside of Dobby (freed by Harry), not one of them wants anything to do with freedom. For all the others, liberation would be a dire fate, a source of shame. They are *happy* with the status quo.

However, Hermione persists relentlessly in her S.P.E.W.[5] efforts, spending every spare moment knitting hats for the Hogwarts house-elves to liberate them. When the hats disappear, she is sure the elves have snapped them up. But one day, *voilà*—there is Dobby, happily free, sporting—one atop the other—all the hats that Hermione so painstakingly knit.

Now when socially aware readers find Ron, Harry, and the author herself, poking fun at a well meaning Hermione, a number of them are, understandably, put off.[6] But Rowling, although opposed to any form of slavery and socially active herself, understands the comic value of a zealous or obsessive fictional character who won't or can't adapt to the reality at hand.

Because Hermione is of great importance to the book and to its hero, and because she is someone readers can identify with, Rowling does not mock her mercilessly but with an understanding smile. To encounter frankly comic characters, however, readers will not have far to look. For the array of laughable caricatures in these pages is wide and varied, including ghosts such as Nearly Headless Nick of the half-severed cranium and Moaning Myrtle the ululating acne ridden damsel who resides in a toilet pipe.

Humor and Irony

As the main characters approach adolescence and Rowling conveys their more complex psychology, the comic element gives way to a more serious type of humor, one that evokes a wry smile in readers—as in Hermione's case—rather than out-and-out laughter.

Freud has seen a close connection between humor and pain, viewing the humorist as someone who jokes about difficulties in order to alleviate them through a sort of catharsis.[7] Bergson too emphasizes the humor-pain relationship, explaining that humor is created when a writer looks at tragedy or evil and zeroes in on concrete details found therein. So it is not surprising that in *Harry Potter* much of the humor revolves around the deep concerns of the characters and the difficulties they undergo.

In *Harry Potter*, especially in the later books, irony constantly comes to the fore as a means of surviving unpleasantness and allaying fears. In this humorous irony the tables are turned; reality is reversed: **1.** something great or fearsome may be described as a mere bagatelle, or **2.** pettiness and stupidity are seen as grand and wonderful. In *Harry Potter*, Rowling most often uses the first approach. When asked what she thought was the funniest moment, she singled out a caustic reply of Ron's toward the end of *The Deathly Hallows*. After Harry's magnificent victory over Voldemort, Peeves the poltergeist reduces the epic event to a bit of doggerel, chanting:

> *"We did it, we bashed them, wee Potter's the one,*
> *And Voldy's gone moldy, so now let's have fun!"*

Upon which, Ron contrasts Peeves' frivolous ditty about the event with the actual hard-won, heroic battle, saying "Really gives a feeling for the scope and tragedy of the thing, doesn't it?" (VII, 746)

Ron, with perpetual jokers Fred and George for older brothers, can be depended on in a number of cases for such satiric remarks. At one point Hermione tries to explain that one's soul can't be physically damaged. When she tells him, "If I picked up a sword right now, Ron, and ran you through with it, I wouldn't damage your soul at all." He answers: "Which would be a real comfort to me, I'm sure." (VII, 104)

Wittier than Ron's ironic comments are Rowling's own asides. Her straight-faced one-liners can take us suddenly from the sublime to the ridiculous. The first example below describes Ron's hand-me-down Quidditch racing broom. The second relates to the game itself:

> [His] old Shooting Star was often outstripped by passing butterflies. (II, 46)
> Although people rarely died playing Quidditch, referees have been known to vanish and turn up months later in the Sahara Desert. (I, 181)

But some of the most amusing instances of witty irony are comments directed at, or about, Professor Sybill Trelawney. Dry, imperious Professor McGonagall takes deadly aim at that self-styled oracle at a Hogwarts Christmas banquet. Fully aware that nearly all Trelawney's predictions are hogwash, the first two words that McGonagall directs at her are: "Tripe, Sybill?" Then, when the Divination teacher inquires "But where is dear Professor Lupin? Dumbledore says he's sick," McGonagall remarks "But surely you already knew that, Sybill?" (III, 229)

Kindly Dumbledore himself cannot resist the temptation to use playful irony at Trelawney's expense. In *The Prisoner of Azkaban*, Harry is highly disconcerted that she seems to have made a real prediction, in a sort of trance, foretelling Pettigrew's return to his old master, Voldemort. When he tells Dumbledore about it, the headmaster, probably to put Harry's concern to rest, says: "Who would have thought of it? That brings her total of real predictions up to two. I should offer her a pay raise." (III, 426)

To be funny at all, irony needs a light touch; when heavy handed, it loses its punch and turns into grim-faced sarcasm. Fortunately, Rowling prefers to keep the characters' retorts and comebacks playful rather than glum.

Ghosts and Gallows Humor

In *Harry Potter*, ghosts have mainly walk-on (or more accurately, float-on) parts, wafting about in hallways or sometimes at banquets. But a few of them play more important roles, and among them we find that oddball, Nearly Headless Nick, a subject of some rather gruesome humor. Nick, the resident ghost of Gryffindor, gets to star in *The Chamber of Secrets*, in a chapter entitled "The Deathday Party." To celebrate the five hundredth anniversary of his death, Nick gives a big party in one of the roomier dungeons of the castle. But a tragi-comic circumstance mars his pleasure: he has received a letter informing him of his ineligibility to enter the annual Headless Hunt, the day of his birthday (or "deathday"), because his head is still somewhat attached to his body. After receiving his letter of rejection from ghost Sir Patrick Delaney-Podmore, he complains banefully,

> "Half an inch of skin and sinew holding my neck on, Harry! Most people would think that's good and beheaded, but oh, no, it's not enough for Sir Properly Decapitated-Podmore." (II, 124)

This inventive transposing and juxtaposing of mourning and celebration, calamity and joy, earthly reality and the sublime, does not stop with Nearly Headless Nick. It continues notably in episodes with another ghostly figure, Moaning Myrtle. Myrtle, a former student at Hogwarts had been teased no end by classmates and constantly cried her eyes out in the girls' bathroom. Stabbed to death by a basilisk there, she returned as a ghost and resided miserably ever after in the lavatory. Throughout the story, her melodramatic bewailing of her fate contrasts humorously with her habitat in the U-bend of a toilet.

Myrtle's contacts with down-to-earth characters make her perpetually an unwitting figure of fun. Here is Rowling's description of her encounter with the nasty poltergeist Peeves. Myrtle begins by lamenting,

> "D'you think I don't know what people call me behind my back? Fat Myrtle! Ugly Myrtle! Miserable, moaning, moping Myrtle!"
>
> "You've forgotten pimply," Peeves hissed in her ear.
>
> Peeves shot after her, pelting her with moldy peanuts, yelling, *"Pimply! Pimply"*

At that point Nick comes up to Harry and a very distressed Hermione, asking, "Enjoying yourselves?" (II, 135)

Not all the ghosts in *Harry Potter* are that amusing. In fact, dull Professor Binns had so little life in him he didn't seem to notice he had died; one morning he simply left his body behind and went to class as usual. The only time we find anything approaching humor in Binns's presence is when Hermione astounds him and his whole History of Magic class by interrupting his droning lecture with a question about the Chamber of Secrets. As if by magic, the students, some of them actually asleep, perk their heads up in amazement at her interruption. Binns tries to ignore Hermione in order to proceed with his droning, but he finally answers her and is astonished that his class is actually looking at him. When others shoot questions at him about the Chamber, he reluctantly replies, addressing each student by the wrong name. Bergson's mechanistic theory of humor comes into play here. All the more so when Binns sharply interrupts his one-time experience of an animated class and reverts to his customary automated, boring procedure, announcing, "That will do...We will return, if you please, to *history*, to solid, believable, verifiable *fact.*"

The incident closes with the author's comment "And within five minutes, the class had sunk into its usual torpor." (II, 152)

Wordplay

At times, Rowling makes us laugh by zeroing on specific words and taking a completely different spin on them. Dumbledore provides a rather silly example of the technique in his opening speech in *The Sorcerer's Stone*. After welcoming new and returning students to school, he announces "I would like to say a few words. And here they are: Nitwit! Blubber! Oddment! Tweak!" And he sits down. (I, 123) The effect of that sally is totally ambiguous; listeners don't know whether to laugh or not, and newcomer Harry wonders if Dumbledore is insane.

However, a less contrived and more humorous instance of Dumbledore's taking words literally occurs at the Hogwarts opening ceremony in *The Goblet of Fire*. Dumbledore stands up to make a momentous announcement: The great Triwizard Tournament, an event that had not taken place in over a century, would be held right there, at Hogwarts, that very year. His audience is flabbergasted by the news. "You're JOKING!" Fred Weasley shouts spontaneously. Without missing a beat, Dumbledore replies,

> "No, I am not joking, Mr. Weasley...Though now that you mention it, I did hear an excellent one over the summer about a troll, a hag, and a leprechaun who all go into a bar..."

Bringing Dumbledore back to order, Professor McGonagall clears her throat loudly, and Dumbledore catches himself. "Er...but maybe this is not the time...no...where was I? Ah, yes, the Triwizard Tournament." (IV, 186) This bit of drollery has a lot going for it: it has Dumbledore focusing on a word, "joking," and, automatically, without thinking, going utterly off the track with it. It has that eminent Headmaster suddenly switching from the sublime, the grand message he was delivering, to the familiar, commonplace format of an old Muggles joke ("These three guys go into a bar, see, and the bartender...") but transposing the joke by replacing Muggles with creatures of the magic world. And it has the rug pulled out from under him, as Professor McGonagall quickly brings him back to the important subject at hand.

The Weasley boys are very good at latching onto a word and taking it off the track entirely. When Mrs. Weasley shouts "Ron! Don't you ever let me see you throwing knives again!" he answers "I won't," and then adds under his breath, "Let you see." (VI, 327) Later, when Ron and Harry haven't asked anyone to the upcoming Yule Ball, Ron suggests they get moving before all the good-looking girls are taken and they end up "with a couple of trolls." Hermione, shocked to hear him, asks "So basically, you're going to take the best-looking girl who'll have you, even if she's horrible?" And Ron, taking her literally, replies, "Er—yeah, that sounds about right." (IV, 394-5)

Fred and George love needling their self-important, sanctimonious brother Percy. In the following exchange between Percy and Fred, the latter, first deflates Percy with his "dragon dung" remark, then focuses on the word "personal." Percy starts the dialogue by complaining how terribly (and importantly) busy he is:

> **Percy:** "I *shudder* to think what the state of my in-tray would be if I was away from work for five days."
>
> **Fred:** "Yeah, someone might slip dragon dung in it again, eh, Perce?"
>
> **Percy:** "That was a sample of fertilizer from Norway!...It was nothing *personal*."
>
> But Fred whispers to Harry "It was...We sent it." (IV, 64)

Harry, generally far more serious than the Weasleys, can, nonetheless, come out with the clever put-down. In the following instance, he does it by taking Rita Skeeter literally: That unprincipled, opportunistic reporter accosts Harry after his first Tri-Wizard task and asks, "I wonder if you could give me a quick word? How you felt facing that dragon? How you feel *now* about the fairness of the scoring?" And Harry answers, "Yeah, you can have a word... *goodbye.*" (IV, 362)

The ways in which Rowling creates humor by zeroing in on specific words are varied; there is no set formula involved. In *The Prisoner of Azkaban* after Harry inflates his aunt , he expects to be punished by the Ministry of Magic. But the Minister, Fudge, currently in charge of protecting Harry, tells him, "Oh, my dear boy…We don't send people off to Azkaban just for blowing up their aunts!" (III, 45) Associating the idea of inflating with a lethal attack, Rowling has Fudge blithely interpreting "blowing up" one's relative as a mere bagatelle.

Earlier, in the first book, a letter sent to Harry is addressed to "Mr. H. Potter, The Cupboard under the Stairs, 4 Privet Drive…" (p. 34) The sender, in specifically pinpointing Harry's horrible living quarters and in casually including the location on an envelope for all to see, turns sordid reality into comic relief. And a less subtle technique comes into play in *The Prisoner of Azkaban*. There, books take their titles literally and don't adapt to the fact that they are books: Flourish and Blotts can no longer stock the *Invisible Book of Invisibility* because it "cost a fortune and we never found them," while *The Monster Book of Monsters* takes itself so seriously it has to be locked up in a cage to prevent its attacks on would be readers. (III, 53)

From the Sublime…

Harry Potter's humor depends at times on earthiness and a certain vulgarity. But that does not shock us because Rowling senses where to draw the line and doesn't take ribaldry or grossness too far. Her earthiness serves as a tonic for spiking situations and dialogue, and the dosage is just adequate to the job.

We encounter, a good number of times, characters making "rude hand gestures," never specifically described. (By the time readers are old enough to understand that, they may well have seen or done it themselves.) Ron does it, Draco Malfoy does it, and when Fudge tries to bring about Dumbledore's downfall, even distinguished gentlemen in portraits do it. A bit more graphic is a comment made by the wizard in the floral nightgown at the Quidditch World Cup race. When a friend pleads with him to change into something more suitable, the wizard demurs, saying "I like a healthy breeze 'round my privates, thanks." (IV, 84)

But throughout the series, Rowling obviously prefers scatological humor to bawdiness—a logical choice, since young readers respond delightedly to references to dung or "poo-poo." One of many examples of this earthiness is found in *The Order of the Phoenix*, when Harry, having cleaned Hedwig's cage, throws his bag of owl droppings over Ron's head into the wastebasket, "which swallowed it and belched loudly." (V, 160)

Those eternal wags, Fred and George Weasley use their anal humor to good effect in *The Half-Blood Prince*. When no one in the entire magic community would dare to make light of Voldemort— a figure so threatening he cannot be named but only referred to as "You-Know-Who"—the Weasley twins put up this sign on their joke shop:

WHY ARE YOU WORRYING ABOUT YOU-KNOW-WHO?
YOU SHOULD BE WORRYING ABOUT YOU-NO-POO—
THE CONSTIPATION SENSATION
THAT'S GRIPPING THE NATION! (VI, 116)

Undermining the unthinkable, bursting a huge and fearsome bubble, bringing the unearthly down to earth, at least for a moment—Fred and George manage to do just that by turning Voldemort into a joke about excretion.

Harry and Ron, seeing the sign, laugh heartily, and Ron calls it brilliant. Of course, since it was Rowling's idea in the first place, the laughter and the word "brilliant" can be construed as self-compliments. If so, they are well deserved.

Humor and Style

Since the *Harry Potter* books are an endless source of humor, to cite, categorize and analyze all examples would turn this one chapter into a book. Any relatively harmless minor character may come out with some comic gem—usually unthinkingly. When Dumbledore arranges for Tom Riddle to leave his orphanage and go to Hogwarts, he explains to the director, Mrs. Cole, that she will have to take Tom back during the summer. Mrs. Cole, undoubtedly not delighted at the prospect of seeing the unlikable boy again but besotted with all the gin Dumbledore has plied her with, says, with a slight hiccup: "Oh, well, that's better than a whack on the nose with a rusty poker." (VI, 268)

An entirely different type of character, Stan Shunpike, provides us with his own style of drollery. Stan, the conductor of the magic Knight Bus, recognizes Harry when he boards the bus a second time. Stan has read some of the nasty articles the *Daily Prophet* printed, portraying Harry as either a mental case or a villain, and he says:

> "You keepin' well, then 'arry? I seen your name in the paper loads over the summer, but it weren't never nuffink very nice...I said to Ern, I said, ''e didn't seem like a nutter when we met 'im, just goes to show, dunnit?'" (V, 525)

If we find amusement in the spice and verbal variety of such dialogues, we discover humor also in Rowling's descriptions of human physiognomy, in her comparisons of faces with animals or inanimate objects (a bald bartender "who looked like a toothless walnut.") (I, 68) and in her anthropomorphism, where objects take on human characteristics. A prime example of such personification is seen in descriptions of the Weasley's magic automobile, full of verbs and modifiers that humanize the vehicle: an engine which "began to whine," windshield wipers waving feebly, "as though in protest," a motor that begins to "shudder," rear lights "blazing angrily," as the car disappears with "one last snort..." In fact, when the car comes to their rescue, both Harry and Ron give it a reassuring pat, with Ron saying, at one point, "Well done, car." (II, 72-76)

And every volume furnishes us with a constant stream of comic alliteration, *e.g.: The Adventures of Martin Miggs, the Mad Muggle* (Ron's comic book), *Break With a Banshee, Gadding With Ghouls, Holidays and Hags, Travels With Trolls* (books by Gilderoy Lockhart);

Ton-Tongue Toffee, Decoy Detonators, Weasleys' Wizard Wheezes (inventions of Fred and George).[8]

But the most admirable feature of Rowling's humorous style is her terse delivery. Her cleverness lies less in what she says than in what she will not articulate. And she has a fine sense of where to draw the line between omission and expression. To convey Mrs. Weasley's girlish crush on Gilderoy Lockhart, she simply mentions that, on the point of seeing him at his book signing, Molly sounds out-of-breath and keeps patting her hair.

In *The Goblet of Fire*, someone mentions the fact that Eloise Midgen was desperate enough to try cursing her acne off. Professor Sprout comments: "But Madame Pomfrey fixed her nose back on in the end." (IV, 195) If Rowling had spelled the girl's fate out in more detail, saying "Eloise tried to curse off her acne, and what do you know—her nose fell off!" she would have come up with merely an inane story. By skipping the accident itself and cutting to the finish, she makes the incident comic.

Ginny Weasley, reared with wags like Fred and George, gives proof of her quick and sassy wit as she matures. In *The Goblet of Fire* she does it with only two words and a nod. Her mother, Molly, shares her dislike of Fleur Delacour but unlike Ginny, refuses to cat about her, since Fleur is engaged to Bill Weasley. So she reprimands Ginny for referring to Fleur as "Phlegm." But when Molly Weasley gets close to revealing her own negative feelings about Fleur by making an unfavorable comparison between Fleur and her beloved son, Bill, Ginny interrupts her and chimes in:

> **Mrs. Weasley:** "[Bill's] a hard-working, down-to-earth sort of a person, whereas she's—"
> **Ginny (nodding):** "A cow…But Bill's not that down-to-earth, he's…" (VI, 93)

The humor of the dialogue lies in Ginny's suggesting that her mother, despite her wish to be diplomatic, would actually have used the word "cow" and Ginny's *nodding*, to indicate that she agrees with Mrs. Weasley's (unvoiced) insult. Without giving her mother time to object, Ginny doesn't skip a beat but immediately continues talking.

If just two words and a nod can illicit humor, earlier in the story Ginny makes us laugh without uttering even one word. In *The Chamber of Secrets*, the usually talkative Ginny, just eleven years old, sits completely mute in the presence of her idol, Harry. At one point he actually addresses a question to the smitten girl. Here is Rowling's full description of Ginny's response to Harry:

> She nodded, blushing to the roots of her hair and put her elbow in the butter dish. (p. 44)

Using the fewest words for the greatest comic effect, Rowling demonstrates artistry in the tradition of a Voltaire or an Oscar Wilde.

* * *

Rowling's use of comedy, wit and humor has not been sufficiently recognized or discussed by critics. However their role in the cycle is an important one. For one thing, they lend a welcome variety to the work, serving as a respite and a catharsis amid dark and dangerous adventures that perpetually generate tension. And Rowling's use of humor enhances *Harry Potter*'s popularity among readers of varying ages, since it can be appreciated at different levels, from the slapstick sight gag to mature witty remarks.

The humorous techniques found throughout *Harry Potter* add to the originality of the work. For they are rarely important features of other adventure or fantasy stories geared to young people, or ever used to such advantage. As apparent from the above illustrations, thanks to her cleverness, her deft touch, discrimination and sense of timing, Rowling's humor is an irresistible feature of the *Harry Potter* cycle.

---

[1] Interview of October 16, 2000. www.accio-quote.org/articles/2000/1000-scholastic-chat.htm

[2] "Le mécanique plaqué sur du vivant," *Le Rire.*"

[3] Incident cited in above, p. 70.

[4] Bergson makes this point in his analysis of comedy.

[5] Society for the Protection of Elvish Welfare. See Chapter Two, p. 38*ff.*

[6] See, for example, Eliza Dresang's essay in *The Ivory Tower*, p. 211*ff.*

[7] "Wit and its Relation to the Unconscious." *The Basic Writings of Sigmund Freud.*

[8] Most alliteration, including "Butterbeer," Whomping Willow" and "Shrieking hack," is lost in translations into other languages. For instance, in the Spanish version, "Whomping Willow" becomes "boxing willow" which translates as "sauce boxeador."

10

A Way With Words

"A simple style is like white light. It is complex
but its complexity is not obvious."
—Anatole France

Rowling's style of writing has received little attention and provoked hardly any discussion to speak of. Fans of *Harry Potter* enthuse about her clever plotting but are generally not concerned with—perhaps not even aware of—her use of words. As for the professionals, when they do focus on Rowling's prose, it is very often to disparage it. Writer Ursula Le Guin called it "stylistically ordinary."[1] Critic Anthony Holden judged it "pedestrian" and "ungrammatical."[2] For Harold Bloom, "Rowling's mind is so governed by clichés and dead metaphors that she has no other style of writing."[3]

It is true that individually most of the sentences and paragraphs of *Harry Potter* are not impressively beautiful or polished. In fact, if Rowling submitted sample pages in a writing class, a professor might well fault her for such things as an unnecessary repetition of words, unoriginal phrases, abundance of adverbs or overuse of the verb "to be" and the passive mode.

None of that matters a whit. For although Rowling's style may not satisfy the experts, it is eminently suited to the story. As critic Yvonne Zipp put it:

> It's true a reader rarely pauses to parse the beauty of a
> sentence (that would slow you down!). But she tells her

tale with such vividness that the words almost vanish as the story pours directly into your consciousness.[4]

What sort of prestidigitation has *Harry Potter's* author conjured up, to make a "bad" style so fascinating? The answer lies in the style itself. Ideally tailored for a tale of adventure, it is simple and clear, lacking in strong metaphors that would call attention to themselves and devoid of descriptive passages to divert readers from the action. Sentences are rarely more than three and a half lines long, and exposition is constantly interrupted by dialogue.

But above all, Rowling's style has the cadence of a master storyteller—a series of short phrases imbued with rhythm to propel readers on relentlessly. If we read aloud a typical passage such as the following, we can see that Rowling—with a history of inventing and telling stories to childhood friends—can bind an audience in the tradition of the African tale-spinning *griot* or the medieval troubadour of southern France.

> He didn't stop to think. Plunging a hand down the neck of his robes, he whipped out his wand and roared, *"Expecto Patronum!"*
>
> Something silver-white, something enormous, erupted from the end of his wand. He knew it had shot directly at the dementors but didn't pause to watch; His mind still miraculously clear, he looked ahead—he was nearly there. He stretched out the hand still grasping his wand and just managed to close his fingers around the small, struggling Snitch.
>
> Madam Hooch's whistle sounded. (III, 262)

The style of some other popular fantasy stories may be more poetic, more mystical or more impressively technical and scientific.[5] Yet the success of *Harry Potter* is in large part due to its clarity of expression and the phrasing and rhythm that build dramatically, engaging readers in page after page.

One of the most admirable features of the work is the unusual authenticity of its dialogue.

A Manner of Speaking

Natural. Realistic. Nuanced. Such words distinguish the dialogue in *Harry Potter* from that of most other fantasy stories. Rowling has endowed her characters with the ability to communicate with each other as ordinary people communicate in real life. A prime example of such realism may be seen in *The Order of the Phoenix*. It is the first meeting of a student group, the future "Dumbledore's Army." Hermione wants to convince the students she rounded up to take lessons in self-defense from Harry. But she is obviously nervous. Are they friends? Will they go along with the idea? She has no speech prepared but addresses her peers off the cuff. Her anxiety comes through in her "ers, her tone of voice and her unrehearsed phrases:

> "Er," said Hermione, her voice slightly higher than usual...Well—er—hi...well, you know why you're here. Erm...well Harry here had the idea—I mean"—Harry had thrown her a sharp look—"I had the idea—that it might be good if people who wanted to study Defense Against the Dark Arts—and I mean, really study it, you know, not the rubbish that Umbridge is doing with us"—(Hermione's voice became suddenly much stronger and more confident)—"because nobody could call that Defense Against the Dark Arts..." (V, 339)

This whole scene, including a back-and-forth between Harry and his schoolmates, is too long to quote here, but throughout we find this same authenticity of verbal expression.

The way in which the characters speak to each other is psychologically on target not only in what they articulate but in what they try to suppress. When Hermione tells Ron not to let Malfoy get to him, he tries to give her an I-could-care-less answer, but but his squashing gesture lets readers know his words are only bravado.

> "Him! Get to me? As if!" said Ron, picking up one of the remaining Cauldron Cakes and squashing it into a pulp. (IV, 170)

And the following lines offer a perfect illustration of a dialogue that realistically balances the expressed and the implicit, Harry happens to be holding Ron's prefect badge when Hermione, who has also been named prefect, spots it. Assuming, of course, that Harry has made the grade, and never imagining the honor could have gone instead to Ron, she cries excitedly,

> "I knew it!…Me too, Harry, me too!"
> "No," said Harry quickly, pushing the badge back into Ron's hand. "It's Ron, not me."
> "It—what?"
> "Ron's prefect, not me," Harry said.
> *"Ron?"* said Hermione, her jaw dropping. "But…are you sure? I mean—"

She turned red as Ron looked around at her with a defiant expression on his face.

> "It's my name on the letter," he said.
> "I…" said Hermione, looking thoroughly bewildered. "I…well…wow! Well done, Ron! That's really—"
> "Unexpected," said George, nodding.
> "No," said Hermione, blushing harder than ever. "No, it's not…Ron's done loads of…"

Fortunately for Hermione, she was saved by Mrs. Weasley backing into the room with a load of laundry. (V, 162-3)

As for Harry, being a friend of Ron and Hermione, he could not express his own deep resentment at winding up the only one of the three not to be chosen for prefect.

For some reason, Harry found that he did not want to look at Hermione. He turned to his bed, picked up the pile of clean robes…and crossed the room to his trunk.

> "Harry?" said Hermione tentatively.
> "Well done," said Harry, so heartily it did not sound like his voice at all, and still not looking at her, "Brilliant. Prefect. Great." (V, 165)

To cite one last example of a natural conversation that hides as much as it reveals, this passage starts with an on-the-surface exchange between Sirius and Molly Weasley.

> **Sirius:** "Well, Molly, I'm pretty sure this is a boggart...it could be something much worse."
> **Molly:** "Right you are, Sirius."
> They were both speaking in carefully light, polite voices that told Harry quite plainly that neither had forgotten their disagreement of the night before. (V, 102)

The dialogue in *Harry Potter* is all the more believable for the fact that individual characters have their own particular style. Very often a reader opening one of the volumes at random can determine right away who is speaking. Of the three friends, Ron can be spotted by his frequent use of "Dunno," "that git," "blimey" and other bits of his favorite slang. It could only be Ron who exclaims as he twiddles the replay knob of a magic gadget, "Wild! I can make that old bloke down there pick his nose again...and again...and again." (IV, 99) It could only be Hermione talking about library books and proudly spouting out the correct answers in class.

Harry is completely aware of how the two others voice their thoughts and opinions. When his scar pains him badly early in *The Goblet of Fire*, he considers asking them for advice. But he can well imagine what Hermione would typically say:

> *"Your scar hurts? Harry, that's really serious...Write to Professor Dumbledore! And I'll go and check* Common Magical Ailments and Afflictions..." (p. 21)

And when Harry imagines Ron's answer, it is pure Ron.

> *Your scar hurt? But...but You-Know-Who can't be near you now, can he? I mean...you'd know, wouldn't you? He'd be trying to do you in again, wouldn't he? I dunno, Harry, maybe curse scars always twinge a bit...I'll ask Dad." (p. 22)

Since Harry himself is intended for universal appeal, his style is sober and straightforward, thus less recognizable. But the same cannot be said for Professor Quirrell, who assumes a stutter throughout Book One, or Stan Shunpike with his cockney dialect, or Rubeus Hagrid and his use of "yeh" for "you," "ter" for "to" and contractions like "an'" and "em."

Rowling has an ear for a wide variety of conversational styles and transposes them deftly into her story. Not every character has specific mannerisms of speech, but each speaks believably in a style befitting that person.

Less is More

Considering *Harry Potter's* seven volumes, covering over 4,000 pages, no one could accuse J. K. Rowling of being short-winded. Yet in her language and style, her descriptions and dialogue, she might be compared to a Chinese artist who uses a minimum of brush strokes to conjure up a range of high mountains or a storm-ravaged sea. For she succeeds in evoking the thoughts, reactions and emotions of her characters in the fewest possible words.

Where the main characters are concerned, understatement is the rule. When Harry must begin the first of three dangerous tasks in the Tri-Wizard Tournament, rather than make his terror explicit, Rowling merely mentions his impression that time has flown by too fast. And when Professor McGonagall tells him it's time to start, rather than describe his feelings, Rowling conveys his fear simply by mentioning his falling fork and the strange sound of his voice:

> "You have to get ready for your first task."
> "Okay," said Harry, standing up, his fork falling onto his plate with a clatter.
> "Good luck, Harry," Hermione whispered. "You'll be fine!"
> "Yeah," said Harry in a voice that was most unlike his own. (IV, 348)

After Harry comes out of the contest victorious but wounded, Ron, who has been unjustly holding a grudge against his best friend, comes to eat humble pie. Harry first answers him coldly. Hermione is worried they won't make up. But when Harry sees that a nervous Ron is about to deliver an apology, he "suddenly finds that he doesn't need to hear it."

> "It's okay," he said, before Ron could get the words out. "Forget it."
> "No," said Ron, "I shouldn't've—"
> "*Forget it*," Harry said.
> Ron grinned nervously at him, and Harry grinned back.
> (p. 358)

Just three brief exchanges—or non-exchanges—constitute the whole of their reconciliation scene. It is immediately followed by Hermione bursting into tears (to their great bewilderment), calling them "stupid," hugging them and rushing away sobbing.

In some cases, just one or two words suffice to describe a multitude of thoughts, intentions or emotions. Mid-way through *The Half-Blood Prince*, when Scrimgeour, the Minister of Magic asks to speak privately with Harry, his friends, Remus Lupin and Arthur Weasley, are worried; although it is not explicitly stated in the book, readers can gather from their brief reactions that they mistrust the Minister and want to prevent him from cornering Harry. The two start to rise, but Harry, confident he can handle the situation, reassures them by murmuring a mere two words on his way out: "It's fine," (p. 342) and they sit down again.

Far more significant and dramatic is an understated exchange between Dumbledore and Snape in chapter thirty-three of *The Deathly Hallows*.[6] Snape is shocked when he learns that after protecting Harry for so long the boy is destined to be killed by Voldemort. Dumbledore, surprised at Snape's reaction, asks him if he has grown to care for Harry after all. Of course that is not the case. "For *him*?" Snape shouts, and cries out "*Expecto Patronum!*" He has conjured up his personal protective charm, and it appears in the form of a silver doe; it is exactly the same Patronus as the one belonging to Harry's mother, Lily Potter. Dumbledore understands. He is amazed and deeply moved that Snape has maintained his love for Lily for so many years—ever since their childhood.

But none of that is mentioned here. It is all contained in these five words:

Dumbledore: "After all this time?"

Snape: "Always." (p. 687)

End of scene. No explanation. No description, but with that one word, "Always," the reader's view of Snape is upended: the villain becomes a human being.

Although understatement is the rule, at times no words are pronounced at all. Instead, the characters convey thoughts and feelings solely through meaningful looks. Hermione, articulate and often quite voluble, sends Ron angry messages silently through withering glances. Or when words will not help, she shows concern for her friends by quietly watching them. Early in *The Deathly Hallows*, Mrs. Weasley, terribly worried about what will happen to Harry, Ron and Hermione if they leave school to set out on their dangerous mission, forces herself to make cheerful conversation with Harry. After which, "she looked at him, a long, searching look, then smiled a little sadly, straightened up, and walked away." Harry watches her as she leaves and feels a wave of remorse for the pain he has been giving her. (p. 110)

Surprisingly, at the start of the same book, Harry's Aunt Petunia appears to give one silent inkling of humanity, one brief, unspoken sign of seeing Harry as a human being, after he has spent ten years plus six summers in her house. Although aware that they will never see each other again, she utters a curt "Good-bye" and marches to the door without looking at him. Then she suddenly stops and looks back at him.

> For a moment Harry had the strangest feeling that she wanted to say something to him: She gave him an odd, tremulous look and seemed to teeter on the edge of speech, but then, with a little jerk of her head, she bustled out of the room... (p. 42)

Was Petunia about to impart her first caring words to Harry? Did she suddenly remember that she was his only living blood

bands in this county, so she's got nothing to occupy her mind. If she wasn't such a lady at heart, she'd be downright common.... Was Will telling the truth about marrying Suellen?"

"Yes," said Scarlett, looking the old lady full in the eye. Goodness, she could remember the time when she was scared to death of Grandma Fontaine! Well, she'd grown up since then and she'd just as soon as not tell her to go to the devil if she meddled in affairs at Tara.

"He could do better," said Grandma candidly.

"Indeed?" said Scarlett haughtily.

"Come off your high horse, Miss," said the old lady tartly. "I shan't attack your precious sister, though I might have if I'd stayed at the burying ground. What I mean is with the scarcity of men in the neighborhood, Will could marry most any of the girls. There's Beetrice's four wild cats and the Munroe girls and the McRae—"

"He's going to marry Sue and that's that."

"She's lucky to get him."

"Tara is lucky to get him."

"You love this place, don't you?"

"Yes."

"So much that you don't mind your sister marrying out of her class as long as you have a man around to care for Tara?"

"Class?" said Scarlett, startled at the idea. "Class? What does class matter now, so long as a girl gets a husband who can take care of her?"

"That's a debatable question," said Old Miss. "Some folks would say you were talking common sense. Others would say you were letting down bars that ought never be lowered one inch. Will's certainly not quality folks and some of your people were."

Her sharp old eyes went to the portrait of Grandma Robillard.

Scarlett thought of Will, lank, unimpressive, mild, eternally chewing a straw, his whole appearance deceptively devoid of energy, like that of most Crackers. He did not have behind him a long line of ancestors of wealth, prominence and blood. The first of Will's family to set foot on Georgia soil might even have been one of Oglethorpe's debtors or a bond servant. Will had not been to college. In fact, four years in a backwoods school was all the education he had ever had. He was honest and he was loyal, he was patient and he was hard working, but certainly he was not quality. Undoubtedly by Robillard standards, Suellen was coming down in the world.

"So you approve of Will coming into your family?"

"Yes," answered Scarlett fiercely, ready to pounce upon the old lady at the first words of condemnation.

"You may kiss me," said Grandma surprisingly, and she smiled in her most approving manner. "I never liked you much till now, Scarlett. You were always hard as a hickory nut, even as a child, and I don't like hard females, barring myself. But I do like the way you meet things. You don't make a fuss about things that can't be helped, even if they are disagreeable. You take your fences cleanly like a good hunter."

Scarlett smiled uncertainly and pecked obediently at the withered cheek presented to her. It was pleasant to hear approving words again, even if she had little idea what they meant.

"There's plenty of folks hereabouts who'll have something to say about you letting Sue marry a Cracker—for all that everybody likes Will. They'll say in one breath what a fine man he is and how terrible it is for an O'Hara girl to marry beneath her. But don't you let it bother you."

"I've never bothered about what people said."

"So I've heard." There was a hint of acid in the old voice. "Well, don't bother about what folks say. It'll probably be a very successful marriage. Of course, Will's always going to look like a Cracker and marriage won't improve his grammar any. And, even if he makes a mint of money, he'll never lend any shine and sparkle to Tara, like your father did. Crackers are short on sparkle. But Will's a gentleman at heart. He's got the right instincts. Nobody but a born gentleman could have put his finger on what is wrong with us as accurately as he just did, down there at the burying. The whole world can't lick us but we can lick ourselves by longing too hard for things we haven't got any more—and by remembering too much. Yes, Will will do well by Suellen and by Tara."

"Then you approve of me letting him marry her?"

"God, no!" The old voice was tired and bitter but vigorous. "Approve of Crackers marrying into old families? Bah! Would I approve of breeding scrub stock to thoroughbreds? Oh, Crackers are good and solid and honest but—"

"But you said you thought it would be a successful match!" cried Scarlett bewildered.

"Oh, I think it's good for Suellen to marry Will—to marry anybody for that matter, because she needs a husband bad. And where else could she get one? And where else could you get as good a manager for Tara? But that doesn't mean I like the situation any better than you do."

But I do like it, thought Scarlett trying to grasp the old lady's meaning. I'm glad Will is going to marry her. Why should she think I minded? She's taking it for granted that I do mind, just like her.

She felt puzzled and a little ashamed, as always when people attributed to her emotions and motives they possessed and thought she shared.

Grandma fanned herself with her palmetto leaf and went on briskly: "I don't approve of the match any more than you do but I'm practical and so are you. And when it comes to something that's unpleasant but can't be helped, I don't see any sense in screaming and kicking about it. That's no way to meet the ups and downs of life. I know because my family and the Old Doctor's family have had more than our share of ups and downs. And if we folks have a motto, it's this: 'Don't holler—smile and bide your time.' We've survived a passel of things that way, smiling and biding our time, and we've gotten to be experts at surviving. We had to be. We've always bet on the wrong horses. Run out of France with the Huguenots, run out of England with the Cavaliers, run out of Scotland with Bonnie Prince Charlie, run out of Haiti by the niggers and now licked by the Yankees. But we always turn up on top in a few years. You know why?"

She cocked her head and Scarlett thought she looked like nothing so much as an old, knowing parrot.

"No, I don't know, I'm sure," she answered politely. But she was heartily bored, even as she had been the day when Grandma launched on her memories of the Creek uprising.

"Well, this is the reason. We bow to the inevitable. We're not wheat, we're buckwheat! When a storm comes along it flattens ripe wheat because it's dry and can't bend with the wind. But ripe buckwheat's got sap in it and it bends. And when the wind has passed, it springs up almost as straight and strong as before. We aren't a stiff-necked tribe. We're mighty limber when a hard wind's blowing, because we know it pays to be limber. When trouble comes we bow to the inevitable without any mouthing, and we work and we smile and we bide our time. And we play along with lesser folks and we take what we can get from them. And when we're strong enough, we kick the folks whose necks we've climbed over. That, my child, is the secret of the survival." And after a pause, she added: "I pass it on to you."

The old lady cackled, as if she were amused by her words, despite the venom in them. She looked as if she expected some comment from Scarlett but the words had made little sense to her and she could think of nothing to say.

"No, sir," Old Miss went on, "our folks get flattened out but they rise up again, and that's more than I can say for plenty of people not so far away from here. Look at Cathleen Calvert. You can see what she's come to. Poor white! And a heap lower than the man she married. Look at the McRae family. Flat to the ground, helpless, don't know what to do, don't know how to do anything. Won't even try. They spend their time whining about the good old days. And look at—well, look at nearly anybody in this County except my Alex and my Sally and you and Jim Tarleton and his girls and some others. The rest have gone under because they didn't have any sap in them, because they didn't have the gumption to rise up again. There never was anything to those folks but money and darkies, and now that the money and darkies are gone, those folks will be Cracker in another generation."

"You forgot the Wilkes."

"No, I didn't forget them. I just thought I'd be polite and not mention them, seeing that Ashley's a guest under this roof. But seeing as how you've brought up their names—look at them! There's India who from all I hear is a dried-up old maid already, giving herself all kinds of widowed airs because Stu Tarleton was killed and not making any effort to forget him and try to catch another man. Of course, she's old but she could catch some widower with a big family if she tried. And poor Honey was always a man-crazy fool with no more sense than a guinea hen. And as for Ashley, look at him!"

"Ashley is a very fine man," began Scarlett hotly.

"I never said he wasn't but he's as helpless as a turtle on his back. If the Wilkes family pulls through these hard times, it'll be Melly who pulls them through. Not Ashley."

"Melly! Lord, Grandma! What are you talking about?

Mrs. Tarleton's eager helping hand so strong under Scarlett's elbow that she was almost lifted from the ground at each step.

"Now, why did Will do that?" cried Scarlett heatedly, when they were out of earshot. "He practically said: 'Look at her! She's going to have a baby!'"

"Well, sake's alive, you are, aren't you?" said Mrs. Tarleton. "Will did right. It was foolish of you to stand in the hot sun when you might have fainted and had a miscarriage."

"Will wasn't bothered about her miscarrying," said Grandma, a little breathless as she labored across the front yard toward the steps. There was a grim, knowing smile on her face. "Will's smart. He didn't want either you or me, Beetrice, at the graveside. He was scared of what we'd say and he knew this was the only way to get rid of us. . . . And it was more than that. He didn't want Scarlett to hear the clods dropping on the coffin. And he's right. Just remember, Scarlett, as long as you don't hear that sound, folks aren't actually dead to you. But once you hear it . . . Well, it's the most dreadfully final sound in the world. . . . Help me up the steps, child, and give me a hand, Beetrice. Scarlett don't any more need your arm than she needs crutches and I'm not so peart, as Will observed. . . . Will knew you were your father's pet and he didn't want to make it worse for you than it already was. He figured it wouldn't be so bad for your sisters. Suellen has her shame to sustain her and Carreen her God. But you've got nothing to sustain you, have you, child?"

"No," answered Scarlett, helping the old lady up the steps, faintly surprised at the truth that sounded in the reedy old voice. "I've never had anything to sustain me—except Mother."

"But when you lost her, you found you could stand alone, didn't you? Well, some folks can't. Your pa was one. Will's right. Don't you grieve. He couldn't get along without Ellen and he's happier where he is. Just like I'll be happier when I join the Old Doctor."

She spoke without any desire for sympathy and the two gave her none. She spoke as briskly and naturally as if her husband were alive and in Jonesboro and a short buggy ride would bring them together. Grandma was too old and had seen too much to fear death.

"But—you can stand alone too," said Scarlett.

"Yes, but it's powerful uncomfortable at times."

"Look here, Grandma," interrupted Mrs. Tarleton, "you ought not to talk to Scarlett like that. She's upset enough already. What with her trip down here and that tight dress and her grief and the heat, she's got enough to make her miscarry without your adding to it, talking grief and sorrow."

"God's nightgown!" cried Scarlett in irritation. "I'm not upset! And I'm not one of those sickly miscarrying fools!"

"You never can tell," said Mrs. Tarleton omnisciently. "I lost my first when I saw a bull gore one of our darkies and—you remember my red mare, Nellie? Now, there was the healthiest-looking mare you ever saw but she was nervous and high strung and if I didn't watch her, she'd—"

"Beetrice, hush," said Grandma. "Scarlett wouldn't miscarry on a bet. Let's us sit here in the hall where it's cool. There's a nice draft through here. Now, you go fetch us a glass of buttermilk, Beetrice, if there's any in the kitchen. Or look in the pantry and see if there's any wine. I could do with a glass. We'll sit here till the folks come up to say goodby."

"Scarlett ought to be in bed," insisted Mrs. Tarleton, running her eyes over her with the expert air of one who calculated a pregnancy to the last-minute of its length.

"Get going," said Grandma, giving her a prod with her cane, and Mrs. Tarleton went toward the kitchen, throwing her hat carelessly on the sideboard and running her hands through her damp red hair.

Scarlett lay back in her chair and unbuttoned the two top buttons of her tight basque. It was cool and dim in the high-ceilinged hall and the vagrant draft that went from back to front of the house was refreshing after the heat of the sun. She looked across the hall into the parlor where Gerald had lain and, wrenching her thoughts from him, looked up at the portrait of Grandma Robillard hanging above the fireplace. The bayonet-scarred portrait with its high-piled hair, half-exposed breasts and cool insolence had, as always, a tonic effect upon her.

"I don't know which hit Beetrice Tarleton worse, losing her boys or her horses," said Grandma Fontaine. "She never did pay much mind to Jim or her girls, you know. She's one of those folks Will was talking about. Her mainspring's busted. Sometimes I wonder if she won't go the way your pa went. She wasn't ever happy unless horses or humans were breeding right in her face and none of her girls are married or got any prospects of catching hus-

relative and they were parting ways forever? As Rowling explained it to her fans, "I think that for one moment she trembled on the verge of wishing Harry luck; that she almost acknowledged that her loathing of his world, and of him, was born out of jealousy."[7]

All that, conveyed in a split second of silence.

Naming

When Adam gave names to the fowl of the air and the beasts of the field, he could not have enjoyed himself as much as Rowling in inventing a nomenclature for people, places, institutions, magic charms and mythical animals. In fact, Rowling's enjoyment must have been greater than Adam's, since she could actually create the entities she named, fabricating a whole menagerie of beasts, a conglomeration of towns and villages, a plethora of charms and spells, a complex educational edifice with its floor plans and classrooms, its professors and syllabi, a detailed system of magic, an imaginary sport with its set rules, and so much more.

As for the names themselves, they are inventive, amusing and apt. Her fictional place names evoke real towns and villages of Britain. The story's "Ottery St. Catchpole," "Little Hangleton," "Tinworth-on-Cornwall" and "Hogsmeade" might remind us of real quaintly named English locales such as Cripplegate, Newcastle-on-Tyne or Chipping Sodbury, a town near Rowling's place of birth. Names of people—in the Dickensian tradition—often reflect their personalities: "Gilderoy Lockhart" for the effeminate teacher in love with himself; "Sybill" as a first name for Professor Trelawney, the self-styled seer; "Severus Snape" for the severe and snake-like potions master.

In the case of Voldemort, naming takes on a darker, more serious, caste. That despicable tyrant despised his unimpressive, plebeian birth name: "Tom Riddle"—a shameful reminder of his Muggle father. So, thanks to Rowling's ingenuity, he can get rid of it by making an anagram out of it, transforming the letters of "Tom Marvolo[8] Riddle" into "I am Lord Voldemort."

Unfortunately for Voldemort, names can kill. The ancient Egyptians, Asians and aboriginal tribal cultures throughout the world understood that. So they traditionally gave children two names. One was for use in public, and the other, the real one, had to be kept secret and not revealed, lest an enemy or malevolent spirits use it to perform evil magic to destroy the person.[9]

But some people did know Voldemort's real name, and Harry Potter was one of them. In their final encounter, as the two circle each other, each determined to win a fight to death, Harry keeps addressing his opponent mercilessly by his birth name.

> "You don't learn from your mistakes, Riddle, do you?"
> *"You dare—"*
> "Yes, I dare," said Harry. "I know things that you don't, Tom Riddle..." (VII, 738)

Nothing could shock and infuriate Voldemort more than that name aimed at deflating him. It is as if the great Lord Voldemort were caught in public with his pants down.

Not all critics would agree on the subject of Rowling's talent for naming. Some have scoffed at the Latinized words she invented for magic charms and her choice of the strange sounding "Quidditch" for a fictional sport. However, her huge mythical vocabulary, savored and adopted by a host of fans, remains a most impressive facet of the cycle.

A Language of the Heart

Rowling is not a sentimental writer. Classic rather than romantic in her approach, she eschews lyricism. Although she renders emotions of her characters convincingly and though, at times, she can touch readers to tears, she does so without the violins and the hearts and flowers.

Her descriptions of young love exude neither passion nor pathos but are most often tinged with an overlay of humor. We recognize the earlier awakening of puberty in girls than in boys, who—like Harry and Ron—don't know what to make of it all or how to behave with those strange, giggling female creatures. We understand and empathize with Harry on his first date, as he worries about whether he can find something to talk about and is horribly aware of his gangling arms. Is he supposed to take Cho's hand? How will he cope if he finally risks reaching for it but she's already removed it? (Irrelevant questions ultimately, since Harry's crush on Cho is eventually squelched by misunderstandings and her prolonged mourning for Cedric.)

In Book Six the portrayal of Harry's evolving love for Ginny befits the more mature sixteen-year old; we no longer see the comic awkwardness previously displayed in his encounters with Cho. But rather than provide detailed descriptions or explanations of emotions, Rowling offers mere impressions—often fleeting ones— in the course of the narration. At times Harry is simply aware of a flowery scent about Ginny. But the first indication that she will inspire something more than friendship occurs when he asks her if she wants to sit with him and others on the Hogwarts Express. When she says she promised to meet Dean, he feels a twinge of annoyance. That in itself would tell us nothing. but Rowling inserts one word that's a giveaway: "strange." And her brief mention of Ginny's hair speaks volumes.

> He felt a strange twinge of annoyance as she walked away, her long red hair dancing behind her. (VI, 136)

Of course Ginny's unavailability raises her stock high, and jealousy intensifies Harry's feelings. He invites her to join him and his friends at Hogsmeade. She can't: she's going with Dean. Harry sees them together and the green-eyed monster takes over. Naturally, we don't read, "Harry felt jealous" or "It upset him terribly to see them together, kissing." Rowling gives us only the impression:

> It was as though something large and scaly erupted into life in Harry's stomach, clawing at his insides: Hot blood seemed to flood his brain, so that all thought was extinguished, replaced by a savage urge to jinx Dean into a jelly. (VI, 286)

However, when he imagines himself kissing Ginny, the monster in his chest "purrs." He fights the feeling when he remembers that Ron, his best friend, can't abide his sister's "snogging" boys. Then the actual outcome-the Ginny-Harry romance—happens in a natural, spontaneous way. After an exciting Gryffindor victory at Quidditch, Ginny rushes up to hug Harry and he finds himself kissing her. Ron sees them and finally shrugs his shoulders as if to say, *"Well—if you must…"* (p. 534)

As we might expect, in describing developing feelings between Ron and Hermione, Rowling follows a different trajectory. Those two, so different from each other, have a stormy love-hate relationship flavored with heavy doses of jealousy and spite. Rowling does not present that relationship linearly but lets it build in isolated episodes from Books Four through Seven. And unlike her treatment of Harry's love for Ginny, she provides no descriptions of emotions churning within Ron or Hermione. They can only be assumed from words, gestures or outward behavior.

In any case, romantic love is not a source of great emotion in *Harry Potter.* Rowling always presents it in an open-eyed manner, often distancing it from us with ironic humor. There is, however, another sort of love with the capacity to move us deeply, that is a yearning for a lost loved one: a dead parent, cherished family member or loyal friend. That is undoubtedly a reflection of the profound affect on Rowling of her own mother's death. In the story, we can empathize with Harry's longing for his murdered parents, reflected in the Mirror of Erised. Or with Dumbledore's desire to have his sister and family back, a desire so intense it lures him into wearing the Resurrection Stone ring and ultimately leads to his demise.

Harry's frustrated yearning for his parents and his loss of the two important father figures in his life, Dumbledore and Sirius, have a far greater impact on us than his love life. But even in such tragic circumstances, Rowling refuses to play to the gallery with out-and-out sentimentality or pathos. Consider Harry's burial of Dobby. Dobby, eternally grateful to Harry for setting him free from slavery as a house-elf, risks and loses his life saving Harry and his friends

from death. As Rowling tells it, when Harry sets about burying
Dobby, he refuses to do it the easy, sensible way: by conjuring a pit
with his magic wand. Instead, he digs it laboriously himself, burying
his grief with each push of the shovel. Ron and Dean join him, and
Harry is sure they will ask why he hasn't used magic. But they don't;
they step into the pit and shovel alongside him in silence. Bill,
Fleur, Hermione and Luna arrive, and—in the simplest of words
and the soberest of styles—here is how the scene ends.

> Luna...crouched down and placed her fingers tenderly
> upon each of the elf's eyelids, sliding them over his glassy
> stare.
>
> "There," she said softly. "Now he could be sleeping."
>
> Harry placed the elf into the grave, arranged his tiny
> limbs so that he might have been resting, then climbed out
> and gazed for the last time upon the little body. He forced
> himself not to break down as he remembered
> Dumbledore's funeral and...the stateliness of the white
> marble tomb. He felt that Dobby deserved just as grand a
> funeral, and here the elf lay between bushes in a roughly
> dug hole.
>
> "I think we ought to say something," piped up Luna. "I'll
> go first, shall I?"
>
> And as everybody looked at her, she addressed the dead
> elf at the bottom of the grave.
>
> "Thank you so much, Dobby, for rescuing me from that
> cellar. It's so unfair that you had to die, when you were so
> good and brave. I'll always remember what you did for us.
> I hope you're happy now."
>
> She turned and looked expectantly at Ron, who cleared his
> throat and said in a thick voice, "Yeah...thanks, Dobby."
>
> Harry swallowed.
>
> "Goodbye, Dobby," he said. It was all he could manage,
> but Luna had said it all for him.

After the grave is filled in, Harry asks, "D'you mind if I stay here a moment?"

They murmur words he doesn't catch; he feels gentle pats upon his back, and they all traipse back toward the cottage while Harry remains alone with the elf. He needs to do one thing more. He finds a rock for Dobby's tombstone, places it at the head of the grave, points a wand at it and etches letters into its surface. They spell out:

HERE LIES DOBBY, A FREE ELF (VII, 480-1)

Portraits

Rowling's thumbnail descriptions of characters are exactly in the tradition of the seventeenth-century Duke of Saint-Simon, who bequeathed to posterity some deadly verbal portraits of his contemporaries in the court of Louis XIV. In his *Mémoires*, Saint-Simon describes a politician who resembles an angry cat; another man named Rion, short, fat and pimply, whose face amounts to an abscess; a certain Madame de Monchevreuil who looks like a parrot, with big bulging eyes that can't see a thing and who even walks like a parrot.

Sound a bit like J. K. Rowling?

From among the kaleidoscope of colorful characters in the cycle, one could cite example after example of her own satirical sketches. To mention only a few, there is forbidding **Severus Snape** with his sallow face, hooked nose, jagged yellow teeth and long, greasy black hair;[10] **Rita Skeeter.** whose insidiousness is reflected in her resemblance to a beetle[11] with jeweled spectacles, her hair set "in elaborate and curiously rigid curls that contrasted oddly with her heavy-jawed face…The thick fingers clutching her crocodile-skin handbag ended in two-inch nails, painted crimson;" (IV, 303) preening **Gilderoy Lockhart,** with blond, wavy hair and dazzling white teeth, first seen "wearing robes of forget-me-not blue that exactly matched his eyes;" (II, 59) **Sybill Trelawney,** ensconced in her dark heavily perfumed tower, described as "very thin, her large glasses magnified her eyes to several times their natural size… draped in a gauzy spangled shawl. Innumerable chains and beads hung around her spindly neck, and her arms and hands were encrusted with bangles and rings;" (III, 102) evil **Dolores Umbridge,** with a face like a large, pale toad, who "looked like somebody's maiden aunt, squat, with short, curly, mouse-brown hair in which she had placed a horrible pink Alice band that matched the fluffy pink cardigan she wore..." (V, 203)

And as a final example, **Mad-Eye Moony** wins the prize for weirder-than-weird. His face "looked as though it had been carved out of weathered wood by someone who had only the vaguest idea of what human faces are supposed to look like...Every inch of skin seemed to be scarred. The mouth looked like a diagonal gash, and a large chunk of the nose was missing. But it was the man's eyes that made him frightening. One of them was small, dark, and beady. The other was large, round as a coin, and a vivid, electric blue. The blue eye was moving ceaselessly, without blinking, and was rolling up and down, and from side to side, quite independently of the normal eye—and then it rolled over, pointing into the back of the man's head..." (IV, 184-5)

Many more portraits could be added to the gallery, including other faculty, students, the Dursley family or ghosts like Moaning Myrtle and Nearly Headless Nick. There are also what one might call "portraits within portraits." That is, personalities who appear, move and speak in pictures on walls, such as the Fat Lady, Sirius Black's mother—a screaming, vituperative harpy—and Sir Cadogan, the oddball knight in armor featured above in the chapter on comedy, Or one of this writer's favorites, sarcastic, jaundiced Phineas Nigellus, a former Hogwarts headmaster who utters biting opinions from his portrait in Dumbledore's office.

In her use of the verbal caricature Rowling succeeds in distilling the essence of characters, their personalities and their physical appearance. Such a method is well suited to the terseness of her style. For like the sketcher of visual caricatures, she likes to concentrate only on the prominent features of a character and to exaggerate those features while omitting the rest of the details. Of course such caricature would be out of place in treating Harry, the trio and Dumbledore, whom Rowling, fortunately, develops more fully. But in applying it to others throughout the story, she created a whole panoply of originals.

* * *

It should be obvious from the above illustrations that Rowling's style contributes greatly to the value and charm of the series. Her talent as a seasoned storyteller, ever impelling the action on; the classical clarity and conciseness of her narration, along with her sense of knowing just the right choice and amount of words to convey feelings; the cadence, variety and pacing of her sentences; the realism of her dialogue, her gift for caricature—these features add immeasurably to the work's readability and its fascination for so many millions of children and adults.

---

[1] "Chronicals of *Earthsea.*" *Guardian.* February 9, 2004.

[2] "Why Harry Potter Doesn't Cast a Spell Over Me." *The Observer.* June 25, 2000.

[3] *Op. cit.* See Introduction, above, p. viii.

[4] "Harry's Back." *Christian Science Monitor.* June 26, 2003.

[5] See, for example, Philip Pullman's *His Dark Materials.*

[6] The scene is contained in Snape's memory, viewed by Harry in Dumbledore's Pensieve.

[7] See Bloomsbury's Official Website, 2007. Or www.mugglenet.com/app/news/full_story/1156.

[8] Marvolo, Voldemort's maternal grandfather, was an heir of Slytherin.

[9] The tradition of a private pet name and an official one for the public is maintained today in many cultures, although in places like India most people are unaware of the custom's origin.

[10] It should be noted that as the story progresses we discover that Snape is far more than this one-dimensional caricature.

[11] As it happens, she can transform herself into a beetle.

PART IV

BEYOND
THE CYCLE

11

THE SPIN-OFFS

"It is important to remember that we
all have magic inside us."
—J. K. Rowling

Rowling followed *Harry Potter* with three slim publications, each of them an offshoot of her cycle. Two of the volumes, *Fantastic Beasts and Where to Find them* and *Quidditch Through the Ages*, appeared in 2001, and the somewhat lengthier *Tales of Beedle the Bard*, in 2007.[1] Weighing in at a mere 42 to 100 pages, these are hardly major works. They can even be seen as appendices to the Opus. Yet they are well worth reading for their charm and humor and for what they add to our knowledge of J. K. Rowling.

The first two books are pastiches, take-offs on a specific genre. *Fantastic Beasts* masquerades as a zoological compendium, an A-to-Z encyclopedia of magical creatures. *Quidditch Through The Ages* purports to be the history of a popular sport. *Tales of Beedle the Bard* is a collection of five fairy tales supposedly ancient but composed by Rowling herself. Although they differ in substance, the three publications have a great deal in common.

Most obviously, they all have direct ties to *Harry Potter* and, in a sense, feed on the cycle. *Fantastic Beasts* is presumably an actual Hogwarts textbook owned by Harry Potter, with the words "Property of Harry Potter" featured prominently on the cover and with marginalia scribbled throughout by Harry, Ron and, at one point, Hermione. A source of inside jokes, it includes references to such Hogwarts personalities as Hagrid, Snape and Lupin. *Quidditch*

Through the Ages is purportedly a Hogwarts library book, and "The Tale of the Three Brothers," the last story in *Tales of Beedle the Bard*, plays an important part in Harry's search for the Deathly Hallows in Book Seven. Not only that, Hogwarts alum, Hermione Granger, is said to have translated the tales from the original runes. Cementing the link between the spin-offs and *Harry Potter*, Dumbledore himself adds his observations to each of the three books.

Curiously, such connections with the original fiction serve as a stamp of authenticity—or "pseudo-authenticity"—for Rowling's three extra-*Potter* inventions. They are, supposedly, not mere fabrications but genuine original works. Why should we believe that? Because **A.** *Harry Potter* is real and true. **B.** The spin-offs have roots in *Harry Potter.* **C.** Ergo the spin-offs are real and true. A scholarly approach, especially in the first two books, adds to Rowling's literary sleight of hand, conveying the message: "Make no mistake: this is all very serious and these fakes are genuine."

Through the Looking Glass

In these publications Rowling reverses our customary idea of the mundane and the magical. As in the cycle itself, she humorously dislocates our everyday perspective and relegates reality to the other side of the mirror. Magic now becomes the norm, while we Muggles are seen as the oddity—alien creatures, relatively ignorant, if harmless. In the spin-offs, wizards view us much as the snake liberated by Harry[2] views the strange humans peering at him from outside his cage.

This transposition of our own ordinary perspective concerning the magic and Muggle worlds provides the "authors"[3] of the spin-offs an opportunity to clarify a big mystery: Why aren't Muggles aware of all the magic occurring in close proximity to them? As luck would have it, they all agree on the answer, to wit: Centuries ago witches and wizards were persecuted by Muggles for performing magic.[4] So in 1692, the International Confederation of Wizards drew up rules for the safety and security of magicians, so that all magic would be hidden from view, or, if not, completely forgotten, thanks to memory charms and the like. As a result of such precautions, few Muggles now realize that magical beasts, flying brooms and other such phenomena actually exist. With that said, it is understandable that the spin-offs and their magic are intended strictly for the wizard community.

Wizards in these stories express no bitterness, no resentment of past persecution by Muggles. As in *Harry Potter*, hostility toward Muggles arises instead from disdainful bigotry, from the belief that those who cannot perform magic are an "untouchable" caste, unworthy to inhabit the same planet as pure-blooded wizards. Given Rowling's hatred of intolerance, it is not surprising that in her *Tales of Beedle the Bard*, admirable figures are accepting of Muggles, while dislikable ones reject them. In Dumbledore's commentaries to the book, for instance, he cites this statement issued in 1675 by one of Draco Malfoy's xenophobic ancestors, Brutus Malfoy, in reference to the pro-Muggle tale, "The Wizard and the Hopping Pot."

> This we may state for certainty. Any wizard who shows fondness for the society of Muggles is of low intelligence, with magic so feeble and pitiful that he can only feel himself superior if surrounded by Muggle pig-men.
>
> Nothing is a surer sign of weak magic than a weakness for non-magical company. (p. 16)

Centuries later, Draco's father would write to the Hogwarts Board of Governors, insisting the book be banned from the school library on the grounds that it included a marriage between a sorcerer and a ordinary Muggle, writing "I do not wish my son to be influenced into sullying the purity of his bloodline by reading stories that promote wizard-Muggle marriage." (p. 40) Unsurprisingly, Dumbledore responded by taking issue with the Malfoys and their arrant bigotry. With Rowling's blessing of course.

In these works Rowling's liberalism does not end with her stance against intolerance. It includes a feminist approach already reflected in the volumes of *Harry Potter*. In *Quidditch Through the Ages*, we learn that from its very beginnings, as early as 962 A.D., witches as well as wizards played the game, the women on an equal footing with the men. In *Tales of Beedle the Bard*, as Rowling points out in her introduction to the book, females play a far more proactive role than in our Muggle fairy tales. They seek their fortune and take their fate into their own hands, "rather than taking a prolonged nap or waiting for someone to return a lost shoe." (p. ix)

Seriously Funny

The main value of these works lies in their humor. In *Fantastic Beasts*, that humor surfaces immediately, before we even get to the author's introduction. Inside the cover, just below the bookmark with "This book belongs to Harry Potter," we find an addendum by Ron: "Shared by Ron Weasley because his fell apart." This is followed by Hermione's words, "Why don't you buy a new one then?" To which Ron replies, "Write on your own book Hermione."

> **Hermione's note:** "You bought all those dungbombs on Saturday. You could have bought a new book instead."
>
> **Ron's answer:** "Dungbombs <u>rule</u>."

Another early page displays an unfinished game of tac-tac-toe, a stick figure of Ron on a guillotine menaced by a spider with the words "You die, Weasley," and "Harry loves Moaning Myrtle," with her name doubly crossed out. At the start of a chapter entitled "A Brief History of Muggle Awareness of Fantastic Beasts," Harry has circled the word "Brief," adding "you liar" directly above it. Sarcastic teenage marginalia found throughout the book continually puncture holes in the scholarly approach of the zoologist (or "magi-zoologist") presumably authoring the book.

In all three spin-offs the humor derives mainly from this irreverent deflation or demystification of the high-sounding and serious. In *Quidditch Through the Ages*, the author discusses the famous Chuddley Cannons team (of which Ron Weasley is a fervent fan). He speaks of the team's triumphs, its "glory days," but adds that their last win took place in 1892 and notes that they changed their club motto in 1972 from "We shall conquer" to "Let's all just keep our fingers crossed and hope for the best." (p. 34)

And in a similar vein, Dumbledore writes in his footnotes to *Tales of Beedle the Bard*,

> "As the eminent wizarding philosopher Bertrand de Pensées Profondes writes in his celebrated work *A Study into the Possibility of Reversing the Actual and Metaphysical Effects of Natural Death, with Particular Regard to the Reintegration of Essence and Matter:* 'Give it up. It's never going to happen.'" (pp. 79-80)

Dumbledore's footnotes and forewords are laden with irony, as he delivers the most outrageous statements cheerfully and with a perfectly straight face. One example is seen in his account of procuring a copy of *Quidditch Through the Ages* from the forbidding school librarian.

> "It was with some difficulty, I must own, that I persuaded Madame Pince to part with [it] so that it might be copied for wider consumption. Indeed, when I told her it was to be made available to Muggles, she was rendered temporarily speechless and neither moved nor blinked for several minutes. When she came to herself she was thoughtful enough to ask whether I had taken leave of my senses..." (p. vii)

Rowling did well to regale us with Dumbledore's dry-witted comments. She even managed to do so in *Tales of Beedle the Bard*, even though at the time of the book's publication the Headmaster was long under ground and in no condition to joke. She solved the problem more or less in by explaining that he had written his commentary to the tales well before his death, and his notes had been fortuitously preserved.

From the examples above, one can see that the humor of the spin-offs is born largely of contrasts and the interplay of opposites: the serious upended by the ridiculous and high-minded scholarship vanquished by down-to-earth reality. In the same vein, anachronisms come into play, when today's culture and political correctness intrude humorously on the history of magic. For instance, we find that back in the early years of Quidditch games, a bird, the golden snidget was so injured by its captors that it was finally declared a "protected species" (*Quidditch*, p. 14) and replaced in the game by the inanimate Snitch.[5] According to *Fantastic Beasts*, the creation of new and untamable monsters was outlawed by a "ban on experimental breeding." (p. vi) And in the realm of psychological self-help, a purported best-seller, inspired by one of Beedle the Bard's old tales, "*The Hairy Heart,*" is entitled, "*The Hairy Heart: a Guide to Wizards Who Won't Commit.*" (*Tales*, p. 60)

Ironically, some of our present-day theories might seem as strange to us as the reasoning in the spin-offs. In *Fantastic Beasts*, a chapter entitled "What is a Beast?" describes the difficulties magicians faced in deciding whom or what to include in their category of "beings." Did a creature have to have two legs? Be capable of speech? Have understanding? Is a centaur or a Muggle a being or a beast? In exactly the same vein, Professor Thomas I. White of Loyola Marymount University recently proposed that playful otters fulfill enough criteria to be placed in the category of "non-human persons."[6]

One might well wonder: on which side of the mirror does that put us?

A Way With Words

The spin-offs provide example after example of Rowling's linguistic inventiveness. They demonstrate her obvious delight in creating names of people, places and institutions. *Quidditch Through the Ages* and *Fantastic Beasts* are especially remarkable sources of her creativity with words.

In Quidditch, Rowling amuses us with a series of deadpan philological explanations. In discussing the etymology of Quidditch, she takes us back to the eleventh century when the game had its beginnings on Queerditch Marsh—an excellent choice, since "queer ditch" would easily elide over the years into "Quidditch." The modern Bludger derived from "Blooder," and the Snitch from the Golden Snidget bird, in another case of elision. Listing locales of English or Irish Quidditch teams, Rowling provides typically quaint names such as Ballycastle and Puddlemere. Her fondness for alliteration is seen in her labeling of teams like the Falmouth Falcons, the Hollyhead Harpies or the Wimbourne Wasps.

Rowling's linguistic virtuosity is at its cleverest and most amusing in the area of foreign languages. Her pseudo-scholarly analyses extend well beyond England, and she dauntlessly adapts them to other cultures. Tracing the game of Quidditch to the Middle Ages, she refers alliteratively to a "famous painting of Günther der Gewalttätige ist der Gewinner ("Gunther the Violent is the Winner"), dated 1105 [which] shows the ancient German game of Stitchstock." (p. 4) Ireland's forerunner of Quidditch is the Celtic sounding game, "Aingingein," and Scotland's, the multi-voweled "Creaothceann."

In describing the spread of Quidditch worldwide, Rowling refers to a fifteenth-century Norwegian poet, "Ingolfr the Iambic" and to his French contemporary, "Malécrit" ("badly written"), who penned these very mortal lines in his play "Hélas, je me suis transfiguré les pieds" ("Alas, I've Transfigured My Feet").

> **Grenouille:** "I cannot go to the market with you today, Crapaud."
>
> **Crapaud:** "But Grenouille, I cannot carry the cow alone."
>
> **Grenouille:** "You know, Crapaud, that I am to be Keeper this morning. Who will stop the Quaffle if I do not?" (p. 39)

In this take-off on a foreign style, Rowling offers a spoof of some inane early French drama. At the same time she is merrily shredding the fabric of her own pseudo-serious history of Quidditch.

Rowling's inventive terminology amounts to a running stream of neologisms in *Fantastic Beasts and Where to Find Them*. In the main body of the book, every page exhibits her choice of unusual names of extraordinary magic creatures: "flobberworm," "graphorn," "grindylow," "jobberknoll," "kneazle," "occamy," to mention but a few. Some of these beasts were already featured in *Harry Potter*; others appear for the first time in this book. To help give them credence, Rowling lists them alongside familiar magic creatures such as pixies, centaurs, unicorns, trolls and the yeti. And her descriptions conform exactly to the style of actual zoological reference books or popular studies in natural history. To illustrate, here is a short section describing one species of dragon:

> "The Norwegian Ridgeback resembles the Horntail in most respects, though instead of tail spikes it sports particularly prominent jet-black ridges along its back. Exceptionally aggressive to its own kind, the Ridgeback is nowadays one of the rarer dragon breeds. It has been known to attack most kinds of large land mammal and, unusually for a dragon, the Ridgeback will feed on water-dwelling creatures..." (p. 13)

* * *

In the three offshoots of *Harry Potter*, a serious, scholarly approach is undermined by an irreverent irony running throughout the texts. For these lighthearted books are designed to keep readers smiling, to amuse rather than impress them as masterworks. Clearly, these days their most likely audience would be fans of the *Harry Potter* cycle, readers who welcome the chance to live once again in Harry's world.[7]

---

[1] Profits from these publications benefited two of Rowling's pet charities: Comic Relief U.K. and the Children's High Level Group.

[2] *The Sorcerer's Stone*, pp. 27-8.

[3] Of course the author in each case is Rowling, but she attributes *Fantastic Beasts* to a certain Newt Scamander, *Quidditch Through the Ages* to Kennilworthy Whisp and the *Tales* to Beedle the Bard.

[4] Witness the trials and persecution of the medieval Inquisition, or the delusive Salem witchcraft trials of 1692, the same year Rowling has her International Confederation of Wizards institute their first anti-Muggle precautions.

[5] Argentina's national sport, *pato*, played by gauchos on horseback in the 17th century, originally made goals by flinging a live duck, later replaced by a ball.

[6] *In Defense of Dolphins: The New Moral Frontier.* Hoboken, N. J., Wiley-Blackwell, 2007.

[7] Theoretically, Rowling could continue spinning off *Harry Potter* by offering books such as *Hogwarts, a History, A First Course in Muggle Studies, A Brief History of Magic*, or Gilderoy Lockhart's *Magical Me*. But at present, that option appears unlikely.

12

FROM STORY TO FILM

"Novels do not have constraints of time and
budget; I can create dazzling effects relying on
nothing but the interaction of my own and my
readers' imagination."

—J. K. Rowling[1]

It is commonly agreed that watching a film demands less effort
than reading a book. Reading calls for a certain amount of
concentration, imagination, a dose of mental energy and an
investment in time. In viewing a film, whether in a cinema or at
home, we settle back for a couple of hours, more or less passive
spectators, while the story is handed to us boxed, wrapped and tied.
The major work has been accomplished beforehand. Director,
screenwriter, photographer and the rest of a competent team have
already processed the ingredients of the story, made them easily
digestible for a wide audience and packaged them with expertise.
On the other hand, reading the original text comes down to a face-
off between just two people, the author and the reader. And the
reader is obliged to "recreate" the author's text. As one person put
it, "Reading stimulates the creative area of the mind to produce
alternate realities."[2]

Many know *Harry Potter* exclusively through movies or DVDs,
without having dipped into a single page of the original. In a sense,
their experience seeing the films is virginal, unspoiled by intimacy
with the text. On the other hand, avid readers of the books, those
who lived with and relished them for long hours, are more likely to

come to the films with pre-conceived ideas. Chances are they would want the movies to keep close to the story they read and savored and to their own vision of the tale and its characters. The film producers were well aware of that point of view.

Early on, Producer David Heyman made a promise to Rowling that the films would remain faithful to the books, and in the main, that goal was achieved. Of course, a literal adherence to Rowling's text would have been impossible. As she herself well knew, there are huge differences between what can be accomplished by a good writer and what can be realized by a competent team of filmmakers. Film has its own exigencies, and some alterations to the original would have to be made, especially where the volumes became longer and more complex. Understanding this, Rowling essentially let go of her work. And as proprietary as she may have felt about her brainchild, she did not hang around the studio lot and interfere. (In any case, she was too hard at work writing later volumes to "hang around.") In the last analysis, to accomplish the job, the final choices had to be the filmmakers,' the ones responsible for the finished product.

Filming such a globally admired work as *Harry Potter* must have presented a huge challenge to those who took on the task. For one thing, unlike the author, they could not describe a character's inner thoughts and motivations (without using a voice-over—or reviving the Greek chorus). As a result, much of the inner suspense would have to be lost; viewers could not truly know what Harry is feeling in the face of danger, or what he thinks and feels in a race against time. And in the main, emotions could only be grasped by watching actors' facial expressions or listening to their words and tone of voice.

Beyond that, the creators could not transpose to the screen some of the most important aspects of the book—Rowling's style and wit—for they would not be able to take up film time quoting passages from the text at any length. In any case, the author's wry wit would have been wasted on the very young and moviegoers who would have greater appreciation for Hagrid's putting a tail on Dudley or

Harry's inflating his aunt. Unsurprisingly, the films had to sacrifice much of Rowling's interior development or replace it with action.

And producers and directors had commercial realities to contend with. They needed to create a product that would appeal to a huge cross-section of the public, to people of all ages and walks of life, fans and non-fans alike. To compete with other films, *Harry Potter* had to have a good enough dose of violence, the latest in special effects and at least a hint of romance and sexuality. Above all, with an enormous investment of time, work, personnel, equipment and all things requiring money, eyes had to be fixed on the bottom line. With all that in mind, the filmmakers needed to know how and where to compromise without compromising integrity.

How well was the challenge fulfilled? Judging from the reactions of the general public and critics, very well indeed. The films have enjoyed great success and garnered enthusiastic reviews internationally in newspapers and magazines. But what about the devotees of the original story, those who enthusiastically read and reread each volume? Specifically, do the films add positively to their reading experience or fail to measure up?

Enhancing the Story

Although readers' reactions to the *Harry Potter* films have been mixed, many of them have relished seeing Rowling's fanciful world come alive on the screen through the added dimensions of sight and sound. Visual images of people and places hitherto only imagined, music to reflect and enhance emotions, speech and sound effects— all of that contributes to transforming the virtual reality of Rowling's text into a more immediate, concrete and graspable brand of reality.

Viewing *The Sorcerer's Stone*, fans of the book can experience the thrills of discovery and recognition as the story comes to life. In the film, Diagon Alley is the epitome of the book's narrow cobble-stoned passage brimming with characters in colorful nineteenth-century garb. Ollivander's shop is that shop to perfection; Gringotts, exactly Gringotts. And there is the utter charm of being transported over water and experiencing a first view of rambling, turreted Hogwarts castle, to the strains of John Williams' hauntingly lyrical "Hedwig's Theme."

Photographic art adds immeasurably in animating and enriching the story. Loving views of the castle, its circular stairwells, Gothic archways, surrounding lake and hills, birds whooshing across clouds, green fields transforming impressionistically into snowy expanses and hazy mountains that resemble delicate Chinese ink drawings. The Forbidden Forest menaces with its tangles of brush and serpentine roots snaking in every direction. Particularly striking (if a bit literal at times) is the photographic symbolism of *The Prisoner of Azkaban*, in which a host of black carrion crows foreshadow Buckbeak's execution. In that film, where time and its reversal play such an important role, there are repeated shots of a large moving pendulum. And just before Hermione and Harry physically retrace past events, our last view is of a set of huge toothed wheels, black gears slowly rotating against the backdrop of a floor-to-ceiling window.[3] As succeeding films, like the novels, get darker, so does the photography, with its deep greens, grays, threatening skies, storms and cloudy mists. Finally, thanks to Eduardo Serra, *The Deathly Hallows* provides some of the most spectacular photography of the series.

Of course in a magical setting full of fantastic creatures and supernatural phenomena, special effects are indispensable. Computer-generated imagery (CGI), animatronics, prosthetics and robotics animate objects and creatures such as the sorting hat, vicious three-headed Fluffy, a spider with motorized legs, eerie dementors and the tiny goblins of Gringotts Bank. *The Order of the Phoenix* alone contained over 1,400 special effects, created by a large number of specialists from various companies.

But for dedicated *Harry Potter* readers, far more important than the expected fireworks of modern technical wizardry is the fact that the films put faces on the imagined characters. It is nothing less than a miracle that three unknown pre-teen actors not only became Harry, Ron and Hermione but that the same three returned in the films year after year, maturing more or less at the same pace as their characters. And that they remained eminently suitable for their parts, while growing as actors, throughout the decade of filming the seven-volume cycle.

It is remarkable too that so many of the story's fictional personalities were interpreted by the finest of British stage actors: Kenneth Branagh, a wonderfully detestable, perfectly timed, Gilderoy Lockhart; Robbie Coltrane, the very embodiment of Hagrid; Maggie Smith, the one and only choice for stern Professor McGonagall; Alan Rickman, a snake-like Snape with deadly articulation; Ralph Fiennes brilliantly cast as Voldemort—and more. Their interpretations have been so memorable that some fans have found it difficult to re-read the books without visualizing the characters as these on-screen interpreters.

Given the films' impressive assemblage of gifted actors, some of the casting might surprise readers. Helena Bonham Carter offers an inspired interpretation of Bellatrix Lestrange as a voluptuous, wildly insane creature one might not imagine from the story. Emma Thompson, one of Britain's most gifted actresses, while superb as always, appears on screen a bit robust for the frail, ethereal Trelawney we may visualize in the reading. Their performances, however, are dependably first-rate.

Transforming the Text

In filming a book a producer's first concern is normally with the plot, that is, a plot capable of holding a viewer's attention from start to finish. So with *Harry Potter,* as with other adventure stories, the story had to be filmed and presented in the most accessible and most exciting way possible. With that goal in mind, various changes were made. Most obviously, the books, especially some longer ones, had to be substantially condensed, obliging directors and screenwriters to cut certain episodes, retain the ones they deemed most important or dramatic and knit them together logically. But additionally, with the general public in mind, the filmmakers felt obliged to make a number of other modifications.

Notably, they often changed the books' endings. In the cycle, every volume through the sixth finishes at the end of each school year, with Harry, Ron and Hermione heading home on the Hogwarts Express and arriving at King's Cross Station. That works very well in the reading, for in each case, Harry has just been through some tumultuous, grueling adventure. Customarily, the books end on a note of relief, with the three friends relaxing together and most often with the prospect of Harry joining the other two during the summer. In an adventure film, however, the mere repetition of a homebound trip would not be seen as effective, and other alternatives were substituted.

At the end of first film, *The Sorcerer's Stone*, Harry pauses before boarding the school train and has a heart-stirring moment with Hagrid, who presents him with precious photographs of his deceased mother and father. In the second one, *The Chamber of Secrets*, the invented final scene has Hagrid, newly exonerated and released from Azkaban prison, making a grand entrance into Hogwarts. The scene ends with Hagrid surrounded and loudly applauded by hundreds of students (except, naturally, by Draco and cohorts). Of course that event would never have taken place in Rowling's story, since few students outside of Harry, Ron and Hermione had a lot of enthusiasm for Hagrid, and many were frightened of his exposing them to dangerous beasts. But it did make a rousing ending for the movie. As did the last scene of film three, *The Prisoner of Azkaban*, with Harry riding high in the sky on a broom that he had supposedly just acquired.

Such liberties do not severely detract from the story, and one can understand the rationale behind the changes. It is also understandable that the filmmakers did not pick a Hermione identical to the books' character with brown bushy hair and large front teeth—or a Harry with an untamable mop of hair. The public, after all, has a right to its attractive, well-kempt idols. And few *Harry Potter* aficionados would object to—or even notice—a number of on-screen changes such as certain characters mouthing lines originally spoken by others. They might also not be aware of minor alterations such as Harry speaking with the sorting hat or Ron and Hermione explaining to him that he is a "Parseltongue" *(The Chamber of Secrets).* And they might not notice such differences in the filmed *Prisoner of Azkaban* as Harry spotting Pettigrew on the Marauder's Map or Malfoy getting smacked by an invisible Harry after calling Hermione a "mudblood."[4] These and other minor deviations from the text might well have been made for the sake of expedience or because they seemed more appealing than the original. But no real harm done.

Readers can also accept more visceral modifications, made for the sake of excitement and increased dramatic impact. Since the films cannot convey the inner intensity and suspense of the books, in which we can read Harry's mind and share his anxiety and terror, they can at least overwhelm us visually by creating frightful scenes of chases and battles. Such is the case near the end of the *Chamber of Secrets,* with the film greatly prolonging the deadly basilisk's pursuit of Harry. Or in the *Prisoner of Azkaban,* in which viewers witness a lengthy battle between Remus Lupin as a werewolf and Sirius as a dog. Or in *The Goblet of Fire,* when a dragon, earthbound in the story, pursues Harry on a wild chase in the air. Changes and additions like these are the norm in filmmaking, not only accepted but expected by viewers used to being assaulted by turbulent imagery and shattering sound.

One of the most striking examples of violent footage added by a *Harry Potter* movie occurs at the start of the sixth film, *The Half Blood Prince,* with the explosion of the Millennium Bridge over London's Thames River. In the book the event was not described at all but only mentioned in passing in a conversation between the Minister of Magic and England's Prime Minister. Yet an enormous amount of time, money, energy, expertise and teamwork went into creating the disaster. As a point of departure, special effects technicians obtained and used the original architectural plans for the 1,241-foot steel suspension bridge. In order to blow it up, they re-created the bridge with computer software, up to the last nut and bolt. The London based visual effects company, Double Negative, used High-Dynamic-Range-Image (HDRI) photography,[5] in a process that took months—for a scene of just thirty seconds!

Why go through all that trouble? When asked why he climbed Mt. Everest, Hillary's answer was "Because it was there." The filmmakers could give the same answer. The technology was there. Using it might not be as impressive as climbing Mt. Everest but impressive all the same. And as an opening, the latest in digital explosions would set a brilliant tone for the action-packed sixth *Harry Potter* movie.

Taking Liberties

Even ardent Harry Potter fans who have read and re-read the cycle can understand that some features of the books have had to be altered and adapted in the films. They may even recognize that the filmmakers' modifications can prove quite successful. In fact, what many critics favored in *The Deathly Hallows, Part I* (which generally followed the original plot), was an invented scene of Harry and Hermione dancing together. However, elsewhere, in a number of cases, the *Harry Potter* films deviate from the story markedly by misinterpreting important characters and changing the meaning of the text. Although some of these changes are not radical ones, they can be disconcerting.

In the case of Snape, for example, readers might well wonder why, in the fourth and fifth film, he is pictured as banging students over the head or knocking noggins together. Such actions might make little children howl in delight, but they could not have been performed by Snape. That hateful man would never stoop to actually *touching* the lowly students. In any event, why bother, when he can terrify them with a glance, freeze them with a word or petrify them with a pregnant pause.

Other misinterpretations, while relatively unimportant, may give the careful reader pause. Originally, in Book Two, *The Chamber of Secrets*, Hermione interrupts Professor Binn's boring class to ask about the chamber. The filmmakers, understandably avoiding a scene with a yawn-inducing professor, have Hermione pose the question in Professor McGonagall's class instead. Completely out of character, the stern, no-nonsense professor unbelievably puts her lesson aside and obliges with a thorough history of the chamber. In the same film, Lucius Malfoy mercilessly insults Arthur Weasley in front of his family and friends. In the book, Weasley jumps up and pins Malfoy against the wall; in the film he simply stands there, a bit bland, with only a mild comeback.

In this same category of relatively inconsequential changes are the movies' interpretations of Hermione and Ron. In Hermione's case, her social activism and misguided attempts to liberate the house-elves with her organization, S.P.E.W., are eliminated from the filmed version. According to Producer David Heyman, Hermione's S.P.E.W. was cut since it didn't "relate to Harry's story."[6] In any case, including it might have made the movie too complex and unwieldy. And as much as the omission is regretted by fans, the filmed version is hardly to be faulted for it.

As for Ron, although he is courageous throughout the Rowling's cycle, the films make him out to be a sheer coward, shrinking, shrieking or complaining in the face of danger. For instance, in the original text of *The Prisoner of Azkaban*, Ron, convinced that Sirius wants to kill Harry, shouts, "You'll have to kill all three of us!" (p. 339) But in the film, it is Hermione who pronounces those words. At the end of *The Half Blood Prince*, when Harry confides that he must leave school to go on a dangerous quest, Ron says, "We'll be there, Harry…We'll go with you wherever you're going." (p. 651) Again, it is Hermione, not Ron, who makes that statement in the film. And although, in *The Chamber of Secrets*, Ron immediately agrees to follow the spiders into the Forbidden Forest (despite his arachnophobia), the film has him whining, "I don't like this; I don't like it at all!" and "Can we go back now?" Still, having Ron act the craven must have made good sense to director and screenwriter, especially since the actor who plays him, Rupert Grint, is the perfect lily-livered sidekick, with his fearful facial expressions and terrified squeaks.

However, more serious deviations do occur in the films, and when it comes to any radical changes, readers have been quick to object. Hundreds of bloggers have expressed dismay at the films' perceived distortion of the "canon." With *The Half Blood Prince*, the least literal film of the first six[7]—they all but cried "Sacrilege!" Whom did they blame? Early on, some expressed anger at the screenwriter, Steve Kloves. It soon became clear, however, that Kloves, an ardent *Harry Potter* fan, had stuck close to the original in his script until director David Yates worked with him on a major re-editing.[8] Once aware of the director's crucial impact, online petitions appeared requesting signatures to block Yates from future work on the series, one going so far as demanding: "Kill Yates."

Meanwhile, the filmmakers themselves have explained their viewpoint to interviewers, justifying their re-creation of the text. Producer David Heyman, who was involved in the workings of the films from start to finish, has said the important motivating factors were mainly to be true to Harry and true to the spirit of Rowling's text. Yates has maintained, among other things, that changes had to be made for the "rhythm" of the films and that they needed to please not just the fans but a "wider global audience as well, who haven't read the books."[9] He further mentioned that Steve Kloves did not write for Rowling's characters but for the film actors, their strengths and weaknesses.[10]

But what about J. K. Rowling? After a wait of two years,[11] when she finally consented to have her cycle filmed, she insisted on the following: being given script approval, having British characters portrayed by British actors and assurance that the films would remain faithful to her characters. Her stipulations were readily accepted. She was made an executive producer and consulted on every script for each of the films. Producer, screenwriters and directors listened to her and made changes she felt strongly about.

Rowling's initial input had largely to do with the appearance and décor of Hogwarts, Diagon Alley and surroundings. She also successfully proposed actor Robbie Coltrane to play Hagrid—a perfect choice (although her suggestion of Terry Gilliam as director was not taken). Only because she requested it, Yates included the house-elf Kreacher in *The Order of the Phoenix*, and for *The Half Blood Prince*, she had Kloves delete a passage about Dumbledore reminiscing about a female lover, explaining to him—and the world—that the Headmaster was gay.

Yet despite such input, she never thought of herself as having any real control but spoke in terms of being "allowed" to have her say: "I've been allowed a lot of input. They have been very generous in allowing me to make my opinions heard."[12] From start to finish, she approved of dialogue that directors and screenwriters added to films. She even accepted a completely invented attack on the Burrows inserted in the sixth film. In short, her attitude was surprisingly *laissez-faire*. She repeatedly said that the filmmakers' alterations to her text were fine, even welcome, since she didn't expect—or even want—the movies to duplicate her story as written. She just wanted them to be good. And, in fact, she was delighted with them.

So if Rowling herself had no problem with major film changes to her work, does it make sense for her readers to complain? Actually, yes. After years of gestation and labor, with a huge mental and emotional investment, Rowling created *Harry Potter*. Then once it was fully formed and ready to go, she released it to millions who adopted and immediately loved it. It is now, in a sense, their baby too. If they think something egregiously wrong is happening to it, a betrayal or corruption—*e.g.:* a film that transforms it into something else entirely—understandably, justifiably, they protest.

Crossing the Line

Question: When does a film adaptation of *Harry Potter* betray the text?

Answer: When it unnecessarily changes the essence of the story and gratuitously alters the thinking, behavior, speech and interactions of the principal characters.

Unfortunately, all too often unwarranted changes do occur, notably in the behavior, speech and actions of major characters like Harry, Ginny and Dumbledore.

Take Harry, for instance. Since he is the most important figure of the series, admired by a vast readership, to make fundamental changes in his character with no apparent reason might strike us not as a practical, normal adaptation to the screen but as a case of tampering. Some *Harry Potter* readers, carried along by the momentum of the films, may not be shocked, or even aware, of certain changes. But fans who have read and re-read the books may well notice them and wonder at them.

As early as the second film, *The Chamber of Secrets*, Harry comes out with words that his model, the "real" Harry, would never have uttered. After the boy helps expose a vile deed committed by Lucius Malfoy, Malfoy says sarcastically, "Let's hope that Mr. Harry Potter will always be around to save the day." Now there is no good answer to that remark, but the director or scriptwriter[13] obviously wanted Harry to have the last word. He replies, "Don't worry, I will." That bit of bravado is simply not Harry Potter; he never brags, but, on the contrary, underplays his qualities and achievements.

In the following film, *The Prisoner of Azkaban*, Harry, overhearing that Sirius treacherously killed his parents, sits down in the snow and sobs audibly. Hermione discovers him and puts her arms around him comfortingly. Again, not Harry Potter. In the book, as soon as he learns that shocking bit of news, he has no wish to connect with his friends but rushes back to his dorm where he can be alone with his thoughts and emotions. And no matter how dark his situation, in the books he never, ever cries. Besides, a sympathetic embrace by Hermione would have embarrassed him no end. But clearly, the moviemakers wanted to touch audiences with such heartwarming inventions.

The Half Blood Prince, whether intentionally or not, goes farther in skewing Harry's character. Before explaining how, let me stress the fact that the film itself is excellent. The scene of the unbreakable vow alone, with its impeccably timed interplay of its three seasoned actors, is worth the price of admission. Jim Broadbent's interpretation of Slughorn is topnotch, and Daniel Radcliffe demonstrates an increasing maturity and competence in handling the complexities of Harry's older persona. Photography by Bruno Dubonnel adds immeasurably (it earned the French photographer an Academy award in 2010). And Director David Yates made it all happen. With that said, let us point out what *Harry Potter* fans could reasonably object to.

At the start of the movie, a fabricated scene shows sixteen-year-old Harry setting up a late night date with an attractive waitress. As it turns out, circumstances prevent him from meeting her. However, the whole idea of this after hours pick-up—perhaps aimed at pleasing hormonal adolescents in the audience—is unrealistic, gratuitous and out of place. As for hormones, it's not that Rowling's Harry is a prude or unattracted to females. But in the context of the story, imagining him planning a tryst with an unknown older woman is like picturing the hero of *Tom Brown's School Days* out on the make.

Later in the same film, in another unlikely scene, Harry's natural impulses are stifled, and he behaves as he would never do in the original story. In the book, when Draco and the Death Eaters come to kill Dumbledore, the Headmaster casts a spell on Harry, temporarily immobilizing him and making him mute. Harry, hidden under his invisibility cloak, can do or say nothing to prevent Dumbledore's downfall. In the film, Dumbledore simply tells Harry to stay out of the way and not do anything to help. So we see Harry, hidden, listening and watching, as his powerless friend and mentor slowly meets his doom. Quite likely the director and/or screenwriter thought it simpler and more expedient not to have the boy hexed and petrified. The only hitch is that Rowling's Harry would not have just stood there quietly. He would have immediately acted in Dumbledore's defense.

In each of these cases, such modifications were not necessary alternatives and lead us to question the filmmakers' assertions that they were concerned with Harry's point of view.

The same problem occurs in *The Half Blood Prince's* interpretation of Harry's relationship with Ginny. One might well wonder why the movie turned it into a series of artificial romantic scenes rather than use Rowling' down-to-earth, believable story of how Harry fell in love and connected with Ginny. *Washington Post* critic Dan Kois noted that "[The film] doesn't make the budding romance between Harry and Ginny feel inevitable and true."[14] He was entirely right.

For one thing, a filmgoer unfamiliar with the text would have no idea that Ginny is a great choice for Harry. In the original, besides being "gutsy,"[15] (Rowling's word for her), she is funny and fun, sprightly, with a lot of personality, quick with a comeback like her lively brothers, Fred and George. Early in the book, she does a take-off on Fleur (or "Phlegm," as she insists on calling her), wafting out of the room with arms high, like a ballerina. Later she does imitations of Ron bobbing up and down in Quidditch and—to Harry's great delight—of Harry's shouting orders to the team. That Ginny is absent in the film.

Harry's growing attraction to her is missing as well. In the book he spent enough time in her company during the previous summer to want to see more of her once back at Hogwarts. But Ginny, who long carried a torch for Harry, is now dating other boys, and whenever he asks her to go some place with his group, she explains she's made another commitment. He realizes that Ginny, a year behind him, never did hang out with his circle, but he's not happy about it, especially when he sees her "snogging" another guy. Compounding the problem is the fact that his best friend Ron is Ginny's brother, and Ron gets furious when he sees Ginny making out with guys. So in the course of the book, Harry daydreams about being together with Ginny, but between her unavailability and Ron's negative attitude about her having boyfriends, he can't really hope.

The book's build-up of Harry's growing but frustrated love for Ginny is entirely missing from the film. Also missing is how it was all resolved: with Ginny becoming disenchanted with her latest boyfriend, Dean, and, finally, available to connect with Harry. And the grand climax, is unfortunately omitted from the film as well. In a Quidditch match, Harry's team (minus Harry but including Ginny) has a spectacular win. Ginny, thoroughly excited, comes running into the Gryffindor lounge, runs up to Harry, a hard, blazing look in her eyes, and gives him a big hug. Without realizing it, Harry finds himself kissing her. When they break apart the room becomes hushed. Some students wolf-whistle and others giggle. Time for a quiet stroll alone together.

Now consider the film. Bonnie Wright, who played Ginny from the start was perfect as the ten-year-old in awe of Harry. But we find her in *The Half Blood Prince* dead serious and devoid of personality. She was given no clever lines and no opportunity to cut up. And rather than show her popularity and unavailability to Harry, we find her only once in a tête-à-tête with a boyfriend (Dean). At other times she is seen uncharacteristically hanging out with the trio or moving herself close to Harry.

The film romance includes these scenes, not found in the book: At the Burrow Ginny walks in with a tray of nutmeats, sits down next to Harry and puts one lovingly in his mouth. Later, in pajamas and bathrobe, she notices his shoelace is untied and she bends over and laces it up. Then after making sure Ron is not around, she draws up to Harry, wishes him "Merry Christmas" and zeroes in on him for what would have been a kiss if not for the arrival of Death Eaters (also an invented scene). When Harry rushes out to fight them, Ginny runs out as well, waves her wand around a few times at the Death Eaters, nearly gets captured by a werewolf but is saved by Harry. All that while she is still, presumably dating other guys.

So there is no logical building of the relationship and no believable reason for Harry to be interested in this particular Ginny in the first place. Yet she is given a large presence in this film. In a Quidditch match she is seen at Harry's side facing the team, as if she were co-captain. She makes a grand entrance into Slughorn's party wearing an elegant long black gown and locks eyes with Harry. And finally, she leads Harry into the Room of Requirement so he can hide Snape's potions text there (in the book Harry hides it unaccompanied). She says meaningfully, "Take my hand" and physically leads him there, tells him to close his eyes, then, after hiding the book herself she slowly approaches him in classic Hollywood style and they sort of rub lips.

This was obviously the filmmakers' idea of giving the public what it wants. Would it have been better to keep to the original? Yes. Would it have been practical for the filmmakers to do so? Yes again, and probably a better solution. Had the real story's build-up been presented convincingly, there would have been no need for the film's interpolated soulful Ginny episodes or added violence such as the fabricated episode of the attack on the Burrow. The original story could certainly have generated enough feeling to hold the audience's interest.

But let us leave the remake of Harry and Ginny's story for some future re-filming of the cycle. Meanwhile, there is Dumbledore to consider.

Richard Harris, who played Dumbledore in the first two films, passed away from Hodgkins disease before he could continue in the third. He was replaced by Sir Michael Gambon. Both men had trained in acting in London, and both had won success in a variety of roles on stage and in films. But their interpretation of the Hogwarts Headmaster could not have been more different. Richard Harris's version of Dumbledore, while understated, had variety, timing, empathy and humor. In his performance, despite the camouflage of abundant facial hair, a distinct personality came through.[16] On the other hand, Michael Gambon played his character more as your standard bearded Grand Old Man. He could have transposed his performance to Gandalf or any number of wise ancient wizards.

In interviews, Gambon claimed he had never read *Harry Potter,* that he simply played himself[17] and that, in any case, he would be working with the script, not the original. But as competent an actor as he is, studying the original Dumbledore carefully would have helped greatly in informing and enriching his portrayal. One has the feeling Sir Michael is doing his thing rather than understanding, embodying and conveying the character.

But the onus is not entirely Gambon's, for the directors and screenwriters had much to do with the Dumbledore's on-screen image. They have him speaking and behaving in ways completely antithetical to Rowling's original character. In *The Goblet of Fire*, for instance, he shakes Harry fiercely to find out if the boy put his name in the goblet. As quite a few bloggers pointed out, Dumbledore would never have condoned any such manhandling of a student.

In *The Half Blood Prince*, he makes a statement the text's Dumbledore would certainly not have made. In the book, Harry, noticing Dumbledore's blackened hand, asks, "What happened to your...?" He answers simply, "Later, Harry." (p. 48) But in the film, Dumbledore says, à propos of the hand, "The tale is thrilling—if I say so myself." The "real" Dumbledore would never have uttered such words. As anyone who has read the story knows, the black hand meant a tragic end for the Headmaster. It was not the by-product of a thrilling adventure but the result of an impossible obsession: Dumbledore's yearning for the Resurrection Stone as a way to bring his mother and sister back to life. He was not proud of it and would find no reason to boast of it. On the contrary, he would warn others not to make the same fatal mistake.

Later in the same film, Dumbledore noses into Harry's private affairs, wanting to know if there's anything going on between him and Hermione (Dumbledore would not have stooped to that!), and he comes out with the soupy exclamation, "Oh, to be young and to feel love's keen sting!" Again, definitely not Dumbledore.

What no one seemed to consider, or, rather, *want* to consider, is that Rowling's Dumbledore is a class act. The man is witty, urbane, knowledgeable, above the fray but very much down to earth. A man of many dimensions. As the above quoted character Phineas Nigellus said of him, "He's got style." (V, 623)

In the films, Dumbledore's lines tend to be preachy and tendentious. One can imagine him on a grandstand or behind a pulpit, as he utters the words, "As I stand looking out on you all tonight..." Among his lofty pronouncements and homilies are "Happiness can be found even in the darkest of times if one only remembers to turn on the light;" "In dreams we enter a world that is entirely our own. [We can] swim in the deepest ocean or glide over the highest mountain." *(Prisoner of Azkaban)*; "Dark and difficult times lie ahead." *(Goblet of Fire)*. In the same film, when he stands before the students and says "I'd like to say a few words," we might have hoped he would let his hair down and follow that phrase with utter nonsense as he did in *The Sorcerer's Stone*. Instead, he thunders: "ETERNAL GLORY!" meaning that such a destiny awaits the person who wins the Tri-wizard Tournament.

But perhaps the best way to show the difference between the style of the films' Dumbledore and the original is to consider the speech that character makes in *The Goblet of Fire*, after Cedric Diggory's death. Here is the film's version of the first part:

> "Today we acknowledge a really terrible loss. Cedric Dig-gory was, as you all know, exceptionally hard-working, infinitely fair-minded, and, most importantly, a fierce, fierce friend. Now I think therefore you have the right to know exactly how he died. You see, Cedric Diggory was MURDERED [shouted]—BY LORD VOLDEMORT! The Ministry of Magic doesn't know which way to tell you this. But not to do so, I think, would be an insult to his memory."

And this is the original:

> "There is much to say to you all tonight. But I first must acknowledge the loss of a very fine person who should be sitting here...enjoying our feast with us. I would like you all, please, to stand, and raise your glasses, to Cedric Diggory. [They do.] ...Cedric was a person who exemplified many of the qualities that distinguish Hufflepuff House...He was a good and loyal friend, a hard worker, he valued fair play. His death has affected you all, whether you knew him well or not. I think you have the right, therefore, to know exactly how it came about. Cedric Diggory was murdered by Lord Voldemort...The Ministry of Magic does not wish me to tell you this...It is my belief, however, that any attempt to pretend that Cedric died as the result of an accident, or some sort of blunder on his own, is an insult to his memory." (pp. 721-2)

The film, understandably, had to shorten and edit Rowling's text. However, in the process it did considerable damage to it. Where the original Dumbledore says, "But first I must acknowledge the loss," the film's words "Today we acknowledge a really terrible loss" make far less sense. In this context of a eulogy, "acknowledge" (recognize, register) is far too weak. "We are grieved by the loss" would have been more appropriate. And adding "really terrible" diminishes that loss. As for "fierce, fierce friend," there was nothing in the text to indicate that Cedric was any more than easygoing and pleasant. And saying that the Ministry of Magic "doesn't know which way to tell you this"—whether the actor's improvisation or words from a script—is incongruous.

The rest of the original speech as relayed in the film presents other problems. To put it briefly, the screen's Dumbledore moralizes and sentimentalizes with a certain banality.

> "Now the pain we all feel at this dreadful loss reminds me—reminds us—that while we may come from different places and speak in different tongues, our hearts beat as one. In light of recent events, the bonds of friendship we made this year will be more important than ever. Remember that. Cedric Diggory will not have died in vain. You remember that."

The book's Dumbledore, on the other hand, delivers a message that is not inspirational but practical: we can only win if we work as a team.

> "In the light of Lord Voldmort's return, we are only as strong as we are united, as weak as we are divided. Lord Voldemort's gift for spreading discord and enmity is very great. We can only fight it by showing an equally strong bond of friendship and trust… Differences of habit and language are nothing at all if our aims are identical and our hearts are open."

Finally, when Dumbledore speaks of Cedric again, his "Remember Cedric" is not soulful nostalgia but a call to arms, as in "Remember the Alamo," "Remember Pearl Harbor."

> "Remember Cedric. Remember, if the time should come when you have to make a choice between what is right and what is easy, remember what happened to a boy who was good, and kind, and brave, because he strayed across the path of Lord Voldemort. Remember Cedric Diggory." (721-2)

In condensing Dumbledore's speech, the film watered it down and made changes that warped its meaning and ignored its militancy. Where the original comes across as open-eyed and relatively straight-from-the-shoulder, the film's version is abstract, sentimental and spiritual, without touching us directly (as does Dumbledore's "Remember Diggory" passage). Although religion as such had nothing to do with the story, film viewers could imagine themselves in church listening to a high-sounding eulogy. In fact, the speech, accompanied by soft, plaintive music, ends with the camera panning up to a cathedral-like ceiling.

Ironically, the great disparity between Rowling's Dumbledore and his film counterpart is anticipated near the end of the sixth book. Harry, sitting at the Headmaster's funeral, vaguely hears a little man in black pronounce a eulogy with abstract phrases like "nobility of spirit," "intellectual contribution," "greatness of heart," and for him "It did not mean very much. It had little to do with Dumbledore as Harry had known him." (VI, 644)[18]

If Harry saw the film, undoubtedly he would have the same reaction: that's not Dumbledore.

* * *

The discrepancies between the filmed interpretation of characters and Rowling's fictional models may well offend people who love and feel proprietary about the original *Harry Potter*. Yet despite those discrepancies and despite all the obstacles facing the filmmakers, they gave readers much to be pleased about.

Throughout, they presented actors who, in almost every case, gave excellent, at times masterful, interpretations of the original characters. They offered a brilliant décor that made the story's setting come alive. Against all odds, they managed to maintain an impressive consistency for a decade, with nearly all the same actors and much of the same set (kept in London's Leavesden Studio). They provided admirable enhancers in the realms of music and photography. And even with their alterations, overall, they did their best to stay with the original story. All in all, their team effort was a highly creative one and their success well deserved.

---

[1] J. K. Rowling, official site. Retrieved Oct. 8, 2008.

[2] Anthony Megna.*www.helium.com/knowledge/122154/-essays-reading-a-book-vs-watching-a-movie.*

[3] Director of Photography: Michael Seresin.

[4] Harry did throw mud at Draco at Hogsmeade, while under his Invisibility Cloak, but that was for Draco's insulting remarks about Hagrid.

[5] For more information about the process, see Erin McCarthy's "Inside the New Harry Potter," *Popular Mechanics*, July 15, 2009.

[6] Online interview on *www.empireonline.com/interviews/intervew.asp?110=368*

[7] See next section.

[8] Kloves worked on every film but the fifth. He said he pushed hard when he thought characters were being violated by directorial changes. He specifically mentioned hating the applause for Hagrid as an ending for *The Chamber of Secrets*. See "Harry Potter Countdown," in *Los Angeles Times* of June 17, 2009.

[9] www.darkhorizons.com/interviews/1448/david-yates-for-harry-potter-and-the-half-blood-prince

[10] *www.comingsoon.net/news/movienews.php?id=56882*

[11] Between the publication of Book I in 1997 and the sale of film rights to Warner Brothers in 1999.

[12] *www.scholastic.com/harypotter/book/author/interview2.htm* February, 2000.

[13] Without being privy to decisions made behind the scenes, it is impossible to pinpoint the person or persons responsible for many of these changes.

[14] "Bewitched, Bewildered and Hot and Bothered." July 14, 2009.

[15] Rowling's word for her in an interview with Melissa Anelli and Emerson Sparts, July 16, 2005. See footnote #8, Chapter Five.

[16] Viewers have particularly noted the "twinkle in his eyes."

[17] Sir Michael can be flippant in interviews, so it is conceivable he said that in jest.

[18] In fact, what comes to Harry's mind is Dumbledore's idea of "saying a few words" in addressing the students—"nitwit," "oddment," "blubber" and "tweak."

CONCLUSIONS

The previous chapters demonstrate how J. K. Rowling's mastery of character development, plotting and style lies at the heart of *Harry Potter*'s great success.

Throughout the study I have emphasized the quality and value of Rowling's storytelling and highlighted her cleverness. Given the positive tone of my book, readers may well assume that I am an ardent admirer, convinced that Rowling can do no wrong. That is only half correct. I am obviously a fervent fan but would never claim that the work is perfect; *Harry Potter*, like any good book, has its weak points.

One problem arises with the story's division into several volumes. Especially in Books Two, Three and Four, Rowling felt obliged to summarize key features of the previous volumes, to explain who the characters are and to identify places and institutions. After all, a reader with no familiarity of Books One and Two might start off the *Harry Potter* experience with Book Three or Four. And even those who read the early books might appreciate reminders about past events or characters, since time may have elapsed between readings with important details forgotten.

However, for many fans who know the cycle intimately, that frequent recapitulation may seem intrusive. For instance, at one point in *The Prisoner of Azkaban*, Harry and his friends look up to see the Hogwarts Express, and Rowling stops to tell readers that the Express is a steam engine that puffs smoke.[1] Then to come across an explanation of Quidditch and its rules in book after book or be told repeatedly that Harry has a scar or that Draco Malfoy is

Harry's enemy and Professor McGonagall a "stern-faced witch" could make us wonder if we qualify as amnesiacs.

Others might object that some events in *Harry Potter* are too preposterous, even in the framework of magic and fantasy. Doesn't Dolores Umbridge's sadism—her setting herself up as Grand Inquisitor, her torture of Harry—stretch the imagination? How can Barty Crouch behave exactly like Mad-Eye Moody all throughout *The Goblet of Fire* when the "polyjuice potion" he took is only supposed to make him look and sound like Moody but not absorb his personality?

But of course none of that matters. A reader carried away by the story might be completely unaware of such things or register them only as a vague smudge on the frosting of the layer cake.

However, there is one criticism of the cycle that bears discussion. Some critics have maintained that *Harry Potter*, unlike other stories they admire, has only one level of meaning. According to William Safire, *Harry Potter*, unlike *Huckleberry Finn* and *Alice in Wonderland*, "is not written on two levels, entertaining one generation while instructing another."[2]

In a *Wall Street Journal* article, Leslie Baynes. comparing Philip Pullman's *His Dark Materials* to *Harry Potter*, also focuses on the value of an instructive level—at Rowling's expense. Professor Baynes writes that unlike Rowling's cycle, Pullman's books are "real literature," that Pullman, "a graduate of Oxford University, with a degree in English, knows his stuff." Although his work is marred by a dogmatic atheism, it should be taken seriously, for it is "loaded with allusions to Greek mythology and philosophy, Milton, Blake and the Bible..." She adds, "Indeed, a child who investigates them would begin to gain the rudiments of a classical education."[3]

Both critics hark back to Horace's precept of *utile dulci*: reading should not only be pleasant but also useful, instructive. According to Horace's *Ars poetica*, the best author aims to delight and edify readers at the same time:

> *Omne tulit punctum qui miscuit utile dulci,*
> *lectorem delectando pariterque monendo.*[4]

As we see, the two critics find *Harry Potter* lacking in the instructive, "useful" level. Yet certainly, if Rowling had wanted to edify and impress readers by including classical allusions, she could easily have done so; she earned her degree in French and Classics at Exeter University and obviously "knows her stuff." As we have seen, however, that is not at all her style. When she demonstrates erudition in the books, she does so in jest, as in the amusing parodies of the spin-offs.[5] Her emphasis is clearly on the *dulci* side of the equation, as she aims foremost to please and entertain readers.

On the other hand, Pullman, a fascinating writer, working in a different genre, presents a mix of fantasy and science fiction in a dense, poetic style. His erudition permeates his works. The phrase, "his dark materials" comes from Milton's *Paradise Lost*. References to Greek mythology and the Bible are ever present.[6] His knowledge of science, astronomy and mathematics underpins the semi-scientific explanations his characters give for fictional phenomena (such as "dust" or the "alethiometer").

Pullman's erudition imparts density and dimension to his work. However, we may well wonder how much of it is "useful" to readers. For much of his scholarship—such as the references to Milton, mythology or the Bible—is skewed, purposely misinterpreted and turned upside-down in the service of atheism and anti-clericalism. In any case, even if all the erudite allusions were faithful to the originals, most young readers would not be able to understand their meaning without the guidance of a qualified teacher.

This calls into question the whole concept of the *utile dulci* when applied to tales for children and young adults. For instance, if Rowling had, in all seriousness, filled her pages with allusions to Greek mythology or the Bible, would that have enlightened young readers, broadened their minds and given them the basics for an understanding of antiquity? Would it have made them better persons? And, practically speaking, would it have improved the story? After decades of teaching and research in literature, my own conviction is that a "useful" level aimed at instructing does not alter the minds and souls of readers. Nor does it enhance the quality of a fictional work.

Still, a number of critics have discovered strong evidence of the *utile dulci* in *Harry Potter*, most notably, in Christian symbolism.[7] Among other things, they see the self-sacrifice of Jesus, his willingness to die for others, mirrored in Lily Potter's sacrificing herself to spare Harry—or in Harry's own willingness to be killed for the sake of humanity. They point to Harry's apparent "resurrection" at the end of the story. And they place the contest between Harry and Voldemort (good and evil) in a religious context.

Such symbolism can enrich the reading of *Harry Potter*. It can also serve as a reassuring bulwark against those critics who have demonized Rowling and her work for corrupting the minds of young people with dark satanic magic. But was the religious symbolism meant to instruct or proselytize readers?

Rowling herself has assured the world that she is no satanic atheist but believes in God. Nonetheless, as we have seen, religion as such plays no role whatever in the lives or thinking of her characters. From all we know of her and her work, it seems unlikely that her aim was to make Harry a Jesus figure or have her story reflect the teachings of the Gospels. Although she recognizes the religious symbolism—especially in Book VII—she maintains, "I am not trying to convert people."[8]

The instructive level is most certainly present throughout the cycle, and a number of edifying lessons lie in store for the reader. But those lessons are presented on a moral, rather than religious level. Their context is not the Bible but our own modern society and the injustices that permeate it.

One of the most obvious moral lessons is the vehement rejection of tyranny and the horrors that accompany it. Despotic Voldemort could be likened to any number of present-day dictators, but especially in the later books of the cycle, he is a twenty-first-century reincarnation of Adolf Hitler and his baneful Nazism. The motto engraved on the dictatorial Ministry of Magic's headquarters: "Magic is Might,"[8] suggests the words *Arbeit Macht Frei* (work makes us free), over the entrance to the Nazi concentration camp at Auschwitz.[9] And Rowling's phrase, "For the Greater Good,"[10] carved on the entrance to a Nurmengard[11] prison built by tyrannical Grundelwald, evokes the high-flown mottoes that justified Nazi persecution.

Other analogies with the Hitler era abound, for instance the persecution of people of "impure" blood. At the height of Voldemort's power, Muggles, disdained as "Mudbloods" by xenophobic wizards, were being "rounded up," like Jews in Hitler's time who were forced to identify themselves before a registration committee because of their non-Aryan blood. And like the resistance groups organized during the Second World War, Harry and his friends formed their subversive "Defense Against the Dark Arts" alliance against Voldemort's powerful Death Eaters. Finally, in *The Deathly Hallows*, the underground radio program, "Potterwatch," evokes the Voice of America shortwave broadcasts of the early forties, radio programs that gave solace and hope to millions under the yoke of the Axis powers. Forcefully underpinning the fight against despotism is this recurring analogy between Voldemort's cause and the Nazism that embodied the worst aspects of a heartless dictatorship.

The ideal of tolerance, born of this hatred of despotism, is another key lesson to be drawn from the story. Reflecting Rowling's liberalism, as many have noted, a whole variety of ethnic groups are included at Hogwarts, with females as active and competent as males. And when it comes to people who scorn Muggles because they lack the "pure blood" of wizards with a proper magic genealogy, right-minded characters in the story naturally root for the Muggles.

A prime spokesman for many of the story's lessons is Headmaster Albus Dumbledore, with his stress on freedom of choice, making the world a better place and, above all, the power of love. However, any moral messages apt to impress a young readership will come not from pronouncements by this ancient sage but from the experiences and actions of Harry and his friends, the characters that readers spontaneously identify with. If Dumbledore speaks of intolerance, it is only an abstract concept, But it truly hits home to us when we find our sensitive Hermione insulted and defenseless in the face of Draco Malfoy's snide taunts about her family's Muggle background and his labeling her "Mudblood."

It is Harry who most powerfully and persuasively conveys the moral messages of Rowling's work. For readers can relate to him quite naturally: he is not some abstract model of perfection, a hero who can do no wrong, but an ordinary teenager, human with understandable foibles. And rather than incorporating the Hollywood ideal of a Michelangelo physique and perfectly chiseled features, he is of medium height and a bit nerdy looking—your average Joe. Because they can easily identify with him, pre-teens and teenagers are touched by Harry. Because they make the journey with him every inch of the way, they are partners with him as much as Ron or Hermione are. They root for him in his attempts to meet his exemplary goals.

Along the way they can be impressed by this ordinary boy who has so much going against him, so many obstacles in his path but who perseveres nonetheless. They can admire his courage, his searching for truth and his attempts to be truthful with himself. They can be convinced by his realization that he is free to choose his course and by his decision to fight the tyranny that threatens his world. They can be inspired by his loyalty, his capacity for friendship and love.

These lessons, all of them positive ones, will not change a coward into a brave warrior nor an immoral reader into a moral one, but they demonstrate that—critics aside—Rowling has imbued *Harry Potter* with a most instructive level indeed.

* * *

It is laudable that Rowling set such a high moral standard for her reading public. However, what counts foremost in a story is not what it teaches but how well it is told. Rowling has told hers in a way that reaches several generations of readers. Older readers appreciate it on a more sophisticated level. They can recognize the allusions to bureaucracy and corruption in the Ministry of Magic, to commercialism and hype in the World Cup extravaganza or to censorship and slanted journalism in *The Daily Prophet*. And unlike the very young,[12] they can savor the subtler aspects of Rowling's humor, the wry wit and irony of her commentary or of Dumbledore's repartee.

But most important is how the cycle speaks to the younger generation. For children, the real value of a work of fiction lies in its power to charm, to hold their interest and capture their imagination. It is the capacity to delight them so fully as to imbue them with the joy of reading, with the desire—the *need*—to continue immersing themselves in other books.

And that, of course, is the miracle of *Harry Potter.*

---

[1] She might have written more casually, "They looked up to see their familiar Hogwarts Express, puffing smoke…"

[2] "Besotted with Potter," *New York Times.* January 27, 2000.

[3] "His Dark Materials." *Wall Street Journal.* February 9, 2008. In fact, the main thrust of this article was a criticism of Pullman's obvious anti-religious bias.

[4] The winner of all the points is the one who mixes usefulness with entertainment, delighting and instructing the reader at the same time.

[5] See Chapter 11, above.

[6] In *The Amber Spyglass,* Lyra is ferried to the Land of the Dead by an oarsman similar to Charon, who rowed people to Hades on the river Styx. Toward the end of the trilogy, she becomes a latter day Eve.

[7] See, for example, the views of Professor Scott Moore, Denise Roper and others online, with the search: "Harry Potter, religious symbolism."

[8] Interview with Oprah Winfrey, CBS, Oct. 1, 2010.

[9] Mentioned in *The Deathly Hallows.*

[10] As for work making people free, the S.S. camp supervisor at Auschwitz greeted new inmates with these words: "You have arrived not at a sanatorium but a German concentration camp from which the only exit is through the chimney of its crematorium." Most died within a few weeks from overwork, beatings, torture, starvation, typhus or dysentery, or were executed.

[11] *The Deathly Hallows.*

[12] An invented place name evocative of Nuremberg, Germany. In 1935, Hitler introduced his "Nuremberg Laws," stripping Jews of their citizenship and civil rights. They were a first step toward his goal of total extermination of the Jews (the "final solution").

[13] Primary school children, for instance.

APPENDIX

CHRONOLOGY AND CREDITS

JOANNE KATHLEEN ROWLING:
b. July 31, 1965.

HARRY JAMES POTTER

Parents James and Lily Potter: **b. 1960**
James, Lily, Severus Snape, Sirius Black, Remus Lupin and Peter
    Pettigrew enroll at Hogwarts: **September, 1971.**
    (Dumbledore Headmaster as of 1970.)
Harry: **b. July 31, 1980.**
Voldemort murders Harry's parents but fails to kill Harry:
    October 31, 1981.
Harry is delivered to the Dursleys for safekeeping:
    November 1, 1981.
Harry enrolls at Hogwarts at age eleven: **September 1, 1991.**
End of Harry's seven-year series of adventures: **June, 1998.**
Epilogue: Harry's son Albus enrolls at Hogwarts,
    September, 2017.

PUBLICATION TIMELINE

Volume I, *Philosopher's Stone*, U.K., Bloomsbury: **1997.**
I. *Sorcerer's Stone*, U.S. edition, Scholastic: **1998**
Volume II, *The Chamber of Secrets:* **1998** (UK), **1999** (US).
Volume III, *The Prisoner of Azkaban:* **1999.**
Volume IV, *The Goblet of Fire:* **2000.**

Volume V, *The Order of the Phoenix:* **2003.**
Volume VI, *The Half Blood Prince:* **2005.**
Volume VII, *The Deathly Hallows:* **2007.**

FILM TIMELINE

The Sorcerer's (Philosopher's) Stone: **2001.**
The Chamber of Secrets: **2002.**
The Prisoner of Azkaban: **2004.**
The Goblet of Fire: **2005.**
The Order of the Phoenix: **2007.**
The Half Blood Prince: **2009.**
The Deathly Hallows: **2010, 2011.**

FILM PRODUCTION CREDITS

PRODUCER: David Heyman

DIRECTORS: Chris Columbus, I and II
Alfonso Cuarón, III
Mike Newell, IV
David Yates, V, VI and both films of VII

SCREENWRITERS: Steve Kloves, all films but *The Order of the Phoenix* (scripted by Michael Rosenberg)

MUSIC: John Williams, principal composer. Other composers: William Ross (II), Patrick Doyle (IV), Nicholas Hooper (V and VI), Alexandre Desplat (VII)

PHOTOGRAPHY: *The Sorcerer's Stone,* John Seale
The Chamber of Secrets, Roger Pratt
The Prisoner of Azkaban, Michael Seresin
The Goblet of Fire, Roger Pratt
The Order of the Phoenix, Slawomir Idziak
The Half Blood Prince, Bruno Delbonnel
The Deathly Hallows, Eduardo Serra

CAST OF CHARACTERS

Harry Potter: Daniel Radcliffe
Ron Weasley: Rupert Grint
Hermione Granger: Emma Watson

FRIENDS AND ALLIES OF HARRY

Sirius Black: Gary Oldman
Cho Chang: Katie Leung
Fleur Delacour: Clémence Poésy
Cedric Diggory: Robert Pattinson
Dobby: Toby Jones
Elphias Doge: Peter Cartwright
Aberforth Dumbledore: Jim McManus
Albus Dumbledore: Richard Harris (films I and II)
Michael Gambon (the others)
Arabella Figg: Kathryn Hunter
Firenze: Ray Fearon
Grawp: Tony Maudsley
Rubeus Hagrid: Robbie Coltrane
Neville Longbottom: Matthew Lewis
Luna Lovegood: Evanna Lynch
Remus Lupin: David Thewlis
Minerva McGonagall: Maggie Smith
Alistor Moody: Brendan Gleeson
James Potter: Adrian Rawlins
Lily Potter: Geraldine Somerville
Kinglsey Shacklebolt: George Harris
Horace Slughorn: Jim Broadbent
Nymphadora Tonks: Natalia Tena
Arthur Weasley: Mark Williams
Bill Weasley: Richard Fish
Charlie Weasley: Alex Crockford
Fred Weasley: James Phelps
George Weasley: Oliver Phelps
Ginny Weasley: Bonnie Wright
Molly Weasley: Julie Walters

NASTY OR NEUTRAL

Alecto Carrow: Suzie Toase
Amycus Carrow: Ralph Ineson
Vincent Crabbe: Jamie Waylett
(does not appear in *Deathly Hallows*)
Barty Crouch, Jr.: David Tennant
Antonin Dolohov: Richard Cubison
Dudley Dursley: Harry Melling
(Aunt) Marge Dursley: Pam Ferris
Petunia Dursley: Fiona Shaw
Vernon Dursley: Richard Griffiths
Argus Filch: David Bradley
Mundungus Fletcher: Andy Linden
Cornelius Fudge: Robert Hardy
Gregory Goyle: Joshua Herdman
Fenrir Greyback: Dave Legeno
Gellert Grindelwald: Jamie Campbell Bower
Griphook: Verne Troyer and Warwick Davis (*Deathly Hallows)*
Bellatrix Lestrange: Helena Bonham Carter
Gilderoy Lockhart: Kenneth Branagh
Walden Macnair: Peter Best
Draco Malfoy: Tom Felton
Lucius Malfoy: Jason Isaacs
Narcissa Malfoy: Helen McCrory
Peeves: Rick Mayal
Peter Pettigrew: Timothy Spall
Quirinus Quirrell: Ian Hart
Rufus Scrimgeour: Bill Nighy
Rita Skeeter: Miranda Richardson
Severus Snape: Alan Rickman
Dolores Umbridge: Imelda Staunton
Lord Voldemort: Ralph Fiennes
Percy Weasley: Chris Rankin

AROUND HOGWARTS

Katie Bell: Emily Dale
Phineas Nigellus Black: John Atterbury
Penelope Clearwater: Gemma Padley
Colin Creevy: Hugh Mitchell
The Fat Lady: Elizabeth Spriggs, Dawn French
Justin Finch-Fletchley: Edward Randell
Seamus Finnigan: Devon Murray
Filius Flitwick: Warwick Davis
Wilhelmina Grubbly-Plank: Apple Brook
Rolanda Hooch: Zoë Wanamaker
Angelina Johnson: Danielle Tabor, Tiana Benjamin
Lee Jordan: Luke Youngblood
Ernie Macmillan: Louis Doyle
Cormac McGlaggen: Freddie Stroma
Moaning Myrtle: Shirley Henderson
Nearly Headless Nick: John Cleese
Pansy Parkinson: Genevieve Gaunt, Scarlett Byrne
Padma Patil: Afshan Azad
Pavarti Patil: Sitara Shah, Shefali Chowdhury
Irma Pince: Sally Mortemore
Poppy Pomfrey: Gemma Jones
Pomona Sprout: Miriam Margolyes
Dean Thomas: Alfred Enoch
Sybill Trelawney: Emma Thompson
Romilda Vane: Anna Shaffer
Oliver Wood: Sean Biggerstaff

OTHER

Bathilda Bagshot: Hazel Douglas
Amelia Bones: Sian Thomas
Mary Cattermole: Kate Fleetwood
Reg Cattermole: Steffan Rhodri
Barty Crouch, Sr.: Roger Lloyd-Pack
Amos Diggory: Jeff Rawle

Ariana Dumbledore: Hebe Beardsall
Gregorovitch: Rade Serbedzija
Igor Karkaroff: Predrag Bjelac
Kreacher: Timothy Bateson
Viktor Krum: Stanislav Ianevski
Augusta Longbottom: Ninette Finch
Xenophilius Lovegood: Rhys Ifans
Madame Maxime: Frances de la Tour
Auntie Muriel: Matyelok Gibbs
Mr. Ollivander: John Hurt
Madame Rosmerta: Julie Christie
Stan Shunpike: Lee Ingleby
Tom, the Barman: Derek Deadman, Jim Tovare
Waitress: Elarica Gallagher

SELECTED BIBLIOGRAPHY

Books and Articles
(Online publications included in footnotes)

By J. K. Rowling:

Harry Potter. London, Scholastic Press; N.Y., Arthur A. Levine Books.

    I. *Harry Potter and the Sorcerer's (Philosopher's) Stone*, 1998.

    II. *Harry Potter and the Chamber of Secrets*, 1999.

    III. *Harry Potter and the Prisoner of Azkaban*, 1999.

    IV. *Harry Potter and the Goblet of Fire*, 2000.

    V. *Harry Potter and the Order of the Phoenix*, 2003.

    VI. *Harry Potter and the Half Blood Prince*, 2005.

    VI. *Harry Potter and the Deathly Hallows*, 2007.

Fantastic Beasts and Where to Find Them by Newt Scamander. London and N.Y., Scholastic Press and Arthur A. Levine Books, 2001.

Quidditch Through the Ages by Kennilworthy Whisp. London and N.Y., Scholastic Press and Arthur A. Levine Books, 2002.

Tales of Beedle the Bard. London and N.Y., Scholastic Press and Arthur A. Levine Books, 2008.

Appleton, Victor. *Tom Swift and His Flying Boat*. Grosset and Dunlap, c1923.

Baynes, Leslie. "His Dark Materials" *Wall Street Journal*. February 9, 2008.

Bergson, Henri. *Le Rire; Essai sur la signification du comique*. Skira, 1945.

Bloom, Harold. "Can Thirty-Five Million Book Buyers Be Wrong? Yes." *Wall Street Journal*. July 22, 2000.

Carey, Brycchan. "Hermione and the House Elves: The Literary and Historical Context of J. K. Rowling's Anti-Slavery Campaign." *Reading Harry Potter; Critical Essays*. Contributions to the Study of Popular Culture. Giselle Lisa Anatol, Ed. Praeger, 2003.

Dahl Roald. *Fantastic Mr. Fox*. Puffin, 2009.

Dixon, Franklin W. *The Hardy Boys Mystery Stories*. Grosset and Dunlap, 1929-1940.

Dresang, Eliza T., "Hermione Granger and the Heritage of Gender." *The Ivory Tower and Harry Potter; Perspectives on a Literary Phenomenon*. Lana A. Whited, Ed. Univ. of Missouri Press, 2002.

Freud, Sigmund."Wit and its Relation to the Unconscious." *Basic Writings of Sigmund Freud*. Modern Library, 1995.

Furlong, Monica. *Wise Child*. Knopf, 1987.

Grahame, Kenneth. *The Wind and the Willows*. Scribner's, 1981.

Holden, Anthony. "Why Harry Potter Doesn't Cast a Spell Over Me." *The Observer*. June 25, 2000.

Hughes, Thomas. *Tom Brown's School Days*. Dutton, 1972.

Jones, Diana Wynne. *Witch Week*. Greenwillow Books, c1988.

Kois, Dan. "Bewitched, Bewildered and Hot and Bothered." *The Washington Post*. July 14, 2009.

Le Guin, Ursula. "Chronicles of *Earthsea*." *Guardian*. Feb. 9, 2004.

The Earthsea Trilogy. Random House, 1984.

Lewis, C. S. *The Complete Chronicles of Narnia*. HarperCollins, 2000.

McCarthy, Erin. "Inside the New Harry Potter." *Popular Mechanics*. July 15, 2009.

Mendelsohn, Farah. "Crowning the King; Harry Potter and the Construction of Authority." *The Ivory Tower and Harry Potter; Perspectives on a Literary Phenomenon.* Lana A. Whited, Ed. Univ. of Missouri Press, 2002.

Murphy, Jill. *Worst Witch.* Candlewick Press, 2000.

Pharr, Mary. "Harry Potter as Hero-in-Progress," *The Ivory Tower.* 2002.

Provezano, Danielle M. and Rosengren, Emily C. "Harry Potter and the Resilience to Adversity." *The Psychology of Harry Potter; an Unauthorized Examination of the Boy Who Lived.* Neil Mullholland, Ed. Benbella Books, 2007.

Pullman, Philip. *His Dark Materials. (The Golden Compass. The Subtle Knife. The Amber Spyglass)* Laurel Leaf, 2003.

Ridley, Matt. *Genome.* HarperCollins, 1999.

Saphire, William. "Besotted with Potter," *New York Times.* January 27, 2000.

Tolkien, J. R. R. *The Hobbit.* Houghton Mifflin, 1988.

The Lord of the Rings. Houghton Mifflin, 1994.

White, Thomas I., *In Defense of Dolphins; The New Moral Frontier.* Wiley-Blackwell, 2007.

Zip, Yvonne. "Harry's Back." *Christian Science Monitor.* June 26, 2003.